Contents

KV-638-111

Civility and Empire

"Civility," a normative code of behavior in British nineteenth-century society, became a means of imposing control and effecting exclusion when transferred to the colonial domain.

This study examines the manner in which "civility" emerged as the ethos of the British colonial state in the Indian subcontinent and formed as a key discursive idea around which questions about citizenship, education, gender, race, labor, and bureaucratic or civil authority were negotiated.

This discourse of civility, Anindyo Roy argues, provided the basis for disciplinary mechanisms essential to managing the historical exigencies confronting the British empire in India. He traces the genealogy of civility in nineteenth- and early twentieth-century literature and culture, covering a wide array of texts by authors such as Scott, Trelawny, Mill, Kipling, E. M. Forster, and Leonard Woolf, late Victorian Anglo-Indian poetry as well as colonial archives relating to parliamentary debates, cadetship in the East India Company, and policies on education, industry, and commerce.

Anindyo Roy is Associate Professor in English at Colby College, Maine, USA, where he teaches critical and postcolonial theory, and postcolonial and modern British literature.

Postcolonial Literatures

Edited in collaboration with the Centre for Colonial and Postcolonial Studies, University of Kent at Canterbury, this series presents a wide range of research into postcolonial literatures by specialists in the field. Volumes will concentrate on writers and writing originating in previously (or presently) colonized areas, and will include material from non-anglophone as well as anglophone colonies and literatures. The series will also include collections of important essays from older journals, and re-issues of classic texts on postcolonial subjects. Routledge is pleased to invite proposals for new books in the series. Interested authors should contact Lyn Innes or Rod Edmond at the Centre for Colonial and Postcolonial Studies, University of Kent at Canterbury, or Routledge's Commissioning Editor for Literature.

The series comprises three strands.

Routledge Research in Postcolonial Literatures is a forum for innovative new research intended for a specialist readership. Published in hardback, titles include:

1. *Magical Realism in West African Fiction: Seeing with a Third Eye* by Brenda Cooper
2. *The Postcolonial Jane Austen* edited by You-Me Park and Rajeswari Sunder Rajan
3. *Contemporary Caribbean Women's Poetry: Making Style* by Denise deCaires Narain
4. *African Literature, Animism and Politics* by Caroline Rooney
5. *Caribbean-English Passages: Intertextuality in a Postcolonial Tradition* by Tobias Döring
6. *Islands in History and Representation* edited by Rod Edmond and Vanessa Smith
7. *Civility and Empire: Literature and Culture in British India, 1822–1922* by Anindyo Roy
8. *Women Writing the West Indies, 1804–1939: 'A Hot Place, Belonging To Us'* by Evelyn O'Callaghan
9. *Postcolonial Pacific Writing: Representations of the Body* by Michelle Keown
10. *Writing Woman, Writing Place: Contemporary Australian and South African Fiction* by Sue Kossew

Postcolonial Literatures makes available in paperback important work in the field. Hardback editions of these titles are also available, some published earlier in the Routledge Research strand of the series. Titles in paperback include:

Postcolonial Studies: A Materialist Critique by Benita Parry
Magical Realism in West African Fiction: Seeing with a Third Eye by Brenda Cooper
The Postcolonial Jane Austen edited by You-Me Park and Rajeswari Sunder Rajan
Contemporary Caribbean Women's Poetry: Making Style by Denise deCaires Narain

Readings in Postcolonial Literatures offers collections of important essays from journals or classic texts in the field. Titles include:

1. *Selected Essays of Wilson Harris* edited by Andrew Bundy

Civility and Empire

Literature and culture in British India, 1822–1922

Anindyo Roy

Routledge
Taylor & Francis Group

LONDON AND NEW YORK

First published 2005
by Routledge
2 Park Square, Milton Park, Abingdon, Oxfordshire OX14 4RN

Simultaneously published in the USA and Canada
by Routledge
711 Third Avenue, New York, NY 10017

First issued in paperback 2014

Routledge is an imprint of the Taylor and Francis Group, an informa business

Typeset in Baskerville by
BOOK NOW Ltd

British Library Cataloguing in Publication Data
A catalogue record for this book is available from the British Library

Library of Congress Cataloging in Publication Data
Roy, Anindyo, 1959–
    Civility and empire: literature and culture in British India, 1822–1922/Anindyo
Roy.
        p. cm. – (Routledge research in postcolonial literatures)
        Includes bibliographical references and index.
    1. Anglo-Indian literature–History and criticism. 2. Literature and society–
India–History–19th century. 3. Literature and society–India–History–20th
century. 4. English literature–Indic influences. 5. British–India–Intellectual
life. 6. Imperialism in literature. 7. Courtesy in literature. 8. Colonies in
literature. 9. India–In literature. I. Title. II. Series.
        PR129.I5R69 2005
        820.9′954–dc22   2004009296

ISBN 13: 978-0-415-30435-1 (hbk)
ISBN 13: 978-0-415-64666-6 (pbk)

Acknowledgments

This book was conceived, written, and revised over a period of nearly six years—with many anticipated and unanticipated detours—in Waterville, Boston, London, Delhi, and Calcutta. My special thanks go to Geeta Patel, whose special skills as a rigorous intellectual mentor are exceeded only by her special generosity and good humor. Much of the study was conducted in the spirit of rethinking the complex histories of colonialism by revisiting the scattered sites of the colonial archive, both in the UK and in India. For this, I owe a special debt to Colby College for its generous support of my research through its humanities research grants. I also offer my deep thanks to my colleagues at Colby College, particularly to the members of the Humanities Grant Committee who approved generous funding for my work; to David Suchoff who patiently read sections of my chapters and offered his incisive critiques; and to other members of the Colby faculty, including Michelle Chilcoat, John Beusterien, Katherine Stubbs, Mary Beth Mills, James Barrett, Carmen Muro-Perez, Meriwynn Grothe, Jorge Olivares, Steven Nuss, and Nikky Singh. To Anjali Arondekar, Jyotsna Singh, and Kath Weston, I offer my sincerest thanks for their spirit and intellectual verve, which continue to inspire me in ways that are hard to enumerate; and to Prajna Parasher, Maria Koundoura, Robert Dulgerian, Harry Walker, Sanjay Talreja, and Andrew Feffer, for conversations that made me sit up and think. To my students in my critical theory, modern British, and postcolonial literature classes, particularly to Zahid Chaudhury, Mike Reilly, and John Sullivan. To my friends from my "undergraduate days" at Delhi University—Samidha Garg, Anil Sethi, Dilip Saxena, Padmanabh Mishra, Gaura Narayan, Amrita Bhalla, Lalita Subbu, Renuka Subbu, and Nirmalya Samanta; to the late Shantha Kadambi of the Department of English at Delhi University, who first instilled in me the love of intellectual labor; and to my friends in the UK—Jonathan Hardy, Gary Lewis, and Megha Chand—for accompanying me for midday lunches and walks through London's parks.

To my mother Meena Roy, and to Arup Roy, Swati Vijh, Harish Vijh, Shanti Roy, Rina Dass, Ratna Sen, and Chandrima Das Gupta—all of whom provided the emotional support for engaging in the long labors of writing and rewriting, and without whom returning to India to conduct "archival work" would have been unthinkable. I thank the library staff at the British Library in London, the National

Archives in New Delhi, the National Library in Calcutta, and the Colby College Library, and my editor. I am also grateful to Gayatri Chakravarty Spivak for her support and encouragement.

Special thanks to *Boundary 2*, *Criticism*, *Journal X*, and *Colby Quarterly* for allowing me to republish some of the revised material:

Reprinted material of Anindyo Roy, "Telling Brutal Things: Colonialism, Bloomsbury, and the Crisis of Narration in Leonard Woolf's 'A Tale Told by Moonlight'," in *Criticism* vol. 43:2, with the permission of the Wayne State University Press © 2002, Wayne State University Press, Detroit, Michigan.

Reprinted material of Anindyo Roy, "Savage Pursuit: The Shaping of Colonial Civility in E. M. Forster's 'The Life to Come'," in *Boundary 2* 28:2 © 2001 by Duke University Press.

Reprinted material of Anindyo Roy, "Metropolitan Civility, Bloomsbury, and the Power of the Modern Colonial State: Leonard Woolf's 'Pearls and Swine'," in *Journal X: A Biannual Journal in Culture and Criticism* 6:1 © 2001 by the University of Mississippi.

Introduction

The nineteenth century, the era from which we date our civility . . .

Lamb, *Elia* (1823)

The great need of "education" in our colleges . . . is to stimulate and foster, in all ways possible, the growth of a real University life, which may develop in those who share it loyalty, disinterestedness and public spirit, together with what, in default of a recognized name, we might, perhaps, call "civility."

"Indian Universities," *Calcutta Review* (1897)

We to-day are haunted and beset by Babu English, enlightened discontent, and insolence of University degrees.

Calcutta Review (1893)

Decidedly this fellow is an original. . . . He is like the nightmare of a Viennese courier.

Kipling, *Kim*

This book is concerned with revisiting the concept of civility, which served as an implicit component in the British colonial project of the nineteenth and the early twentieth century. The power of civility lay in its ability subtly to impose control or effect exclusion by establishing a normative code of imperial Britishness that operated on the variables of nationality, class, and gender. However, the same concept came to acquire an elusive quality when transferred to the colonial domain, and it is this elusiveness, visible in the sometimes fractured rhetorics of civility, that opens up a new history of colonial power relations.

Why "civility?"

Censuring the colonial government for continuing to support the spread of Western education through the recently founded Indian universities, the *Calcutta Review* of 1897 pointed to the pernicious effects of such a policy on the social manners of Indian youth. After acquiring "the small amount of education involved in getting through one or two University examinations," the monthly claimed, the educated youth had adopted "a self-asserting, aggressive and bumptious manner, which is inconsistent either with native or English ideas of what a gentleman ought to be." This crisis, the reviewer further noted, had resulted from the failure of such education to foster the values of civility among the Indian youth, who had not only failed to acquire "the highly-polished manners of their fathers," but had not even benefited from the sobering influence of "the quiet, self-contained and modest demeanour which commonly characterizes the young Englishman" ("Indian Universities," *CR* 1897: 143).[1] Typical of their time, the behavioral attributes listed here represented those ideals of civility that were perceived to be central to the formation of "national" English character; however, their appearance in this colonial context raises the question of their real political meaning. How could an education institutionalized by the colonial state for the betterment of its colonized subjects meet its true hegemonic ends? What effect did the appeal to "civility" have on constituting colonial subjecthood? Scarcely sixty years before the appearance of this article in the *Calcutta Review*, Thomas Babington Macaulay, the founder of modern Western education in India, had asserted with characteristic equanimity in his speech "Government of India" that it was not "possible to calculate the benefits which we might derive from the diffusion of European civilization among the vast population of the East" (Macaulay 1860: 571).[2] Among these "benefits" was of course "loyalty to the state," which could be elicited from colonized subjects through education. The expectation had been that a people "who had acquired a knowledge of western literature and science" would be motivated as much by "an enlightened conviction that their welfare depended on a continuance of existing relations" as from "a knowledge of those powerful resources at the command of the British Government" ("Review of *Considerations*," *CR* 1861: 204). Protection of the status quo and the belief that education would be "an inestimable safe-guard to our rule" (ibid.) provided the key rationale to the colonial government in the succeeding years to continue supporting Macaulay's vision of Western education in India. It was based on a form of reasoning whose ideological basis clearly lay in the liberal view that colonial rule had successfully supplanted the cruel despotism of the East with an "enlightened despotism" that worked for the benefit of the colonized majority.[3] In other words, a particular class of educated (male) subjects who were possessed with a firm knowledge of their *own* enlightened self-interest could be relied upon to safeguard the interests of the empire as a whole. By being able to identify a common ground between the agenda of the empire and its own survival as a new community of classed citizens, these subjects would serve as ideal mediators between the imperial government and the colonized populace.[4]

A marked change in this viewpoint becomes evident after the 1870s following the opening up of the covenanted civil services, hitherto reserved exclusively for British subjects, which enabled the entry of qualified university-educated Indians to posts. Although the numbers of the latter were few, this policy was soon perceived to be a threat to the privileged spaces of the Anglo-Indian world. One of the ways in which this new threat materialized in Anglo-Indian public culture was through the figure of the "competition *baboo*"–the educated Indian vying for the same privileges promised to the British colonizer. The presence of the *baboo* not only signified the failure of Macaulay's dream of producing a docile community of educated subjects through the diffusion of Western learning, it also gave added impetus to the growing perception that "throwing wide the portals of the University [had] attract[ed] effort into unpredictable channels . . . inevitably provid[ing] for a large and growing class of the discontended" ("Teaching of English," *CR* 1893: 300). That "unpredictability" was in fact the problem for many Anglo-Indian administrators, who felt that this experiment in education had produced a new crisis for colonial administrators, a crisis whose effects were also palpable in the growing disaffection among the educated classes of Indians.[5] The alarmist tone that informed much of the debates about the fiscal and political wisdom of maintaining a publicly supported higher education in English, which were conducted on the pages of the established Anglo-Indian monthly in the final decades of the nineteenth century, can best be understood when placed against this new rhetoric of "crisis" pervading British India. In fact, among political circles, the sentiments evoked by it were widely shared by many India-hands who had succeeded to the legacy of Macaulay, namely Sir Charles Wood, secretary of state, who had deprecated the "employment of a highly crammed Baboo of Calcutta," and Lord Salisbury, who in 1877 had written to the viceroy, Lord Lytton, that he could "imagine no more terrible future for India than that of being governed by Competition Baboos" (quoted in Hira Lal Singh 1963: 16, 28). Ironically, it was Macaulay who had, in the concluding moments of his celebrated speech, anticipated that the political fallout of English education in the future might not be that easy to predict or even to control, given the constraints under which the goals of the new civilizing mission had been set:

> Are we to keep the people of India ignorant in order that we may keep them submissive? Or do we think that we can give them knowledge without awakening ambition? Or do we mean to awaken ambition and to provide it with no legitimate end? Who will answer any of these questions in the affirmative?
>
> (Macaulay 1860: 572)

His concluding words strike a chord of hesitance that symptomizes not only the enormity of the task of governance undertaken by liberal authorities to meet its hegemonic ends, but also the deep discrepancy that lay within the order of "civility" that had been the basis for defining citizenship. In fact, it is this discrepancy that forces our attention back to this particular historical moment as a way to rethink the question of "civility" that emerges in relation to the colonial state and the latter's efforts to define "citizenship." These efforts, exemplified by governmental policies on native education, were aimed at producing "citizenship" as a way to reinscribe and manage the very unevenness upon which the civilizing rationale had been built.

The questions that Macaulay had posed in his 1833 speech continued to hound Anglo-Indian public opinion in the last three decades of the nineteenth century, culminating in the bitter controversy of the Ilbert Bill in 1883. In the dispute generated by the Bill that had proposed that Indian judges should be allowed to preside over Europeans in native courts, the founder of English education in India came to be regarded by the Anglo-Indian community as a "seditious author" (Kincaid 1938: 195). The strange twist of irony discernible here is magnified by the fact that the *Calcutta Review* of 1895, while repeating Macaulay's dictum that English "might form a bond of union between the ruler and the ruled, the Aryans of the land and Aryans from over the sea" ("Indian Universities," *CR* 1895: 387), only stressed the impossibility of that union. The emergent mind-view was that Macaulay's "English" education had only produced what the Russian agent in Kipling's *Kim* would call "the monstrous hybridism of East and West." Embodied in the *baboo*, the Western educated colonial counterpart of the Victorian gentleman, this abnormal hybridity had to be acknowledged, at some level, as a historically inevitable condition: as the Russian agent comments, Hurree Babu "represents in little India *in transition*" (Kipling [1901] 1998: 288; emphasis added). However, equally powerful was the need to ensure that this historical inevitability did not jeopardize the existing relations of power between the colonial authorities and native subjects. As a consequence, the *baboo* had to be represented as "un-civil" subject: whether employed as a native clerk or a petty government official, he was produced endlessly as a caricature of the "original," and enters the nineteenth-century imperial imagination with a kind of wild flamboyance that is clearly discernable in Kipling's creation in *Kim*, the Calcutta University educated Hurree Chunder Mookherji, and in F. Anstey's caricature of the Bengali gentleman, "Baboo Jabberjee."[6]

The figure of the Western-educated "competition *baboo*" not only came to represent the new threat to the status quo following the introduction and gradual implementation of the Indian Civil Services Act of 1861 (the piece of legislative reform resulting from the recommendations of the Macaulay Committee of 1854 permitting Indians to compete for entry into the civil services), but that threat itself worked in tandem with the representation of the *baboo* as a "translated" figure. In fact, in a work such as *Kim*, the *baboo*'s peculiar relationship with the English language is represented in terms of the power of "translation." What emerges powerfully in the literature about the *baboo* is the utilization of translation as a two-pronged political strategy: on the one hand, it designated the power to use the master language, as Kipling does, to define and make visible an authentic "translated" object, and on the other, that translated subject is made to "speak" the master language in a manner where the transgression of linguistic norms and competence becomes the key criterion for marking and calibrating his civility. This "subject–object" dynamic was therefore crucial to the consolidation of civility in colonial discourse.

The colonial subject's inability to be truly "civil" could be embodied only in terms of the inherent impossibility written into the concept of civility. However, although the *baboo*'s imperfect efforts at translating the master language only produced a hybrid and aberrant form, that form could be rendered in all its visibility, providing colonial authorities with the rationale that the "Government should be careful not to continue their stimulating process for too long or carry it too far" ("The Native Press," *CR* 1866: 378). In fact, the very incitement to speak about the elusive civility of the *baboo* takes on a particular discursive form at the heart of which is the question about his hybrid language. Despite the efforts to map out this hybridity, and to mock and parody it endlessly, colonial authorities could never fully comprehend the "educated" mind of the colonial subject. As Kipling shows, deep within the layers of the *baboo*'s docile mind lay the seeds of chaos and treasonous thought. On the one hand, the unorthodox combination of "Herbert Spencer," "Shakespeare," "Wordsworth," "Burke and Hare," and Hindu *shastras* (Kipling [1901] 1998: 211) in his vocabulary seemed merely funny. On the other hand, the treasonous thoughts often appeared too embedded in the ludicrous irrationality of his "educated" mind to be isolated and identified in any measurable form. What remains representable in the colonial narrative is this strange hybridity, one that seemed to reproduce itself endlessly in the behavior of the *baboo*. Constructed as an enigma, the *baboo* is therefore subject to a whole range of contradictions: even when acquiescent, his civility was perceived to be merely a mask concealing an aggressive and deceptively ambitious mind. But since that mask could not be completely exposed, the *baboo* is shown to vacillate between being aggressive and being excessively civil and obsequious. In other words, the *baboo*'s aberrant "hybridism" had to be constantly described, deciphered, and monitored but the core of his mind could never be exposed, which explains in part the nineteenth-century fascination with the *baboo*'s language—with its "polyglot character" (Wright 1891: 8), its ostensible penchant for "bombast and grandiloquence," and its "injudicious use of metaphors" (ibid.: 16).

Described as "the curious and remarkable" product that had resulted from "this English graft on Indian soil" ("The Teaching of English," *CR* 1893: 294), the *baboo*'s language became an object of constant surveillance. Kipling's representation of it, including the often distorted pronunciation of common English words, is therefore to be seen as part of this preoccupation with his strange hybridism.[7] The 1890 *"Baboo English": On our Mother-Tongue as our Aryan Brethren Understand It*, a collection of "amusing specimens" from native usage of the English tongue, is only one example, among many, of this interest in scrutinizing the fate of the English language seen as somehow corrupted by the *baboo*'s flagrant disregard for the norms of linguistic civility.[8] Such preoccupation with the *baboo*'s language enabled a reassessment and reconsolidation of the centrality of British racial and national identity at a time when the dissemination of Western learning had resulted in creating new shifts in the existing colonial power relations. While the rapidly increasing middle classes in a province such as Bengal had taken advantage of the new possibilities opened to them by Western learning, their emergent aspirations and achievements could now be represented only through the monstrous figure of the *baboo* with his ridiculously inflated English, a language which, in the words of a writer in the *Calcutta Review*, failed to "make angels," and had "philologists weeping" ("The Teaching of English," *CR* 1893: 294). Apart from the concern about language, the many narratives involving the *baboo* in the nineteenth century undeniably point to the fact that, failing to be the "angel," he was beginning to serve as the figure on whom all of the anxieties produced by the shifting power relations could most easily be projected. Therefore, he remained an intractable presence in the Anglo-Indian world, a reminder of the government's failure, despite its best intentions, to inculcate "civility" among its subjects through education.

In the nineteenth century, civility was regarded as an unalienable part of the definition of "gentlemanly" character. "Language" and "civility" were tied through a shared space: both relied on hierarchies that invested individuals with different kinds of social and cultural authority. However, as the present study reveals, these hierarchies were not always fixed: generating a range of other distinctions, they often expanded their own boundaries or crossed over to others. For example, the nineteenth-century education debates that had centered on the relevance of teaching "correct language" over the teaching of "literature" were based on an implicit opposition that had been principally structured by class relations existing within metropolitan society. In the colony, however, it was deployed to foster a different political ideology: while the study of literature was aimed at creating an authentic "disinterested" loyalty, the teaching of "correct" language was more explicitly pragmatic, motivated by the desire to inculcate the "loyalty of fear" that could, in addition to "disinterestedness," produce the docile colonial subject. Both of these positions were, of course, anchored in those principles of liberalism that were deployed to encourage public education. One can discern the special relationship established between civility and language in Kipling's *Kim*, especially in the way in which Kipling narrates Kim's strategic relationship with two different languages—the master language, English, and the local Urdu dialect (the "vernacular") he speaks in the company of his fellow Indians. Kim's relationship with languages—and his bilingualism—becomes an important marker of his European civility, one guaranteed both by his remarkably effortless ability to pick up English spoken like a "Sahib" at a missionary school and by his hold over the local Urdu, a language he uses with a kind of playful dexterity. Kipling constantly distinguishes the moments and marks the shifts between these languages, especially when he describes Kim speaking one language while "thinking" in another. Because of this ability, Kim is able consciously to choose between the two languages, and, despite the changing situations in which he finds himself, his fluency in the vernacular does not in any way diminish his ability to recognize standard English even when he avoids speaking in it. Kim's special "European" status is also assured by the fact that, although he often embraces the vernacular—described as the language of the "native born, mixed with quaint reflections" (Kipling [1901] 1998: 172)—his efforts are always the result of his conscious decision to "translate" from it. Unlike the *baboo*'s inflated language, Kim's translation is never dissonant; quite the contrary, this particular competence—to "shift speech" (ibid.: 196)—endows him with an air of "authenticity" that he utilizes strategically to project the vernacular. Capable of "remember[ing] with both kinds of faces" (ibid.: 191), Kim is always in control of each shift in language as effectively as he can deploy the power of his "civility" to prove to the world that he is essentially a *sahib*.[9] In this he stands in contrast to the ludicrous Hurree Babu: like Kim he speaks two languages, but unlike Kim he is never in control of the shifts between the two. However, this incapacity—although dramatized in *Kim* through the descriptions of Hurree Babu's floundering language —cannot fully reveal what lies behind the man's mask. The *baboo*'s adoption of master language for the purpose of self-expression may be a sign of the loyalty of fear, although that loyalty is also shown to conflict with his own middle-class aspirations of freedom, aspirations set in place by the introduction of Western learning. It is therefore not surprising that Kipling attributes the *baboo*'s conflict not to the contradiction that lay within the very idea of civility introduced in India but to the *baboo*'s strange hybridity, stemming from the confusion created in his mind by the "dreams of Bengali gods, text-books of education, and the Royal Society, London, England" (Kipling [1901] 1998: 318).

This projection of an internal contradiction within the subjectivity of the *baboo* is rehearsed in myriad forms throughout the colonial era. As clarified earlier, that subjectivity had to be constantly rendered in a visibly objectifiable form—the form of hybridity—so that the *baboo*'s aspirations could be put to the service of the colonial government. Together with his inescapable "Bengali" nature, Hurree Babu's authenticity is produced out of a particular interpretive move on Kipling's part, and it is not surprising that, although it is the *baboo* in Kipling's novel who is presented as the most literate and well-read person working for the imperial government, his world can never meet the Arnoldian standard of cultivated "sweetness and light." His objectified hybridity becomes the visible mark of his subject position—that of a dizzy and muddle-headed "crammed" man who can only follow but never lead.

As that pervasive Victorian norm that had been essential to the formation of key social values in the colonial world, namely "loyalty, disinterestedness and public spirit," civility had its origin in metropolitan ideas of social decorum and class privilege. Not only did the educated *baboo* become, in colonial eyes, the *semi-*educated "native clerk" vying for a limited number of government jobs, even those members of the educated Indian elite who through Western education had aspired for, and gained entry into, higher positions in the civil service were derided for lacking "moral courage which enables a man to act alone in a highly responsible position" (quoted in Hira Lal Singh 1963: 16). It is worth pointing out that, within this rhetoric, all of the desirable traits—"moral courage," "loyalty," "disinterested-ness," and "public spirit"—which promoted social decorum and class privilege were nameable except for "civility," which for this writer of the 1897 edition of *Calcutta Review* could exist only "in default of a recognized name." What was it about civility that in the case of colonials it could not be called by its "recognized name"? "Default" suggests lack or absence, which signifies that in some sense what was recognized as the "civility" of colonized subjects could only stand in for—in an approximate sense—but not really represent the "core" that gave the dominant social norms their true meaning and function in the metropolitan world. Could it be that the very ordinariness of the term "civility" concealed another, more signifi-cant, order that made it much more than what was understood merely as yet another form of outward social behavior? Why had a word that seemed so easy to define in the metropolis become so enigmatic in the colonial world at this historical moment?

These questions provide the starting point for the study of civility that I undertake in my book. In her discussion of an early modern text, Aphra Behn's *The Widow's Ranter*, Margo Hendricks ties civility to the concept of race, arguing that the concept of civility is founded on a paradox with a strategic function: "the more the native becomes assimilated, the more her/his alienness becomes culturally reified" (Hendricks 1994: 227). Though I am in general agreement with Hendricks's analysis of cultural reification, I begin this study with the premise that the deliberate elusiveness ascribed to the term "civility" in the nineteenth century provoked a more densely and amorphously arranged discourse about social behavior, producing the conditions for both incitement and interdiction of a discourse through which colonial power relations were defined and consolidated. These relations provided the basis for the linking of nineteenth-century modernity and colonialism as exemplified by the simultaneous management of material resources and the subjects of governance through—as Arjun Appadurai has suggested—governmental regulation of numbers and "classification activities" (Appadurai 1996: 116).[10] Such consolidation of power indicates that the elusiveness of the colonial subject could be utilized to structure and reinforce the ideologies of civility with the same energy as the material resources of the colony were being utilized to organize the modern state. As I demonstrate in the course of this study, the discourse of civility indicates both the power of the colonial investment in constituting norms of "civil selfhood" and the trouble that it meets over and over again in the confrontation with its own projections of "otherness." However, there are two sides to this process of investment that should be borne in mind. First, the confrontation with this projected "otherness" had to be transformed, through narrativization, from a situation of unreadability to that of visibility so that the norms of civil selfhood could be enunciated and its power manifested across colonial culture. Second, these projections—whether they belonged to the *baboo*, the "Jew," the nautch girl, the tribal potentate, or the native pearl diver—had to be constantly displaced from their historical spaces and made to function within specific *narrative* relations constructed by the colonial imaginary in the nineteenth and twentieth centuries. In other words, these projections are always already historically negotiated entities, instead of being "purely" fictional or ideal types. In fact, my study demonstrates that the roles these projections play within colonial narratives are symptomatic of the historical contestations produced within the discourse of civility in colonial India, contestations that were never fully acknowledged by the colonial powers that authorized these narratives.

My study broadly identifies two periods for examining the construction of civility. In the nineteenth century, the need to mark the "elusiveness" of the colonial subject's "civility" results from a differential relation that is established to assure a stable place for the metropolitan subject and his "civility." In the twentieth century, however, a new tension erupts within this differential dynamic as the civility of the metropolitan subject itself becomes problematic, revealing within its structural stability its own *history*, that is, its own troubled links with the political economy of colonialism and its vision of "modernity." It is therefore not surprising that the discourse of colonial civility found in twentieth-century writers such as E. M. Forster and Leonard Woolf constantly forces our attention to the question of the materiality of the imperial enterprise, thereby allowing us to identify and question those imperatives of civility that the colonial state had put to its own service in the name of "modernity." It is from this broad historical perspective that I contend that what culminated at the end of the nineteenth century in colonial India in the decisive debates about education of the natives (and the monstrosity of the hybrid *baboo*) has a particular genealogy, a genealogy that this book attempts to trace. I also argue that since the term "civility" was perceived to work by "default" in the nineteenth-century colonial situation, the resulting semantic uncertainty allowed for a complex range of positions to be articulated, differential positions on social behavior whose historical fashioning brings to the fore crucial issues concerning the structural relations between the modern British state—established as a paradigm for "representative government"—and the Indian empire, whose existence came to be defined in terms of the state-ordained rationale for the exercise of an "enlightened despotism." In the twentieth century, these relations underwent a specific historical crisis as a result of which the very domain of civility that had been utilized to justify the empire presented itself as the problem. Both Forster and Woolf bring up questions about the historical and political nature of the imperial mission that test the normalizing function of English liberal discourse, and, by rerouting the question of civility back to the metropolis, they render visible the very unevenness upon which the relations of colonial power operated. The projections of "otherness" in Forster's "The Life to Come" and in Leonard Woolf's colonial short stories are therefore always situated within specific material sites that bring out that unevenness.

Homi Bhabha provides one of the theoretical contexts necessary for comprehending this genealogy of civility. In his essay "Sly Civility," Bhabha argues that civility was scripted into the nineteenth-century post-utilitarian colonial text as an enunciatory category that operated through the "dream of a perfect system of recordation . . . underwritten by the practice of utilitarian reforms" (Bhaba 1985: 71). As an enunciatory category rehearsed time and again in different forms of "writing," civility, according to Bhabha, was vulnerable to its own textuality: the liberal investment in the idea of civility—understood as fair and democratic "public discussion" and as the key to the rationale for reform and improvement in the colony—was an impossible dream. Because the difference between "civility" and "despotism," fundamental to colonialism, remained in place, civil discourse could not free itself from this difference. Bhabha further notes that the political effect of this order of difference materialized in the colonial strategies of "surveillance, subjection, and inscription," which were intrinsic to the practices set in place by civil discourse. Given his theoretical bias, it is not surprising that the exclusive emphasis on "agonistic uncertainty" (with its Derridean resonance) remains key to Bhabha's purpose of reading civility as being "sly"; and although his efforts to link that uncertainty to the incompatibility between the British "nation" and "empire" appear to keep the focus on the political, it is not clear from his analysis how the enunciation of civility—with its "ambivalent deferred address of colonial governance" (ibid.: 74)—takes on specific *historical forms* or registers particular political effects in the colonial age. Although Bhabha's example of John Stuart Mill is extremely pertinent to comprehending the political ramifications of this discourse of civility—he is right in suggesting that the role of a philosopher such as Mill in writing and amending colonial dispatches through the East India's Company's Office of Correspondence cannot be seen in isolation from the different economic and political policies that were formulated for the governance of India during the mid-nineteenth century–he appears to be more interested in teasing out the ambivalence intrinsic to the liberal project than on tracing the history that connects this ambivalence to the normative function of civility. It is worth pointing out that "civility" was more than a concept caught up in agonistic textual uncertainty or in unstable enunciatory modes of liberalism: it has a particular genealogy that links it with different, and often competing, discursive rims constituting the idea of the modern British state, with its own politics of class, race, and gender. This is a genealogy that shows that even "contradictions" often had an important productive role in consolidating colonial ideologies. In fact, as Bhabha himself acknowledges, civility possessed "interdictory borders" (ibid.: 75), which supports the contention I made earlier that the idea of civility was built around and operated as a normative discourse, particularly through the processes of incitement and interdiction–processes that are, as Michel Foucault has argued, key to hegemonic discourses of the state.

Before I clarify how civility functioned as a normative idea, it might be worthwhile to draw a more schematic history of the term. Civility has its classical metropolitan base in the idea of "civic virtue" that had been embodied as a norm guiding the social behavior of the citizens of the modern state, the *polis*. Even in the late sixteenth century, Edmund Spenser invokes the "sweet civility" of "an Englishman brought up *naturally*" (Spenser 1983: 78) in England as a way to mark the difference between a "barbarous" Ireland and civilized England, the latter sustained by the rule of the king's law that is "surely most just and most agreeable, both with the government and with the nature of the people" (ibid.: 68). It is in this conjoining of "government" and the "nature of the people" that the *ethos* of civility gets to be defined in the colonial Elizabethan era. By the eighteenth century, the link between "civility" and "civil identity" further reinforced that particular ethos, making it the basis for securing those powerful ideologies for modern citizenship that came to be linked to Britain's status as an emerging imperial power. The history of this emerging identity, driven in part by a fantasy of a guiding providence, allowed Britain to undertake the real tasks of defining the provenance of government both within and outside its borders, simultaneously constructing and regulating the needs and aspirations of Britons who had been exposed to the new historical exigencies of colonialism and those of colonized people who found themselves subject to British civil rule. The ruling order's investment in the idea of civility had a material as well as an ideological basis. In fact, the economic traffic of colonialism depended, to a large measure, on the exchange and traffic of those ideological values that determined the normative function of civility. The viability of establishing a link between the material and the ideological is also underscored by the fact that, within the historical frame of the nineteenth and early twentieth century, colonialism produced a global economic order in relation to the regimes of civil order ordained by the modern state. These regimes were characterized by specific rules of property, law, inheritance, educational opportunity, growth, and accumulation relating to civil behavior, which naturalized this global economic order by inserting the last-named into a unifying national narrative perceived to be part of Europe's providential destiny.[11] Given the fact that the empire had been established out of the sometimes protracted political contestations within Europe, which persisted even in the face of often repeated assertions of imperial power and stability in the latter half of the nineteenth century, it is remarkable that British colonial ideologies not only survived these unpredictable changes, but continued, in the face of these challenges, to be re-energized by the norms enunciated by these regimes. This can be explained, as noted earlier, by the very productive functional nature of these regimes—that is, their constant and fluid restructuring of the norms of civility.

Following Michel Foucault's analysis of modern liberal society constituted in the nineteenth century, I argue in my section on the Bengali *baboo*, and more explicitly in my chapter on John Stuart Mill, that the ability to consolidate the contradictions that were built within it best indicate the normalizing power of the disciplinary regimes of civility set in place during this period. This power can be traced, demonstrated time and again, in its ability to negotiate flexibly the normative function of civil behavior in order to maintain the hegemony of a liberal colonial nation-state. My study also demonstrates that this normativity was produced largely through the reordering of race, gender, and class identities within a wide array of colonial sites: the marketplace, educational institutions, military and civil stations, the frontiers of the empire, the house of the prostitute and the mysterious *zenanas*, aboriginal forest territories and missionary stations, and the pearl fisheries of the Indian subcontinent. Civility materialized at these sites through a range of ideological practices, leading to the formation and legitimization of bourgeois social desire and the ruling ideas of modern progress and mobility that was to shape the modern ethos of the nation.

Take the example of John Warren, Benjamin Disraeli's "obscure adventurer" in the novel *Sybil*: described as being "assiduous, discreet, and very civil" (Disraeli [1845] 1995: 67), Warren voyages to India from London as a gentleman's valet to become in a few years a "financial genius," making his profits through selling rice hoarded during the Indian famines. The important point to note about Warren is that it is his "civility" that initially attracts the attention of the colonial official through whose influence Warren's entry into the arena of colonial profits is facilitated. Warren's other qualities—his "prudence," sense of "adventure," "discretion," and "prescience"—therefore rely on his "civility," an intrinsic trait and a fundamental virtue that helps transform a valet into a successful gentleman. Disraeli's awareness of this change is only heightened by his inimitable irony, as reflected in the following passage: " A provident administration it seems had invested the public revenue in its benevolent purchase; the misery was so excessive that even pestilence was anticipated, when the great forestallers came to the rescue of the people over whose destinies they presided; and at the same time fed, and pocketed, millions" (ibid.). Capturing the link between the colonial government's administrative functioning, its role as the "savior" of colonial subjects in distress, and the financial fates of individuals such as Warren, Disraeli's language brings to the fore the undeniable complicity between private profit and state enterprise, between metropolitan aspiration and state-ordained privilege. Even in Jane Austen's *Sense and Sensibility*, civility and its representative social values, "good breeding and good nature" (Austen 1970: 43), are shown to be linked to the traffic in colonial wealth. However, Austen's representation of Colonel Brandon, the man who had once lived and worked in the East Indies, suggests that for the metropolitan subject the relationship between the domain of "sense" and the legitimacy of wealth acquired from the colonies could be comprehended simultaneously as something that was part of everyday common knowledge (like discussions about the "hot climate" and "mosquitoes") and as a scandal that had to be repressed. When Willoughby asks Elinor if her discussions with Colonel Brandon had "perhaps" included "observations" about "the existence of nabobs, gold mohrs, and palanquins," Elinor, intent on defending the colonel, responds by saying enigmatically: "I may venture to say that *his* observations have stretched farther than *your* candour" (ibid.: 44). Willoughby's reference to "nabobs and gold mohrs" is an indication that he suspects that behind Colonel Brandon's "good breeding" may lie a darker story about his colonial exploits, a story that might challenge the outward show of civility that is so attractive to a woman of sense like Elinor. The manner in which the sensible Elinor responds to Willoughby shows that her finely attuned irony, directed at Willoughby, is a means of deflecting the question by diffusing the moral boundaries between Willoughby's attempt at "candour" and the "truth" about Brandon's civility. In Austen's world of sense, then, the source of Brandon's wealth and stature has no direct bearing on his character; the fact that he "has been abroad; has read, and has a thinking mind" (ibid.: 43) is sufficient to make him worthy of Elinor's devotion.

In the colonial context, this everyday common understanding of civility, particularly the civility of imperial men, is often consolidated by defining and monitoring the social behavior of colonial subjects, such as the native *baboo* and the nautch girl. As I demonstrate in chapter 3, representations of the native nautch girl in the nineteenth century were often based on the knowledge that, despite her marginal status, she was also part of a modern order of aggressive individuality that propelled colonial Englishmen to seek their place in a competitive world. However, unlike her male counterpart, the nautch girl had to be constantly monitored, and her behavior controlled and curbed by the government exercised by white men. In short, her "difference" from these men had to be accounted for by using the normative standards of competitive individuality, and only by identifying and objectifying her in this manner was it possible to differentiate her from the authorized norms of gender and class behavior as defined in the metropolis. Similarly, this difference—between the uncertain civility of the educated Indian subject and the self-evident civility of the British male subject—leaves its traces in the nineteenth- and twentieth-century colonial discourse. At one point in *Kim*, Kipling's narrator makes his Bengali *baboo* confess in a self-deprecating manner that he was "unfortunately Asiatic, which is a serious detriment in some respects" (Kipling [1901] 1998: 272). At another moment, however, Kipling reveals the *baboo*'s deep resentment at being compelled to adopt the norms of metropolitan civility for the sake of surviving in the white man's world. As Kipling shows, the *baboo*'s mask of civility drops off only when he speaks under the influence of alcohol, and in this state he is described as becoming "thickly treasonous" and speaking "in terms of sweeping indecency of a Government which had forced upon him a white man's education and neglected to supply him with a white man's salary" (ibid.: 286). When confronted with his disloyalty to the British government, however, Kipling's *baboo* can only smirk, grin, and leer with "infinite cunning," until he is "beaten out of his defences, and forced to speak—truth" (ibid.: 287). It is significant that Kipling's narrator deliberately leaves out this "truth" that is forced out of the mouth of Hurree Babu. That "truth" could not be represented partly because it could not be made visible in the way in which his hybridity could be exposed, and partly because this "truth" would seriously jeopardize the entire narrative purview of *Kim*.[12]

The difference between Disraeli's John Warren and Kipling's Hurree Babu, explained in the preceding paragraphs, reveals the centrality of civility in the functioning of the colonial state and opens up a highly differentiated space for inquiring into the representation of different forms of social desire that gained ascendancy in the imperial age. The present study undertakes the task of telling their story by identifying and exploring the discourses of civility that were shaped by British colonialism between 1822 and 1922, a period in which the emergence of modern, industrial and colonial Britain coincided with the formation of what Michel Foucault has identified as a "disciplinary" society. My main objective in these explorations is to identify and interpret a diverse body of literary, historical, biographical, and political archives of this colonial period that demonstrates the manifold ways in which the discourses of civility served to consolidate and regulate a normative system of disciplinary practices. Imbricating race, gender, and class identities, these disciplinary practices played a significant role in constituting the body of the nation-state in Britain. What is worth underlining is that historically the disciplinary modalities of the nation-state involved a particular relationship with colonialism and with its economic, educational and administrative institutions, which emerges time and again in the narratives that I explore in this study.

A genealogy of civility: tracing its "normative" function

My study acquired its present unity at that critical hermeneutic juncture when, faced with the daunting task of responding to the heterogeneity of the archival material I had excavated, I was obliged to rethink the relationship between the British nation and Indian colony by identifying and analyzing the ways in which the deployment of civility as a normative category ran parallel to and often intersected with the manner in which race, gender, and class identities were constituted as specific *effects* of a disciplinary system. "Effects" signifies the productive and reproductive processes that accompany signifying practices, some of which may at times be incommensurable with other similar practices, but which are ultimately managed through the "normalizing" processes of civility. The first step in critical analysis therefore necessitated a move beyond a simple and stable binary schema of centers and margins. Like the dispersive power of a lens, the archival material seemed to point to a form of historicity whose understanding rested on a heterogeneity that demanded an attention to its multiple discursive forms and functions. In fact, the seemingly fixed colonial divide itself seemed to be a jagged one, produced out of these competing and at times contradictory signifying practices. It is here that Foucault's theories of archaeology and genealogy seemed most pertinent to my analysis.[13] Responding to this heterogeneity meant not only formulating a discernible unifying theoretical model to account for these signifying practices, but also, more importantly, tracing a genealogy where these disciplinary modalities resonated with historical specificity to reveal the fashioning of race, class, and gender identities in diverse relational terms. In other words, the function of the modern nation-state in consolidating these identities could not be understood without investigating this relationality as a differentiating dynamic, particularly within the framework of colonialism's formation as a disciplinary construct.

The ideas of "discipline" and "normativity" that I adopt in this study are resolutely Foucauldian notions.[14] Although the idea of discipline seems most obviously to be an expression of specific systems of domination—whether conceived as being explicitly coercive or hegemonic—my work points resolutely to what Deepak Kumar has called "an imbricated view of domination in its myriad forms" (Kumar 1997: 23). If, from a standard Saidian "orientalist" perspective, discipline was considered to have formed the very core from which knowledge was defined as a way to exercise control over the colonized, from a post-Althusserian Foucauldian perspective, discipline reveals itself as the effect produced out of specific discursive sites of colonialism where, as Rosemary Hennessy and Rajeswari Mohan have noted in another context, "ideological work is continuously produced out of diverse political and economic interests to disrupt or to re-secure existing social arrangements " (Hennessy and Mohan 1994: 466). This necessarily means that, before colonial authority could be exercised in any form, discipline had to shape the very metropolitan core from which power could be enunciated, and subsequently to invest that power with specific authority. In the colonial context, this ideological work is most clearly discernible in the ways in which social arrangements were both produced—and in turn produced—specific *norms*. Given the two-way productive nature of such "ideological work," singular notions of alterity or otherness again fail to offer an adequate historicist account of the role of civility in the colonial context. Too intransigent and fixed, "the rhetoric of otherness" creates a false division between the "self" and the "other," which, as Sara Suleri has observed, often becomes "a postmodern substitute for the very Orientalism" (Suleri 1992: 13) postcolonial scholars seek to challenge. In my study, I have attempted to subject notions of colonial alterity to an understanding of "disciplinarity" by investigating their formation within a relational field of normativity. The idea of "civility" is central to this critical enterprise since it offers a productive center for identifying and tracing the function of that normativity.

Given the role of the nation-state in regulating different forms of social desire through colonization, it is tempting to see this regulation as functioning through a mechanically causal logic and through an explicitly coercive system. This, however, is not the case: this is because, despite its imagined singularity, the metropolitan "core" of the nation-state that had been established through the dominant economic, social, and cultural institutions was constantly subject to the historical torque of colonialism. In fact, forced to operate under the influence of this torque, the nation-state assumed its metropolitan centrality primarily by defining itself out of an expanding field of social relations and economic possibilities that also included the constraints laid upon it by the ever-changing tasks of imperial governance—constraints emerging from, for example, the tasks of coordinating public policies on native education to those undertaken for the surveillance of prostitutes near army camps. This expanding field of social control therefore required a degree of standardization so that the unevenness created by the expansion is put to the service of producing identifiable objects across which new social relations could again be identified, measured, and regulated. What emerged in this process was the disciplinary face of the nation-state—the powerful field of normativity through which it registered its legitimacy and conducted its ideological work. Therefore, any account of this field of normativity has to take into account the specific sites and those limitations imposed on the nation-state by the unpredictable nature of imperial governance which often called for new negotiations in maintaining the power of its ruling ideologies. It is therefore important to emphasize that it is within this productive field of normativity—one that functioned within the shifting terrains of ideology—that the metropolitan bourgeois identity was constructed during the nineteenth and early twentieth centuries, allowing the metropolitan–colonial divide to be negotiated constantly through specific economic, political, and cultural practices.

An emblematic case in point of the normative operations of civility can be seen in the debates during the 1880s concerning the education of the children of Europeans stationed in India and those of Eurasians and poor Europeans whose increasing numbers had once led Viceroy Lord Lytton to refer to them as "a scandal to the English name and the English Government" ("Eurasians and Poor Europeans," *CR* 1881: 49).[15] Following hard on the heels of the education discussions during the era of Macaulay, these debates raised a new controversy that renewed the focus on those questions about civility, race, and national identity that had attended the former. On the one hand, the justification for setting up schools meant exclusively for European children rested on the rationale that, although Western education in India had brought together the "two divergent streams of Western and Eastern thought"—and in that process created the new enlightened and educated classes—it was felt that "it would be a mistake to prematurely mingle their turbid waters" ("Education Code," *CR* 1887: 383). Even in this metaphorical rhetoric, evoking fluid streams to talk about the relationship between the East and the West, the colonial divide remains in place. On the other hand, the "liberal" opposition to this position was enunciated in the following manner: it was argued that since the term "European" was essentially "undefinable [*sic*]" there was "no reason why those natives and such foreigners as Armenians, Greek, and Burmese, *who have cast off their national characteristics* and are distinctly European in their habits and modes of thought should not be thought worthy of a place in a European School" ("Bengal European Code," *CR* 1887: 112; emphasis added). Asserting that the racial and national category "European" was not immutable, G. S. Gasper, in an article in the *Calcutta Review* of 1887, claimed that "foreign nationals" such as Greeks, Africans, and the Chinese should be allowed to join these schools, since they "were bound together by a common Government, a common religion, a common language, and a common home" (ibid.: 113). It was argued that their origins—their "ancestral" home—had no bearing on their present status as colonial British subjects. In other words, since the civility of these subjects had been assured by their newly constructed shared common status vis-à-vis the master language and civil institutions in place, they were all to be considered to have been "naturalized."

A closer examination of this aspect of civility reveals that the political allegiances ensured by the idea of a common culture were produced by making "naturalization" a normative concept that was capable of calibrating difference while sublating it into another order where that difference could also be negated. The construction of this common criterion can be described as a process of normalization: by making the original term "European" indefinable, a new notion of diversity is posited and the shared interests of diverse citizenship delineated across an idea of civility based on citizenship—that is, participation in the institutions defined by common "government, language, and home." The translation of colonial power from what Louis Althusser calls a repressive state apparatus to a hegemonic ideological one ensured that true civility could be guaranteed only through participation in the institutions of the state, which in turn ensured that the state and its dominant ideologies of "government, language, and home" continued to serve as the central authority for regulating the lives of colonial subjects. Ironically, there is no sense here that education, which was perceived inevitably to lead to the shedding of one's "origins," also meant forfeiting a common inherited civility—or what the 1897 *Calcutta Review* called "the highly polished manners of the[ir] fathers" ("Indian Universities," *CR* 1897: 143). Furthermore, it is worth emphasizing that in this process of "naturalization" the sheer heterogeneity of racial identities of the different non-white communities can be said to have itself produced the norm through which one set of racial categories embodied in the term "national origin" was supplanted by another term, "naturalized citizenship". In other words, once this "naturalization" is given a specific reality and set in place, differences of national origin can be ordered on a new plane for consolidating racial difference.

The question of the *baboo*'s elusive civility can be posed by locating his place within this rhetoric of naturalization found in Gasper. Despite his self-confessed "Asiatic" origins, the *baboo* could not be fully assimilated into the imagined wholeness of a common "government, language, and home." Because his "native" origins marked him as an entity with an indelible racial identity, he remained the unaccommodated man in this "naturalized" world. In fact, the *baboo*'s language and his peculiar class status meant that he had to rely on that image of civility that could only serve as a "mask," an image that always rubbed up against—and therefore stood in difference to–the ideals of naturalized citizenship. It is therefore ironic that in *Kim* the very man–Hurree Babu–who is trained by colonial education to gather ethnographic details about obscure Indian communities (and who also dreams of presenting his research to the Royal Ethnographical Society in London) is himself transformed into an ethnographic object for the narrator.

The fate of the *baboo*, in many ways, was similar to that of the Eurasian: as opposed to those "naturalized" Greeks, Armenians, Burmese and educated Indians, Indian Eurasians of mixed blood were described as possessing "inordinate conceit, and excessive self-confidence, and want of civility" ("Eurasians and Poor Europeans," *CR* 1881: 40). Deliberating the fate of the often poor and destitute community of Eurasians, Edward Thomas, in the 1881 issue of the *Calcutta Review*, discussed their education and employment by recalling their history as racial subjects: "That has happened in India which has occurred in most lands and in all times, wherever and whenever two races at *different stages of civilization have met*. The races have mingled and an amalgam has been produced possessing qualities akin to both" (ibid.: 39). However, according to Thomas, given this racial "difference" that the Eurasians had inherited, there was no possibility for them to be "naturalized"; and, since they did not possess any identifiable and fixed "original" national identity, they could not be considered to have any civility that could be transformed and put to the service of the higher cause of the state. The Eurasian's education therefore presents a "problem" for Anglo-India. When we turn to Kipling's *Kim*, certain parallels between the fate of the Eurasian and that of Kim–"a poor white of the very poorest" (Kipling [1901] 1998: 49)–become obvious. Both suffer from poverty and lack of education. In fact, Kipling's description of Kim sitting astride the gun in front of the Lahore Museum "in defiance of municipal orders" (ibid.) is consonant with the stereotype of the uncivil and untutored poor Eurasian. However, Kim is not of mixed blood, although, like other destitute Europeans, he needs the tutelage of the colonial state. Raised by an untutored Indian woman addicted to opium, Kim has to be placed in the hands of colonial authorities so that he can realize his true potential as a white subject. While Eurasians of mixed blood were considered racially inferior to the "original," having inherited their "less desirable qualities from . . . their [native] mothers" and therefore lacking in the "healthy rivalry and fellowship with the hardy race of their fathers" ("Eurasians and Poor Europeans," *CR* 1881: 39), Kim's less desirable traits can be superseded through the intervention of the state.

In the words of Lord Lytton, the only profession for Eurasians, described as a "profitless, unmanageable community" ("Eurasians and Poor Europeans," *CR* 1881: 48), was "soldiering"–preparing "to submit themselves to all of the hardships and subordinate routine duties implied in a soldier's life in India" (ibid.: 53). "Subordination"–with its colonial implication–here signifies a class bias in addition to a racial one: it formed the key frame of Anglo-Indian perceptions of Eurasians which is evident in the accompanying rhetoric that routinely highlighted the poverty and marginality of this community. It is also worth noting that, once Kim's identity as a pure European is established, he has no problem negotiating the racial and class divide separating the "poor" European (which he is) from the natives (both poor and rich) and from upper-class Anglo-Indians, such as Colonel Creighton. He is endowed with a certain felicity of accessing the privileges endowed by all of these streams of his inherited legacy, including the attractive marginality and hybridity that allow him to mix easily with fellow Indians. As Michael Gorra notes, it is Kim's "Englishness [that] makes [him] at home throughout the subcontinent in a way that no Indian can be" (Gorra 1997: 639). Despite his marginal class status, Kim becomes a key player in Kipling's "Big Game" of military intelligence: it is the white "father's" legacy that enables him to discover and assert his unified identity and to reclaim his rightful place as an upwardly mobile classed citizen within the colonial order. In other words, the "knot" in the question about his own ethnic and religious hybridism that Kim had posed earlier in the novel—"What am I? Mussalman, Hindu, Jain, or Buddhist" (Kipling [1901] 1998: 191)—is ultimately resolved through this passage into the father's legacy marked by the route to "whiteness" from being a "poor white." Of course this passage to "whiteness" is not available to an Indian such as Hurree Babu: unlike Kim, the Bengali has no such access to a father's legacy, and even at the end of the novel, when he has proved his mettle as an effective player in the British government's efforts at political espionage, he can do no better than to confess to his fundamentally "oriental" nature (ibid.: 328).[16]

The question of civility that emerged in these nineteenth-century narratives and educational debates was coterminous with the normalizing effects achieved through the institutionalization of "culture" as advanced in the metropolis by Victorian England's most eminent seer Matthew Arnold.[17] In fact, "culture" offered a new site within the discourse of education in the colonies for producing race and class identities. By subjecting race and class differences to its own disciplinary function, culture allowed these differences to be negotiated at a level where civility came to be endowed with a special aura. First, a distinction had to be made between "men of culture" and "crammed men." Commenting on the true worth of candidates who competed for the civil service examinations, the *Calcutta Review* of 1874 quoted Arnold's words that such individuals could be considered only "crammed men, not formed men" ("Cram and Crammers," *CR* 1874: 293). As opposed to "crammed men," "formed men" were perceived to be individuals committed to the Arnoldian view that literary education was the foundation for "character," and that belief in the transcendent function of culture fostered, through literary and cultural appreciation, the ideals of metropolitan and gentlemanly civility. However, countering Arnold's attack on "crammers"—the colonial "philistines" who had adopted the raw pragmatism of the rising middle classes—the *Calcutta Review* states explicitly that although the "Gospel of sweetness and light—of Geist and anti-Philistinism—is beautiful and abstractedly true," one has to consider the fact "that England owes to Philistinism her place among the Nations" (ibid.).[18] Worth noting is the fact that this defense of middle-class pragmatism is articulated by appealing to English nationalist ideals exemplified by the rising concern about the fate of the English language in India. Since it is not voiced in direct opposition to the Arnoldian vision, this concern for the "fate" of the English language moves the question of "pragmatism" to another level—to the need to protect a "national" legacy. Even those who opposed the Arnoldian vision of the primacy of the study of Western literature claimed that the problem of education in India was not what many considered the "lofty problem of literature, morality, and social custom," but "the simple and elementary problem of plain English speech, the *correct and rational* speaking and writing of the English tongue itself" ("Race and Language," *CR* 1893: 294). Commanding the problem in this direction of "correctness" allowed colonial authorities to define a new measure of determining the efficacy of education in promoting the "rational" ideals of civility, as well as the virtues of "moral courage," "loyalty," "disinterestedness, and "public spirit"—ideals that formed the very core of the rhetoric deployed in the Arnoldian vision of culture, even while acknowledging that education had nothing to do with the "lofty problem" of "morality." This doubleness is evident in the impassioned appeal made by the writer in the *Calcutta Review*: "I am thinking of the English language . . . We owe a debt to the English language and to ourselves which we neglect at our peril" (ibid.: 307). What reanimated this concern with "correct" language can of course be explained by the growing anxiety in Anglo-India triggered by the rise of Indian nationalism, originally expressed in an 1861 issue of the *Calcutta Review* that "no education will give the Bengali the *true, disinterested loyalty,* which in times of peril . . . stirs the breast and nerves the arm of the Englishman . . . It will be in vain for us to expect anything more than the *loyalty of fear*" ("Review of *Considerations,*" *CR* 1861: 209; emphasis added). In other words, civility—in the metropolitan sense—was an impossible ideal in the colony irrespective of the manner in which liberal reformers imagined the role that Western education was to play in the governance of India. Although it was necessary to evoke civility, its foundation in liberal thinking about freedom was not reliable enough to build the structure of disinterested loyalty among Indians; in this sense, therefore, the term could exist only as a "default of a recognized name." For this reason, the civility of Kim and Hurree Babu had to be renarrated and tested in multiple ways in Kipling's novel.[19]

To the extent to which the line separating pure "despotism" from an "enlightened despotism" (based on liberal philosophy) had relied on this tenuous distinction between "disinterested loyalty" and "the loyalty of fear," it can also be said that it is this tenuousness that is "normalized" in the discourses about culture and civility. The effects of this process of normalization can be discerned most clearly in the ways in which race, class, and national ideas punctuated the education debates in the nineteenth century. Those who continued to defend their cause on the basis of the universalist and humanist argument that the goal of Western education was "to impart to India a share in this common heritage of human knowledge, to bestow on her children the freedom of that great intellectual commonwealth which is neither European nor Western, European, Asiatic, or American, but of the world and of the human race" ("A Contribution," *CR* 1892: 350), simultaneously argued that the appeal to this "intellectual commonwealth" could be utilized to manage the lives of Indian subjects, people who "by the laws of heredity" must "remain in leading-strings," since the "mind of young India is in leading strings" (ibid.: 354).

Civility is, therefore, not the mark of an immutable and stable status that mechanically reproduced pre-given divisions; instead it rested on the negotiation of the racial metropolitan–colonial divide that helped constitute the very thresholds where specific standards or norms could be produced in conjunction with the shifting structure of bourgeois social desire and ideals. In that respect, the construction of these thresholds proves to be a dynamic process. Civility can be considered to be the node from which a diverse set of questions can be posed about the normalizing practices of colonial society—whether they relate to economics, gender and sexuality, or the politics of class and race. My attempt to identify and comprehend in the colonial archive the links between these diverse practices, and to trace the accompanying dynamic relations set in place within the domain of a disciplinary nation-state, is therefore aimed at constructing a specific genealogy of civility. This is a "genealogy" that is to be understood in the Foucauldian sense as a history that highlights the heterogeneity and often incommensurable effects produced by the processes of normalization associated with the production of civility within both metropolitan and colonial domains. In fact, it is in the multiple lineaments of the colonial archive that this genealogy becomes visible. Following the impulse of this Foucauldian history—and pushing its questioning into the domain of colonial politics—I suggest that it is only by entering the density of the colonial archive that one can identify the discursively constituted meaning of the normativity underlying civility.[20] My effort is not simply to interpret the colonial archive by deploying Foucault's ideas in a unilateral manner, but rather to think through their logic and to modify them in order to avoid subsuming the heterogeneity of that archive under a single unifying umbrella. Although my work aims at reconstructing the thresholds of normativity, it avoids pursuing a single thematic strand perceived as moving seamlessly through time; instead, it attempts to identify their constitution in their heterogeneity—as written into bodies that are identified in many ways as desiring, laboring, and speaking, and as circumscribed by histories that are produced as official, unofficial, private, or public. Once conceptualized in this manner, the processes of objectifying and projecting difference—recurrent throughout the colonial period—begin to reveal a disciplinary function, one that highlights the processes of normalization produced through the struggle and contestation to define civility. An exploration of this history lies at the heart of my inquiry into colonial civility. In the following sections I will attempt to provide an overview of the five chapters, first by introducing the common concerns of chapters 1, 3, 4 and 5, and then by devoting a separate section to chapter 2 in order to propose an alternative theoretical model for comprehending the link between civility and the discourse of liberalism that Homi Bhabha has explored in his article "Sly Civility."

In chapter 1, I place Walter Scott's oriental tale *The Surgeon's Daughter* in the context of the rise of disciplinary society by showing how social desire in early nineteenth-century colonial Britain was regulated through the production of specific forms of "male civility." This social desire, triggered by colonial traffic, had been grounded on questions of property, wealth, accumulation, and social mobility for middle-class men within the domestic order, which are articulated time and again in many nineteenth-century narratives (such as John Trelawny's

Adventures of a Younger Son). I single out Scott's story about the half-Jewish Richard Middlemas's adventures in India to examine these questions because, in constructing its narrative of civility, the tale constantly tests its own projections of otherness, using them to mark the very boundaries of social desire legitimized by the colonial state for middle-class men. It is not surprising that other figures of alterity—for example, the female adventurer and the Indian despot—are introduced in this tale to locate and objectify the racialized Jew. The colonial context is crucial here: not only is the protagonist whose social desires have to be mapped half "Jewish," his entry into the "Indian" realm is also made to bring out the dark underside of that "Jewishness" that lies concealed under his "Scottish" identity. Constantly monitored, the protagonist's double identity is progressively subsumed under his immutable Jewishness (which the tale attributes to his maternal inheritance). Throughout the Indian sections of the narrative, Richard's social aspirations are simultaneously articulated *and* differentiated from the legitimate forms of "Anglo-Saxon" social behavior—generosity, free play, loyalty, and disinterestedness. Eventually, this renegade figure is eliminated from its narrative in order for the story to re-establish and consolidate the moral center defined by the norms characterizing "Anglo-Saxon" social behavior. My analysis of Walter Scott's tale therefore demonstrates how the normativity of middle-class aspirations was instituted through the process of establishing a stable racial mark at a time when these aspirations were themselves beginning to threaten the authority of the Whig establishment whose economic and social power had been derived from an already instituted colonial traffic. I bring to my analysis various early nineteenth-century materials that include the debates about the "Jewish question" in Britain, John Trelawny's popular adventure romance *Adventures of a Younger Son*, memoirs of cadets in the East India Company, and government and mercantile tracts, as well as popular poems and satires written about Jewish merchants and "stock jobbers." These archival materials enable me to situate Scott's tale within a discursive order that reaches out to the larger domain of metropolitan civil order and renders visible the density of this discursive production of civility as inflected by questions of national identity, class, and gender.

Chapter 3 is devoted to the exploration of the popular Anglo-Indian romances that appeared in the last three decades of the nineteenth century, a period when metropolitan British society witnessed key shifts in existing gender and class relations. I examine the normative processes of civility at work in this domain of nineteenth-century popular culture by focusing on the representations of a threatened masculinity in this popular fictional subgenre. In fact, the repeated assertions of male power enacted at different locales within the colony—at the frontiers of the empire, in the civil station, in the local princely court, and at the *zenana*—signify a crisis of civility, a crisis that had resulted both from the challenges to male authority posed by the rising power of the suffragist movement and from the global competition for power among the various imperial states in Europe. As these romances demonstrate, this crisis was resolved by harnessing the newly found political power of the "New Woman" and the sexual power of native nautch girls. I argue in the course of this chapter that this form of resolution necessitated the use of female figures who were seen to exist on the margins of middle-class morality and who had been traditionally positioned outside the exclusive domain of middle-class patriarchy. Historically, then, one can discern a link between the rise of the suffragist movement and its accompanying polemics in Britain, and the regulative practices of sexual surveillance enforced in the 1860s and 1870s to monitor the bodies of prostitutes in India. While the question of the "New Woman" provided new incitement for talking about the "nature" of womanhood in relation to her role in politics and in the domestic sphere, the practices of sexual surveillance in the colonies provided British men with special access to a hitherto unknown world. Adopted to protect British soldiers from the threat of sexually communicable diseases, sexual surveillance normalized the boundaries of the "interior" and the "exterior," allowing imperial men to consolidate the power of their own civility by transgressing the boundaries and, then, asserting their authority over them. Like the "New Woman," the Indian nautch girl in these romances provided the tantalizing figure of a powerful femininity, whose desires had to be read, comprehended, mastered, and then differentiated from the dominant forms of civility. The circuitry of identification and differentiation established in these popular Anglo-Indian romances between British men, British women, and Indian nautch girls, therefore, held together those forms of civility that worked to secure the power that many middle-class men felt were being eroded by the political and social developments of the period. Again following the methodology of "thick description" adopted in the other chapters, I situate these Anglo-Indian romances within a larger discursive setting that consists of popular Anglo-Indian poetry, imperial histories, and missionary and government tracts.

Chapter 4 is a re-examination of E. M. Forster's posthumously published "A Life to Come," a story set in the aboriginal tribal regions of central India. I place the story's homoerotic narrative of the religious conversion of a tribal leader by an English missionary within the discourse of civility that had been adopted and legitimized by the growing modern industrial state. Unlike the *baboo* or the Eurasian, the aboriginal could be designated racially only in terms of the discourse of the "primitive," a discourse that needed the requisite "difference" with European "modernity"—with all of its economic and cultural ramifications—in order to be representable. I argue that Forster's story of sexual encounter between the tribal leader and the English missionary not only discloses the ruse of that civil order of modernity, conceived as the promise of a Western civilization to ensure through industrialization a better "life to come" for the subject population, but also gestures towards a history of the violent transformation that accompanied the introduction of a disciplinary colonial political economy to parts of India inhabited by indigenous peoples. Taking into account the possible complicity between the projection of a homoerotic fantasy and the desire to create a historical critique of modernity, I locate Forster's narration of desire and its deferral in this story at two levels. First, in terms of the actual story, it reveals the degradation of the tribal subaltern at the hands of a missionary who, while asserting his European civility, continues to exploit the former's passion for him in order to secure the authority of the modern civil state. Second, when placed alongside the long history of colonial incursions into tribal territories that began as early as the mid-Victorian era, Forster's narrative also unveils how colonial civility—depicted as missionary conversion and as the promise of economic transformation—was produced in relation to a political economy that rested on the commodification of the tribal body and lands seized by British authorities. Throughout the story Forster emphasizes this commodifying process by deliberately appropriating the exotic image of the primitive and then gesturing towards the way in which the gradual conversion of tribal forests into the profit-making timber and mining industry paralleled the religious conversion of the pagan into the Christian. Nineteenth- and early twentieth-century colonial missionary and military accounts of the "pacification" of India's indigenous tribes provide a discursive context in this chapter for teasing out this remarkable allegory of colonial commodification.

At the heart of chapter 5 is an assessment of the normative function of civility in relation to body, sexuality, and labor in the colonies. The focus of this chapter is on two stories by Leonard Woolf set in colonial Ceylon and India, namely "A Tale Told by Moonlight" and "Pearls and Swine." Although Leonard Woolf is better known for his Bloomsbury connections, my chapter focuses on another phase of his career when he served as a civil bureaucrat for a period of seven years (1904–11) in the Senior Crown Colony of Ceylon, five years before he embarked on his political career in Britain. The two stories, written after he returned to England in 1911, are powerfully emblematic of the ways in which the authority of male civility functioned within the domain of sexuality and of colonial bureaucratic power. "A Tale Told by Moonlight" deals with the colonial fetishism that re-establishes the often occluded link between the civility of the metropolitan subject and the power of the metropolitan state. Presented as an oriental romance, Woolf's story about the relationship between the Englishman and the native woman opens up the seams of a colonial fantasy and reveals the underlying economic structure of exchange that made that fantasy part of those power relations that helped consolidate the legitimacy of the metropolitan state. Adopting a narrative where the language of fantasy constantly rubs up against its own history of power, Woolf exposes the limits of the order of civility by rendering visible the fetishistic relations established between the colonial state and the bodies that are put into its service. In "Pearls and Swine," Woolf shows how the order of civility adopted by the colonial bureaucratic system depended not only on producing a racial imaginary but also on establishing a form of "biopower" that would ensure the most efficient system of extraction of labor from colonial subjects.[21] The story's setting in the pearl fisheries of the Indian subcontinent therefore signifies a return to a specific site of extraction and accumulation central to a colonial political economy. As in "A Tale Told by Moonlight," the story enacts a particular crisis by placing the metropolitan individual against this site of extraction and accumulation, and by gradually tearing down his mask of civility and bureaucratic decorum. Following the method of historical inquiry adopted in the preceding chapters, I utilize several scientific and managerial tracts about the pearl industry produced in the first decades of the century as a way to place Woolf's rendition of the authority and limits of modern biopower within the domain of the modern state.

In both chapters 4 and 5 I pay special attention to narrative technique and to questions of language, representation, and narratorial authority. This is because, as part of the modernist initiative to experiment with narrative, the stories of E. M. Forster and Leonard Woolf share a persistent concern for these issues. However, this concern with experimentation as a way to renegotiate the relationship between language and representation has to be understood, more importantly, as an effort to engage in a historical critique of modernity and its civil order. It is important to bear in mind that the idea of modernity had been worked through the historical experience of colonialism. For Forster and Woolf, this process of working through meant recognizing that the master language had already been produced by the contestations of cultures and histories, ready to reassert its strange power by fracturing the very seams of metropolitan subjectivity. In some ways, this is not altogether surprising, since language was from the very outset right at the center of the discourse about civility that made the metropolitan subject the sovereign subject of knowledge. Wrenching language away from its purely representational frame allowed both Forster and Woolf to excavate those fugitive places where desire links up with civility and makes it part of the historical process of colonization through which the modern state is imagined. The ruse of that desire is revealed through the appearance of the colonial fetish, the object produced by the colonial man in order to realize his own desires. Punctuating the very movement of narrative, this fetish is embodied in specific figures: in Forster it is the tribal man, and in Woolf it appears as the body of the native prostitute and the bodies of the laboring pearl divers. While Forster works through the palimpsest of the past by excavating the violence behind missionary civility, Woolf adopts a Conradian technique to frame his colonial narratives.[22]

Foucault and Mill: disciplinarity and the liberal discourse of colonialism

A word is in order about a particular switch in focus that happens in chapter 2 in which I direct the reader's attention to the construction of the civility of the metropolitan liberal subject in John Stuart Mill's *Autobiography* by locating it within an explicitly Foucauldian context of "disciplinarity." The need to explicate this context more fully derives in part from my use, in the preceding sections, of Bhabha to discuss the political framework of the liberal discourse of civility. To critics who may ask why a project that initially arises from questions about "civility" requires this specific focus on Foucault's ideas about "governmentality," it is sufficient to remark that the answer to it is provided in the manner in which I begin this chapter and develop my arguments. By addressing the ways in which John Stuart Mill, who served as a colonial bureaucrat with the East India Company, conceived of the authority of the metropolitan liberal subject in relation to civility and its normalizing function in defining the idea of a "national character" with respect to India, I call attention to Foucault's specific theory about the normalizing function of liberalism itself. Central to the processes of self-fashioning described in Mill's *Autobiography* is a metropolitan *Bildungsroman* narrative that for me raises significant questions about civility that had co-emerged with the institutionalizing of liberal practices, namely that of education of the native in India.

The colonial *baboo* is therefore indispensable to the critical reassessment of Mill, along with the Bentham-inspired ideal utilitarian educational agenda that finds its place in Mill's *Autobiography* (one that is satirized, for example, by Charles Dickens in the 1854 novel *Hard Times*). The formal aspect of Mill's *Autobiography* is itself significant: the centrality of the metropolitan liberal self—represented by Mill's own voice—is constituted by the structuring of a self-referential narrative around an "absent center." This allows a dialectical relationship to be established between the self and the world of "others." It is significant that this dialectical relationship could work only by positing the idea of colonial "difference" or "lack"—one that Mill constructs and projects constantly on to the subjectivity of the colonial "other." The fact that the subjectivity of the colonized appears so consistently in his writings about colonialism alerts us to its importance in evaluating the *Autobiography*. While, in the *Autobiography*, that absence or lack is perceived as a source of self-empowerment—a site of self-fashioning from which the freedom gained from education could be enunciated—in the case of the colonial other that absence became the source of deficiency for the colonial subject, one that no amount of education could replenish. This is an idea that Mill often deployed to legitimize the influence of an "enlightened despotism" in governing a colonized people. Historically the power of metropolitan civility had been consolidated through the colonial government's specific engagement with education, and through the project of enlightenment that it promised to Indians. Thus, the issue of education and civility is intrinsic to the formation of the idea of "governance" in Mill—an idea that relates both to individual betterment and to the collective improvement of a people under government. The ideal of "self-representation"—signified as a collective ideal for the metropolis—is echoed in those liberal ideals of selfhood and individuality that are staple to Mill's entire philosophical *oeuvre*. My analysis of the *Autobiography* and Mill's colonial writings show that this ideal of "self-representation" was inseparable from the notion of "governance," whether it is understood as the action of self-regulation or as the regulation of colonial subjects and their aspirations.

Because of this doubleness, the idea of "governance" that I have attempt to trace in Mill provides a suitable site for placing it alongside the ideas of "governmentality" and "disciplinarity" as advanced by Foucault in works such as *Discipline and Punish* and in the essays "The Birth of Biopolitics" and "Governmentality." Bhabha seems to have side-stepped the idea of governmentality in his analysis of civility, which, from a Foucauldian perspective, appears to have played a powerful role in mediating the role of the metropolitan self in constructing the imagined wholeness of the "modern" nation. Furthermore, as noted earlier, Bhabha fails to take a work such as Mill's *Autobiography* into consideration in order fully to tease out the political ramifications of liberal selfhood in constructing and justifying the colonial mode of government. In the following pages I will offer an extended explanation of Foucault's model in order better to locate my own project on colonial civility and to justify why we need to take that model into account to comprehend its jagged genealogies.

Foucault's theorization of disciplinary society extends from *Discipline and Punish* to his essays and interviews on "power/knowledge," finding its clearest and most succinct expression in the brief description of a course he offered entitled "The Birth of Biopolitics." The specific ideas advanced in these works provide a general framework for my own understanding of two significant issues highlighted in my analysis of Mill: first, Foucault's conceptualization of power/knowledge allows us to approach the question of how the "structures of recognition" helped constitute a "subjectivity" that became such a powerful arbitrator of knowledge (Owen 1994: 157); second, Foucault's ideas about "governmentality" offer a suitable site for theorizing the relationship between these structures of recognition and the larger disciplinary mechanisms through which the colonial state exercised its specific administrative power.[23] In *Discipline and Punish*, Foucault explains the ways in which disciplinary mechanisms originated in the modern state. These mechanisms, he suggests, were not simply imposed from a central "sovereign" authority on to the body politic but penetrated and permeated the very forms that constituted modern identity and citizenship as defined by the liberal state and civil society. In "The Birth of Biopolitics," he advances a new understanding of these mechanisms by linking them with the formation of "liberalism." He clarifies that he is concerned not with "'liberalism' . . . as a theory of ideology—and even less, certainly, as a way for 'society' to 'represent' itself," but "rather, as a practice, which is to say, as a 'way of doing things' oriented towards objectives and regulating itself by means of sustained reflection" (Foucault 1997: 73–4). This reflective function lies at the heart of "discipline," providing the key to comprehending the multiple relationships of power forged within the modern liberal imaginary as it emerges in relationship with the colonial enterprise and its civilizing mission.[24] However, the latter point is something that Foucault himself does not take into account or elaborate in any significant manner.

My work shows that, in identifying itself as a "liberal" society, Britain entered a domain that entailed what Foucault calls the "rationalization" of the "exercise of government." The term "government" is crucial here: as Foucault clarifies, "government" is to be understood not as the "institution of government, but the activity that consists in governing human behavior in the framework of, and by means of, state institutions." He insists that "government" indicates not merely the presence of the institutions of government, but also an "effect" produced through specific practices. That "effect" is most noticeable during the period when liberalism "breaks with that 'reason of state' that had sought to justify state power by justifying a growing governmentality." This break from an earlier all-encompassing authoritarian power is significant, because, according to Foucault, it allowed the liberal state to "maximize the effects of the state institutions while diminishing, as far as possible, its costs" (Foucault 1997: 74), starting with the basic assumption that government *could not be its own end* since it acted on behalf of "society" and a collectivity called the "people," both of which were in a sense external to it.

The "self-reflexive" rationalization evident here, Foucault argues, provides a significant condition of possibility for the production of the very idea of "society" that then simultaneously becomes the "object" of governance, or, to put it in a slightly different manner, establishes the "object" where the effects of governance are registered. Foucault claims that it is this rationale that allows society to be perceived as a collectivity, a collectivity that gives government its authority to govern based on the effects of governance it is capable of registering. In fact, it is on behalf of this collectivity ("society") "that one will try to determine why there has to be a government, to what extent it can be done without, and in which cases it is needless or harmful for it to intervene." Foucault further reasons that behind such a conceptualization of society is the notion of the "technology of government," which is founded on the postulate that government is "already 'too much,' 'in excess'—or at least that it is added on as a supplement which can be and must be questioned as to its necessity and usefulness." Thus, the "sustained reflection" takes on the form of a "self-critique" within liberalism, and it is this "self-critique" that becomes the site of a regulative system, constituting "the reason for its polymorphism and its recurrences." Indeed, it is liberalism's "polymorphism" that serves as the basis of its own systemic surveillance and of its constantly negotiable system of checks and balances, providing the rationale for seeing itself as "a tool for criticizing the reality" (this "reality," it is important to note, is the "reality effect" of governmentality). It becomes clear from this simultaneous rationalizing and regulating process built within liberalism that dissenting positions are from time to time leveled against "previous governmentality," or on "current governmentality" that requires reform, or on a governmentality that has to be countered and limited. Therefore, Foucault contends that "we will be able to find liberalism, in different and simultaneous forms, as a regulative scheme of governmental practice and as the theme of a sometimes-radical opposition" (Foucault 1997: 75). Regulation, in this sense, then depends on the co-presence of the controlling *as well as* oppositional practices; in fact, oppositional practices helped create the need for specific tactics of management that formed the basic logic of liberalism. For example, the ceaseless debates about "free trade" and "monopoly" conducted during the nineteenth century were simultaneous with liberalism's own rationalizing and regulating agendas. Before I proceed to articulate the points that arise from Foucault's conceptualization of the liberal notion of "governmentality," I would like to clarify in advance the chief ideas about the nation-state as utilized in the context of the present discussion.

The modern idea of the state rests on the authority conceived as being derived from a "people," presupposing what Lloyd and Thomas have called a "principle of organization in which people and their institutions are expressed in and through the state" (Lloyd and Thomas 1998: 3). The relationship of power between the "sovereign" and people that had characterized the "pre-modern" state is replaced in the modern era by a new relationship of representation between the state and a people designated as a "national" people. According to Foucault, this "expressive" ideal allowed "national" people to be defined as "population"—a new object targeted for analysis and control through specific practices involving health, education, sexuality, and the monitoring of labor, among others. Immanuel Wallerstein has shown that this notion "of peoplehood is a major institutional construct of historical capitalism" (Balibar and Wallerstein 1991: 84), setting into motion what he calls the "manipulable 'rational' processes of the present" (ibid.: 78). Wallerstein emphasizes primarily the temporal aspect of this rationality, arguing that the category of the "people" is defined in accordance with a "temporal dimension of pastness" that is utilized "in the socialization of individuals, in the maintenance of group solidarity, in the establishment of or challenge to social legitimization" (ibid.). In the colonial context, this sense of temporality was linked to the nation-state's phantasmatic "origin" as well as to the idea of a progressive history that was seen to culminate providentially in the colonial enterprise. De-emphasizing the temporal dimension as a reference point in the understanding of the construction of nationality, Foucault sees the processes of socialization and social legitimation as being caught up and implicated in the space of a collectivity called "population." As population, the people become the highly differential object of the state, providing the latter with a whole range of rationales for acting or intervening on its behalf. Therefore, as Joseph Rouse notes, the formation of the modern disciplinary state points to a form of state power that is "far more complex and subtle than the massive and spectacular displays of force" (Rouse 1994: 95) that had characterized the earlier forms of sovereignty.

I wish to return to Foucault's conceptualization of the liberal notion of "govern-mentality" by taking these ideas into account.[25] It is clear that several significant points arise from Foucault's ideas. First, based as it is on a government–society "macro" binary, Foucault's theory about governmentality ignores the site of the colony, and therefore fails to consider how the "supplementarity" of government can be explained in relation to the third term, the "colony." Is it possible to theorize this supplementarity outside the binary proposed by Foucault in order to account for the "disciplinary" nature of liberalism functioning in the era of colonialism? Second, since Foucault asserts that "any rationalization of the exercise of govern-ment aims at maximizing its effects while diminishing, as far as possible, its costs," it might be worthwhile to ponder the question of "costs" in the colonial context, especially since the "political and economic" (Foucault 1997: 74) sense of "costs" bears a global significance that exceeds the narrow domestic sphere of nineteenth-century Britain. For example, the idea of the "market," which Foucault claims provided for liberalism a "locus of privileged experience where one can identify the effects of excessive government" (ibid.: 76), had to include the political and economic costs involved in governing and educating a colony such as India while managing a domestic finance and consolidating those internal ideas about sovereignty and nationality whose fate seemed to depend increasingly on the growing exigencies of colonial developments. David Scott rightly points out:

> It seems to me that the *kind* of investigation Foucault undertakes (in however sketchy and incomplete a manner, and with however narrow a geographical focus) encourages those of us interested in the problem of the specific effects of colonialism on the forms of life of the colonized to historicize European rule in a way that brings into focus the political rationalities in relation to which this rule was effected.
>
> (Scott 1995: 204)

In short, the economy of maximization/minimization effected within metropolitan liberalism needs to be reconceived by taking into account the context of colonial rule.

It is also important to note that the formation of a metropolitan liberal order in Britain had been coterminous with what Gayatri Spivak has called the "scandal of a misshapen and monstrous state," represented by the colonial government which, "although by definition chartered by the state of Britain, burst the boundaries of the metropolitan or mother-state" (Spivak 1999: 220). This bursting of boundaries, I claim, has to be read in conjunction with Foucault's idea of the "excess" attributed to "government," which he claims provided the necessary condition for early nineteenth-century liberalism to rationalize its own disciplinary system. In fact, to push this question in another direction, one could claim that the order of domestic governmentality also existed in a relation of "excess" to both colonial society and the colonial government in India, and therefore the latter (colonial government) had to be constituted in a manner that provided the metropolitan government with the authority to "govern." In the colonial context, then, the "excess" that Foucault theorized as being harnessed through the forms of "regulative scheme of governmental practice" (Foucault 1997: 75) was itself based on the construction of society/government around a discourse of "difference." The simultaneous projection of the excess as both interior and exterior to governmentality is enabled by this discourse; in fact, the reality of colonial markets could be constructed as being intrinsic to the economic status of the British nation only when those markets are identified as lying beyond the pale of the metropolitan order. This is also the case with governance: as evident in John Stuart Mill's thinking about Indian governance, it is India's difference that becomes the basis for the normalizing disciplinary power of the liberal government that is exercised both within the domestic order and on the colony by applying the differentiating principle of "self-representation." As emphasized earlier, this notion of "self-representation" is negotiated in the *Autobiography* by constructing a civility that depends for its existence on liberal institutions, particularly those relating to "culture" and "language," as exemplified by Mill's evocation of Wordsworth.

In Mill's theory of liberty, this differentiating principle finds its own rationale in the "auto-critique" implicit in nineteenth-century liberal ideology of government, a rationale that had been anchored in the philosophical notion of a universal "human fallibility." By asserting that liberty's foundation within the metropolitan order lay in the acknowledgment of the universality of human finiteness and fallibility, British disciplinary society utilized such thinking to regulate and normalize the power of its own (liberal) governmentality. However, such an embedded relationship between acknowledging the limits of a system while regulating its normalizing practices appears to have been registered quite differently on the colonial terrain, especially when it came to providing a specific definition to "colonial society" (as opposed to domestic society). Since, on the domestic front, governmental practices had been rationalized in terms of a reason of "society" or a "national people," that relationship, in the colonial context, had to be instituted around *differences* imputed to the incommensurability of human natures and histories found in the metropolitan space and in the colony. Depending on the exigencies of colonial practice, the "reason" of colonial society had to be fashioned in specific ways that would rely on, and also be capable of, producing colonial difference, irrespective of whether this difference is posited as an *a priori* or *a posteriori* principle. It is in this sense that normativity can be seen as being produced within a threshold where differences are deployed in a disciplinary manner. In other words, the purpose of this deployment of difference is to objectify the colonial space and to utilize that objectification to provide the rationale for metropolitan power. If a colonial bureaucrat such as John Stuart Mill saw the "reason" of a representative government as lying at the heart of British national "character" (which he also perceived as something that was shaped by its own national history), colonial Indian "society," to him, presented a very different picture to what one encountered in Britain. In the colonial context, then, the principle of sanctioned authority of governmentality had to be located *elsewhere* in order to function as normalized disciplinary authority. This *elsewhere*–constituted as *a priori* or *a posteriori* difference–was necessary for liberalism in order to consolidate its normalizing practices. It is clear, moreover, that the asymmetry lying at the center of this "elsewhere" is a productive one, since it also defined a variety of the marginal sites where the norms of civility could be produced.

It can be argued that this asymmetry is also a manifestation of liberalism's own "polymorphousness," one deployed to rationalize/constitute governmentality. Again, in the colonial context, this "polymorphousness" serves to rationalize and manage the practical tasks entrusted upon colonial institutions by being defined along the lines of a "colonial divide" that is both produced through a diverse range of activities and deployed to standardize norms. Of course, as I demonstrate in the chapter on Mill, many liberals challenged this divide, but they did so by assuming the normative function of that divide, and then rationalizing or providing an alternative historical understanding of it in order to counter the prevailing arguments for the status quo. I argue in the chapter that, despite the contestations about the validity of specific forms of colonial governmental authority and prac-tice, this divide served as a normative site by weaving itself into the triangulated structure of state–nation–colony. This divide spurred the institution and growth of governmental practices that depended on, as much as they produced, an array of differences that could be deployed on the colonial terrain. Often objectified in the bodies of subjects identified along class, gender, and racial lines, their identities as "national" or "colonial" produced those differences that became the ground for further regulating the objectives of a disciplinary society. As David Scott has argued so persuasively, "colonial governmentality" reflects the objectives of disciplinary society since it is based on a "rationality" that produces "not so much extractive-effects on colonial bodies as governing-effects on colonial conduct" (Scott 1995: 204). This is again seen most clearly in the education debates of the nineteenth century.

As noted earlier, in a disciplinary society, civility's specific function as a norm did not lie in repeating and reinforcing the already constituted demarcations between the legitimate and the illegitimate, or the "normal" and the "excessive," but rather functioned as something that "by means of which and *through which* society, when it becomes a disciplinary society, communicate[d] *with itself*" (Ewald 170–1; emphasis added). Such "self-communication," as Foucault reminds us, was vital in the age of liberalism, since disciplines were seen to "create" society, not establish partitions by assuming pre-given structures. Foucault's reasoning suggests that, in this paradoxical relationship, British society had to be simultaneously *preconceived* as a "people" in order to define the power and legitimacy of "government" and seen to be produced by the latter's disciplinary function. Thus, the notion of "population" helped standardize the notion of "people," thereby creating a normative function which Foucault's commentator François Ewald has argued *connected* the different "disciplinary institutions of production, with knowledge (*savoir*), wealth and finance and ma[de] them interdisciplinary, homogenizing social space even if it [did] not unify it" (ibid.: 171). Within the colonial context, this form of standardization without unification had to take into account the differences imputed to the colony and its collectivity—the "subject races."

For Partha Chatterjee, "race" is the defining signifier across which the "rule of colonial difference" (Chatterjee 1993: 19) is deployed, a difference by which the colonized is represented. If the norms of civility in Britain can be described as having come into existence by effecting those identifiable measures by which the common measure was produced, and by which different thresholds were identified, my inquiry seeks to ask how this "common measure" was produced at the triangulated site of society–government–colony. Furthermore, if the notion of the "government" had been produced as a "supplement" (Foucault 1997: 75) to domestic society, that supplementarity also functioned *in relation to* the colony, the site that occupied the unstable ground between "society" and "non-society," as defined by metropolitan liberal standards. Once we take this into consideration, we can begin to identify the "threshold" of those sites utilized for specifying the productive dynamics of the norms of a colonial civility. If, as Foucault indicates, the social spaces are homogenized through discipline, this homogenizing (and not unifying) dynamic performed a specific function within the realm of colonial difference, and is registered in multiple forms every time civil authority is invoked.

As indicated earlier in the section on the Bengali *baboo*, this process of homogenization enabled the objectification and containment of colonial Indian society by helping to shape varying forms of surveillance within both the domestic and the colonial order. Surveillance constituted the very boundaries of a normalizing disciplinary structure. As I show in chapter 1, its ubiquity as a disciplinary order begins to establish itself in the nineteenth century by helping provide a powerful tool to shape notions of race within Britain itself. The forms of surveillance proliferate throughout the nineteenth century and the early decades of the twentieth century, and, as I discuss in the Conclusion, the historicity of civility is also intimately tied to the creation of new sites *within* the metropolis that open up supplementary boundaries of conduct over which civility could perform its work of normalization. Therefore, in identifying the discourses of "civility" within these forms of surveillance, I am also attempting to ascertain the location and form of those bodies that become the objects for the institution of civil normativity—those of the "Jew," the mysterious Indian nautch girl, the tribal subaltern, the laboring pearl diver, or the English drawing room (as discussed in my analysis of D. H. Lawrence's *Women in Love*).

The "art of reflective insolence"

Foucault characterized the genealogical project as an "art of reflective insolence." It is therefore not surprising that a study of "civility" should be undertaken in a spirit that challenges as well as historicizes its domain of authority. The shift that I have been attempting to mark—from a binary Foucauldian model implicit in Foucault's critique of liberal governmentality to a triangulated model of society—government—colony—is to be understood primarily as a task of rehistoricization, already attempted by a significant number of studies on colonial discourse in the Indian subcontinent, particularly those by Sara Suleri, Gauri Vishwanathan, Jenny Sharpe, Inderpal Grewal, Antoinette Burton, and, more recently, Parama Roy and Nancy Paxton. All of these studies have, to an extent, been influenced by Edward Said's pathbreaking study of "orientalism," although each of them extends or revises Said's model in significant ways.[26] Despite some critics' objections to Said's conceptualization of the dynamics through which the "Orient" comes into being as an object of knowledge, the critical impulse that informs Said's work opens up a vast array of questions about the relationships of power implicit in disciplinary systems. Gayatri Spivak's Marxist-deconstructive analysis of the postcolonial subaltern experience in relation to the culture of imperialism also enables a new perspective on the function of civility within colonialism.[27]

My focus on clarifying the normative discourses of civility covers a wide range of historical archive—from colonial romances to narratives of cadetship in the East India Company, from imperial biographies to stories about India's aboriginal tribes and pearl fisheries. In tracing a genealogy of civility through the assessment of these colonial archives, produced and circulated in the print culture of the nineteenth and early twentieth centuries, I do not attempt to provide an "epochal" study, one that charts what Michael Donnelly has called the "long term" evolutionary progress of the principles of civility (Donnelly 1991: 200). My genealogical approach forces attention not on the grand continuity of "principles" and "ideas," but on particular discursive formations—or "regimes"—by investigating how discrete elements of the normativity behind the notion of civility come together at specific points in the period between 1822 and 1922.[28] Drawing on a wide variety of material that includes political pamphlets, scientific and administrative manuals, parliamentary reports, suffragist tracts, missionary accounts, oriental tales, popular Anglo-Indian romances, fictional autobiographies of civil servants, colonial poetry and fiction, and travel narratives, I track the discourses of civility by bringing attention to the sites and forms of normativity on and through which colonial Britain established its identity as a colonial disciplinary society, and by marking out the dynamic and often contestatory relationships between society—government—colony through which the normative measures were negotiated. I have therefore followed Gayatri Spivak in blurring the distinction between the "archive" and "literature" by recognizing the ways in which they both produce the "'effects of the real'" through which the colonizer constructs himself as he constructs the colony" (Spivak 1999: 203).

A history of the discursive organization of "civility"—which forms the thematic core of this book—is visible in the jagged continuum that this study attempts to map. The period under consideration includes most of the nineteenth century and the early twentieth century, ending with the era of World War I. Although the chapters are ordered in a chronological sequence, while developing the arguments in this book I have not resorted to a linear account, but have instead favored an approach that allowed me to traverse forwards and backwards, picking up a thread here, dropping a stitch there, while following the main theme. Since the chapters do not assume any progressive order that might be seen to unfold through time, I make no attempt to develop a macro-historical perspective in this book. My effort, therefore, is not simply to "interpret" the colonial archive by deploying Foucault's concepts in a unilateral manner, but rather to think through their logic and to modify them in order to avoid subsuming the heterogeneity of the archive under one unchanging and overarching conceptual umbrella. Also necessary to this reading is a sustained attention to "minor" non-canonical texts, which in my view constitute the necessary archive for this kind of study and which are often over-looked in studies of canonical literature. Being necessarily interdisciplinary, my work employs the insights gained from current literary and cultural criticism and a theoretically informed discourse analysis aimed at situating these archives within the boundaries of specific discursive regularities and irregularities. Consequently, I have not been faithful to any one particular paradigm of critical analysis. I have, however, paid careful attention to the modulating influence of specific histories in shaping and animating these discursive forms, influenced in part by Michel Foucault's work. In so doing, I have also been aware that interdisciplinary work necessarily depends on taking a risk, a risk that comes from what Foucault has called the "art of reflective insolence," and which Parama Roy has called the peril "of never being erudite enough to satisfy the demands of all disciplines that one is using, addressing, and inhabiting" (Roy 1998: 15). Ensuring historical detail as I traverse disciplinary formations, I hope to let my "uncivil" and risky undertaking yield a new understanding of the politics of culture and provide a new perspective on the ways in which we continue to function within, and outside, the normalizing power of "civility" in our own critical discourses.

1 Colonial civility and the regulation of social desire

Walter Scott introduces his little-known Oriental tale *The Surgeon's Daughter* with a short metanarrative in which the fictional author, Mr. Croftangry, while expressing his fears that the Highland theme had lost its romantic appeal for his readers, is advised by his friend and aristocratic patron, Mr. Fairscribe, to do "with your Muse of Fiction, as you call her, as many an honest man does with his own sons in flesh and blood . . . Send her to India" (Scott [1827] 2000: 155).[1] For the desperate Mr. Croftangry, the only way of ensuring the survival of his own literary career in this situation was to "light upon any topic to *supply the place of* the Highlands" (ibid.: 154; emphasis added). Mr. Fairscribe's advice to the author is significant not only because it points to the emerging popularity of the empire as a topic of fiction, but also because the analogy embedded in it is symptomatic of the enmeshing of different strands of social behavior triggered by the economic and cultural politics of early nineteenth-century British colonialism in India. More specifically, within this complex whole is visible the constitutive role of metro-politan civility in establishing and legitimizing the power of the colonial state. The analogy also reflects the dominant belief of the times that Britain's colonies provided the most reliable avenue for profit, investment, and accumulation of capital perceived to be depleting in the domestic sphere, and that the continuity of the nation's patriarchal social order depended on exploiting that potential.[2] This is most clearly visible in the two metanarratorial frames, where a web of inter-connecting links is established between "literary" authorship, the rights and privileges of British Whig patriarchy, and the growing markets for new goods made possible through the colonial traffic. These links also point to the fact that colonialism gained its power and coherence as a social, political, and economic enterprise by organizing itself around specific norms of male civility that had been fashioned according to the logic of an emerging disciplinary nation. That logic, as this chapter attempts to demonstrate, was aimed at both inspiring and restraining those social desires of Britons that were historically linked to nation's rise as a colonial state. It required the production of a racialized discourse of cultural otherness as a way to imagine new definitions of citizenship, inheritance, and nationality, and as a way to manage the social desires triggered by them.

By opening up new possibilities for the market to reshape and regulate the needs of the people, the colonial enterprise created a new traffic between the nation and its colonies. It also helped replace traditional modes of acquiring property in a nation that continued to be propelled by new desires for wealth and social mobility. Faced with the declining interest in conventional Highland adventures, the narrator of *The Surgeon's Daughter* seeks out the exotic Orient to satisfy the demands of his readers. Unlike the adventure romances set in the Highlands novels, the Orient provided a new imaginative space for Scott to test the limits of the expanding field of social desire. As indicated earlier, this was necessary for realizing not only the demands of a post-mercantile ideology of property, but also the modern values of middle-class social mobility that had been spurred on by colonialism. The projection of this Oriental fantasy was, therefore, inextricably linked to its disciplinary role: the limits of social desire could only be defined in so far as those limits produced the "deviant" forms of civility associated with that desire. In short, the idea of deviancy helped establish a discourse of normativity across which notions of class, gender, and racial identity were made available for public scrutiny. This is most clearly brought out in Scott's Oriental tale, which is marked by the co-presence of two contrary impulses—one celebrating the social and material desires of an emerging colonial nation, and the other distancing itself from the undesirable aspects of that desire and projecting them on the "other" within the British social order—the Jew.[3] The semantic uncertainty of the word "civility" that I noted in the Introduction is linked to the co-presence of these impulses. Throughout the narrative Scott regulates these contrary impulses by simultaneously creating and maintaining the boundaries between the "legitimate" and the "illegitimate," and utilizing their discursive flexibility to define and approve the centrality of those civil norms produced by the colonial traffic. This allows the projected duality in British social desire to be differentiated, renegotiated, and, eventually, resolved in ways that are later visible in the figure of the *baboo*. Unlike the *baboo*, however, Scott's renegade protagonist Richard Middlemas serves as the internal "other" who is deployed within a larger economy of alterity in order to generate a "new," supposedly more stable figure—the racialized Jew. This racialized "other" therefore plays a key role in the production of legitimate civil identity in the colonial era, a process that is discernible in other works of the period, most notably in colonial adventure tales, in narratives about company cadets, and in civil and parliamentary discourses. My chapter focuses on some of the psycho-rhetorical mechanisms that can be said to have regulated the narrative of deviancy in Scott's Oriental tale as a way to link this deviancy to the larger discursive circuitry through which notions of civility entered, and were defined by, the social and pathological imagination of the early nineteenth century.

The invention of Whig "aristocracy" and British anti-Semitism

The Surgeon's Daughter has often been dismissed as an inherently flawed work.[4] John Lauber (1966), in explaining Scott's choice of foreign settings in many of his works, contends that it merely indicates the author's desperate attempts to revive his declining popularity among the reading audience. Albert Canning, writing in 1910, however, assessed the tale in more positive terms, contending that Scott's historical imagination was faithful to the events that had led to the establishment of British rule in India, adding that the author had "avowedly read India's history attentively, following British conquests therein with natural pride and gratification" (Canning 1910: 211). Canning also praised "Scott's genius" for showing "what a splendid romance about India he could have given to the world had he ever visited that interesting and extraordinary country" (ibid.: 269). As this present chapter makes clear, this "splendid romance about India" had little to do with historical veracity; instead, it fulfilled a more significant function—that of renegotiating and resolving the contradictory impulses that existed within Britain's own national imaginary in the early decades of the nineteenth century. A specific history of class relations, particularly one that had helped define and consolidate Whig identity, underlies this "historical" romance. On the one hand, Whigs believed that the forces of the market alone justified the expanding capability for economic speculation in the colonies, since a significant amount of their own wealth had originally been generated through mercantile enterprise; on the other hand, however, by creating new wealth among the rising middle classes, these forces threatened the very social structures that had sustained Whig dominance in the economic and cultural politics of the day. Consequently, they were impelled to identify with an aristocratic past, inventing a new genealogy as a way to consolidate their dominance as a class of leaders and visionaries, instead of mere economic pragmatists.

Throughout the late eighteenth century and well into the first two decades of the nineteenth, colonial mercenaries, merchants, and "nabobs," including petty social climbers from the countryside and "foreigners"—primarily Jewish traders— had steadily accumulated power and privilege through their involvement with colonial enterprises, profiting from the vast resources available for trade and early industrial initiatives. The wealth of the established Whig aristocracy had itself been generated to a large extent through such colonial traffic. In fact, its capital had been produced through the mercantile economic initiatives of "free trade," from which it had derived its current wealth and status. As that capital accumulated and flowed into a growing industrial economy, Whigs found themselves in the company of the ruling manufacturing classes whose values of pragmatism and competitiveness seemed to threaten their power. Maaja Stewart has noted that

> in spite of its connection with the landed gentry in the flow of money and blood, mercantile experience would ultimately work against the old feudal estate ideology and in the next century [nineteenth century] would help bring about a shift of the balance of power from the landed gentry and aristocracy to the commercial, industrial, and professional classes.
>
> (Stewart 1993: 14)

It is against these challenges to traditional class identity that Scott fashioned his own aristocratic world-view, returning to a simpler, and hierarchized, version of the social world in which this aristocracy maintained its central status.

This return to an aristocratic world-view had significant repercussions. Scott's interest in imperial narratives, as evidenced in *The Talisman*, can be explained as an attempt to reassert the primacy of an aristocratic heroic order. The turn to the Eastern frontier in these imperial narratives served to dramatize the conflict between rival empires, which was a strategy meant to uphold the providential supremacy of the military classes who had provided the leadership in such struggles. As Ian Duncan has observed, the "complicated relation" existing in Scott's works between "regional representation and a series of metropolitan and imperial horizons" (Duncan 1993: 371) signifies a specific ideological response to the dramatic shifts in class relations in the social order of the late eighteenth and early nineteenth century. The link between the regional and the imperial therefore highlights the struggle for political and economic leadership in a nation faced with the reality of shifting class alliances. Furthermore, the historian J. G. A. Pocock has noted that, although approving of commerce and entrepreneurial leadership of the new industrial classes, key Whigs of the period, most notably Edmund Burke, asserted that the management of such commerce should rest in "aristocratic hands" (Pocock 1985: 281). Raised as the son of a middle-class Edinburgh lawyer, Walter Scott later established his own literary reputation by celebrating the nationalist aristocratic ideals of "passion, gallantry, and death" (Green 1979: 104) found in the Waverley novels. As David Brown has observed, Scott's own political opinions began to harden around this period of transitions—a time that also witnessed the rise of the industrial working class in Britain. Scott's return to the heroic pastoral therefore reflects a wish to hold on to the "old way of life," ensuring a stability in ideological positioning in face of those material changes that threatened the existing social order.

Even the value of "literature"—as a category believed to transcend the changing exigencies of the social world—came under the influence of this new rationale for innovation and manufacture that had fueled social mobility among the various classes. In *Fictions of State*, Patrick Brantlinger has suggested that, during the nineteenth century, the status of literary production had been jeopardized by the pragmatic rationales for industry and manufacture, making their claim to transcendence "dubious." Brantlinger asserts: "The self-contempt that pervades this apology of Scott's for his too-rapid but nonetheless lucrative novel writing exemplifies the ressentiment" (Brantlinger 1996: 153) which becomes pervasive in later nineteenth-century literature. Scott's own narrator, Mr. Croftangry, seems to be caught up in this traffic—between the literary and the financially viable—as he approaches his mentor, Mr. Fairscribe, for a new fictional topic. The sense of unease about literature's links to trade can therefore be explained in the context of this conflictual space in which members of the Whig aristocracy found themselves. Although still dependent on mercantile and manufacturing interests, they resented the rapid entry of more people intent on securing the privileges hitherto enjoyed by the dominant classes.[5] The invention of an aristocratic genealogy by the Whigs, therefore, resulted in part from this sense of resentment for the pragmatic rationale that lay behind the economic power of the "alien" communities, particularly Jewish immigrants who had played a significant role, during this time, in the commerce of the empire, and who had emerged as the single most powerful non-Anglo-Saxon community with a major stake in Britain's colonial economy. Threatened by the latter's economic power, the established Whig gentry appealed to their invented "aristocratic pedigree" as a way to differentiate themselves from these "others," thereby sanctioning new forms of racist ideologies among which was a resurgent anti-Semitism. This development also signified the troubled relations that had resulted from the rising dependence of the Whig aristocracy on the new holders of wealth.

Scott himself appears to have shared some of these anti-Semitic sentiments. As his biographer Sutherland has indicated, Scott's personal grudges towards the Jewish gold merchant Abud, about whom the writer reputedly made some "venomously racist remarks," may have been prompted by Abud's threat to sue him for not repaying his debts (Sutherland 1995: 315). Once again, the gold merchant revived the peril of the blood-sucking Jew. Despite its obscure status in the literary canon, *The Surgeon's Daughter* is a significant work precisely because its fantasy narrative serves as the disciplinary site where the Jew was produced as the racial other, the figure who embodied the undesirable darker underside of those very impulses that had allowed Britain's middle classes to realize their own social desire. By selecting a historical narrative that had already been codified along racial lines as the story of the victorious Europeans over the Orientals, Scott utilizes the imperialist ideologies of an aristo-military class to provide a secure ground for identifying those who could call themselves genuinely "British." To this extent the narrative functions as an ideal "imaginary type" that Abdul JanMuhamed has characterized as a text in which "the subject is eclipsed by his fixation on and fetishization of the Other" (JanMuhamed 1985: 61). It is worth noting that the fetishization of Jewishness occasioned by these aristocratic nationalist ideologies occurs within Scott's retrospective delineation of an eighteenth-century imperial history, a history that had produced the world of military heroes, merchants, and mercenaries. He evokes this particular sense of the past in order to project the history of imperial Britain as a promise of the future—the future of an "aristocratic" nation. Scott could only hope that, if the eighteenth century had confirmed the primacy of the aristo-military world-view for having helped establish the empire, the nineteenth century would continue to consolidate it with the same kind of nationalist vigor. As Eric Stokes has demonstrated, after years of military action dominated by generals of the East India Company, it had been primarily the Whigs who had aligned themselves with imperial administrators and colonial authorities in order to establish new rationales for governing the Indian empire. However, the euphoric vision of the past was also linked in a subterranean manner to the dark legacy of eighteenth-century freebooters and of colonial plunder and violence, which had contributed equally to the material formation of the empire. Since *The Surgeon's Daughter* is infused with this sense of a double history, this legacy had to be projected on to the "other" in order to differentiate it from the "self," so that the latter could continue to uphold its moral authority to assert its claim to a genuine British identity.

History shows that, as the source of British mercantile power in the eighteenth century, India's wealth had filtered through the entire fabric of British society, benefiting alike the aristocrat, the petty bourgeois, and the Jew. If the assertion of an essential Britishness had consisted in defending the life and value system generated by this colonial wealth, it was hard to ignore the claims of the rising communities to assert their own status as contributors to this national wealth. After all, colonial trade and manufacture had also helped them to secure powerful positions within society, a privilege hitherto claimed by the wealthy Whigs. However, as indicated earlier, faced with this inherent conflict between what the colonial past concealed—its inherent rapacity—and what it glorified—its invented aristocratic resourcefulness and benevolent agenda in the nineteenth century—Scott selects a convenient scapegoat to represent the former, and narrates a tale that sets the "bad" colonial apart from the "good" colonial. Unlike the representation of the Jewish Isaac of York in *Ivanhoe*, the scapegoat in this tale is a half-Jewish character singularized as the man bearing the mark of the colonial history of trade, plunder, and political intrigue. It is not coincidental that it is this history that continued to influence other writers of the colonial romance in the nineteenth century, particularly Edward John Trelawny in *Adventures of a Younger Son* (1829), a work to which I will return in the following sections of the present chapter.

Metanarratorial maneuvers in The Surgeon's Daughter

Consistent with the pattern suggested above, the narrative of *The Surgeon's Daughter* is bound to an entire circle of national, class, and racial identifications, a circle that plays a pivotal role in affirming the invented "aristocracy" of the Whigs and legitimizing it as the natural expression of British civility. Part of this interlinked circle begins to emerge in the tale's larger discursive texture—its two "metanarratorial" frames. Although they technically lie outside the "actual" story about the renegade Jew, and are meant to serve only as explanations for the tale's origin and genesis, the specific arrangement and codification of the "story" behind the "story" gesture towards the larger social formation of what Pierre Bourdieu has called "cultural capital" in early nineteenth-century imperial Britain. In a society where class alignments were key to social mobility, the accumulation of such capital signaled new shifts in class identity and class alliance, which were essential to fashioning the self as a productive and mobile agent guided by the norms of civility. As stated earlier, the conversations between Mr. Croftangry and Mr. Fairscribe embody the principles of literary commodification in a colonial market introduced during this period, but, more significantly, these principles are concretized as material exchange items through the series of analogies that commence with the introductory exchange between these two figures. As a merchant aristocrat, Mr. Fairscribe couches his literary advice to the narrator, Mr. Croftangry, in mercantile terms: "I could tell you some *tricks of my own trade*" (Scott [1827] 2000: 155; emphasis added), identifying literary labor with the material institutions of colonialism. Mr. Croftangry willingly follows his aristocratic patron's suggestion to adopt this "trick" of trade and, as the story takes form, Fairscribe—the reader is told—serves as a "zealous coadjutor" to Mr. Croftangry's literary endeavor, "half-ashamed . . . yet half-proud of the *literary stock company* in which he has got a *share*" (ibid.: 158; emphasis added). Although investment in a "literary stock company" and the writing of "fiction" are here both subsumed under a common mercantilist world-view, the combination of "shame" and "pride" signifies the sense of discomfort, on the part of the Whig aristocracy, with the initiatives of industrial production. Incitement and interdiction operate simultaneously in order to justify the potential power of this collaborative endeavor between the two figures. Behind such an exchange lies the fact of sheer profitability promised by Indian stocks and shares, a financial phenomenon of this period to which Scott himself alludes in the tale. Clearly, the literary authorship of the narrative of empire is at first figuratively embodied in mercantile metaphors of investment and wealth, which Scott drew out of his knowledge of the colonial history initiated by the exploits of the East India Company, a history that was also a reminder of the continuities between the holders of old wealth and the promise of newer possibilities of profit from the colonies.

Furthermore, the presence of this legacy of the empire is palpable within the very heart of Scotland. Mr. Croftangry is told by Fairscribe that his own lavish Scottish estate was drawn from a colonial inheritance handed down by Miss Menie Grey, a member of the Fairscribe family. Mr. Croftangry is told that, upon returning to Scotland, Menie Grey had bestowed upon the Fairscribe family a considerable part of her wealth acquired from the Indian ruler Hyder Ali. The tone of the social exchange between the patron and the writer which follows this description suggests an atmosphere of mutual civility that binds the two in an open and yet dependent relationship. Just as the pictorial artist had immortalized the aristocratic image of Menie Gray in the portrait adorning Fairscribe's wealthy interior, the writer, Mr. Croftangry, now seeks to valorize that tradition by binding himself to the task of recovering and giving new meaning and prestige to the Fairscribe family genealogy. Giving fictional life to the story of Menie Gray therefore fulfills Mr. Croftangry's social obligation, but it also allows him to make an entry into the most intimate, interior spaces of the colonial aristocracy represented by Fairscribe. Such an alliance between the old aristocracy and the writer as "manufacturer" serves to create an image of a beneficial co-dependence of people from two classes, where the individual desires of each class mirror the harmony of a seemingly symbiotic social order.[6]

This sense of reciprocal dependence, however, undergoes a significant change. As the pattern of class identification continues to be articulated in these two metanarratorial frames, it becomes apparent that Mr. Croftangry, as the "manufacturer" of the tale, has come to possess a vital part of the cultural capital available within the discursive environment of a post-mercantile nation. This new-found power of the rising middle classes is embodied in the final chapter, where Mr. Croftangry is shown to utilize the metaphorical import of British mercantilism's new power in the indigenous manufacturing sector successfully to mold his own narrative about India. Responding to the question of how he had acquired such extensive knowledge about the Indian settings in his Oriental tale, Mr. Croftangry refers to the conversation that had just taken place about "imitation shawls" then available in English markets. He asserts that these imitation shawls were popular commodities for sale because consumers could not differentiate them "from the actual country shawl, except by some inimitable cross-stitch in the border" (Scott [1827] 2000: 287):

> Like the imitative operatives of Paisley, I have composed my shawl by incorporating into the wool a little Thibet wool which my excellent friend and neighbor, Colonel MacKerris, one of the best fellows who ever trod a Highland Moor, or dived into an Indian jungle, had the goodness to supply me with.
>
> (ibid.: 288)

Mr. Croftangry has learned a new language in order to rationalize his literary enterprise, the language of industrial manufacture that valorized the inventive power to assemble materials derived from colonial commodities in order to produce new commodities that imitated the "original." Although serving as the mark of the new resourcefulness among the industrial classes for initiating home manufacture, such language also suggests the potential deception of the inauthentic commodity that could easily "mimic" the real. It can be read as representing a violation of traditional hierarchies resulting from the gradual erosion of the older values of mercantilism based exclusively on trade rather than on manufacture. Scott, however, presents Mr. Croftangry's literary labor as a seemingly benign effort, one that is still symbiotically dependent on the benevolence of the old mercantile aristocracy. In a sense, Mr. Croftangry is only an imitator, still dependent on the largesse of the aristocracy that allows him access to the latter's symbolic capital. There is no sense of immediate threat to the established order posed by Mr. Croftangry's literary initiative: the social boundaries are maintained and the code of civility ensures that, despite the new mobility on the part of an ascendant class, the aristocracy retains its privileged place. The metanarratorial frames in *The Surgeon's Daughter*, therefore, can be seen to provide the clearest example of the ways in which questions concerning literary effort in this age was concretely embedded in, and intersected by, larger questions about the power of colonial mercantilism as it made way for industrial manufacture. They are also symptomatic of the social, economic, and cultural forces that were reshaping Britain and recasting the traditional class alliances and loyalties, thereby creating the need to justify the new patterns of emergent social desire. In addition to providing the external frames for the tale and elucidating its evolution as fiction, they signify what Fiona Robertson calls "the interplay of different forms of narratorial and historical authority" (Robertson 1994: 3), signaling the making of fiction as a social and discursive phenomenon, where individual literary inspirations for production are closely aligned with an evolving network of national and class interests.

Testing civility and disciplining social desire: the "Jew" and the "Orient"

Unlike the metanarratorial frames, Scott's narrativization of social desire in this Oriental tale is centrally dependent on a racialized discourse about the Jew. Set against the background of the providential history of the empire, and animated by the stories of individual characters who move in that heroic landscape, this narrative is sustained partly through a contrast between the vision of an unchecked mercantilism that, in Scott's view, had fallen prey to its own self-interest, and that of the more cautionary position of nineteenth-century post-mercantile culture, as represented by a "governmental" imperialism with its ethos of reason and management, and its promise of a more restrained sense of social mobility. For Scott, this tidied-up contrast between two kinds of colonial authority also helped consolidate a system of difference across which aristocratic Britain could recognize, reaffirm, and maintain its own values of civility and its own racial and political identity. India's alterity provided a suitable locus for identifying and marking out the "other," necessary to this design. *The Surgeon's Daughter* reveals that the historical perspective offered by the events of the 1770s (the time frame of the story) led Scott, writing in the 1820s, to recast strategically the authority of the colonial legacy. As a result, the history of "trade and plunder" (Mukherjee 1974: 301) that characterized much of mercantile imperialism is recast as a socially sanctioned, providential history. Concurrently, the darker aspects of that history are represented by projecting it on to an "outsider"–the Jew–within the national scene.

National narratives regularly embody the disciplinary function of the state. In his study of *Ivanhoe*, Michael Ragussis has contended that Scott placed the "Jewish question" at the heart of English national identity by "depicting the persecution of the Jews, including the attempt to convert them, at a critical moment in history–the founding of the English nation" (Ragussis 1995: 12). If the story of national origins had been linked to the Jewish presence, Scott's Oriental tale reveals that the "Jewish question" continued to inflect questions about national identity during this time of major historical changes in material relations between the major classes and communities within imperial Britain. The effects of these historical changes– resulting from the colonial enterprise–are palpable in the emergent anti-Semitism. As the hated double, the Jew is produced as the unaccommodated figure, a figure through which the "lack" and the "excess" in the norms of civility guiding social desire could be identified. In this respect, the Jew's identity was key to the disciplinary function of the narrative, since it is around him that the norms of that disciplinarity could be realized. At the same time, the protagonist of *The Surgeon's Daughter*, Richard Middlemas, is only half-Jewish, and right from the beginning of the story Richard's biracial identity is linked with India's alterity as well as with the memory of the eighteenth-century history of British freebooters and colonial plunderers. This is brought out by Scott's delineation of Richard's most intimate yearnings early in the tale:

> To India . . . happy dog–to India! You may well bear with equanimity all disappointments sustained on this side of the globe. Oh, Delhi! oh, Golconda!

have your names no power to conjure idle recollections?—India, where gold is won by steel; where a brave man cannot pitch his desires of fame and wealth so high, but that he may realize it, if he have fortune to his friend!

(Scott [1827] 2000: 198)

As the illegitimate son of a rich Sephardic Jewess named Zilia Moncada and an English mercantile adventurer and traitor named Richard Tresham, Richard Middlemas was raised by Gideon Grey, a local doctor in the Scottish Highlands. Abandoned by his family as an infant, the lonely boy is stirred by his nurse's exaggerated and flattering stories about his glorious parentage, which—the reader is told—excited "the most ambitious visions in the mind of a boy, who naturally felt a strong desire of rising in the world, and was conscious of possessing the powers necessary to his advancement" (Scott [1827] 2000: 181). Like any young English- or Scotsman, Richard decides to get a commission with the East India Company and seek wealth in India after realizing that his dream of upward mobility had very limited prospects in the Highlands. Like Mr. Croftangry, the writer, Richard seeks out "India" to satisfy a desire, and, from the very outset, his dreams are embodied in a rhetoric of wealth deeply entrenched in the value of social mobility. As Richard tells his friend: "To spend two additional years in this infernal wilderness [Scotland], cruizing after crowns and half-crowns, when worse men are making lacs and crores of rupees—it is a sad falling off, Adam" (ibid.: 199).

A significant number of military reminiscences of the period attest to the growing popularity of colonial careers for young men faced with limited opportunities at home.[7] "Griffins"—as these first arrivals in India were popularly called—becomes a common term in the late eighteenth century to describe the young colonial cadets in the service of the East India Company. Although fired by the joy of discovery and the promise of wealth, many of these young cadets took up such careers because they had limited chances at home for improving their status. As many of the narratives of young cadets show, this had been spurred by domestic laws governing property and primogeniture, which left many young men without a future in the country. In *A Cadetship in the Honourable East India's Company's Service*, the author Edward Blagdon recounts the life of a cadet whose father dies prematurely leaving behind three sons. While the first succeeded to the father's acres and the second became a land agent, the third (Edward), left without an inheritance, accepted a cadetship with the East India Company for a sum of £200. Similarly, in *Adventures of a Younger Son*, John Trelawny's hero, a privateer on a merchant ship, describes himself as coming

into the world, branded and denounced as a vagrant, not littered by a drab in a ditch but still worse; for I was a younger son of a family, so proud of their antiquity, that even gout and mortgaged estates were traced, many generations back, on the genealogical tree, as ancient heirlooms of aristocratic origin, and therefore reverenced.

(Trelawny [1831] 1974: 1)

He compares the "atrocious law of primogeniture" (ibid.) to the practices of a Spartan mother killing her own child. In emphasizing the violent inequity of the system of primogeniture, Trelawny conveys not only the promise of freedom that could be secured by young men who dared to step outside the confining borders of home, but also the awesome potential of young Britons to rise above their socially brutal environment and to shape their own future by sheer force of will. Restrained socially and psychologically in this world, the romantic hero of *Adventures of a Younger Son* can simultaneously display extreme emotions of barbarism and compassion. Uncompromising and sensitive, he is capable of wreaking untold violence on his opponents as well as sympathizing with, and fighting on behalf of, the underdog who possesses little power or influence. The popularity of such a work can therefore be ascribed to this romanticization of the renegade, reflecting a particular response, on the part of the reading public, to a fantasy that was tantalizing precisely because it evoked the romance of the aberrant while maintaining the heroic ideal of British masculinity.[8]

In his *Military Reminiscences*, Colonel James Welsh provides an autobiographical account of what he calls a "plain, unlettered Soldier" (Welsh 1830: vii), born of "respectable parents, in the Capital of Scotland," whose fate "early in life [was] to be launched into the world without a pilot. . . . to embark as a Cadet for the East Indies" (ibid.: viii). In addition to furnishing details about the life of a griffin in military cantonments in India, Welsh's autobiography chronicles the numerous military campaigns conducted by the British against the Indian powers, and celebrates the newly found glory of British valor, enterprise, and resourcefulness. Strikingly similar to Welsh's account are the anonymously authored *Twelve Years' Military Adventure in Three Quarters of the Globe*,[9] and *The Cadet: A Poem*. The first describes the life of a young cadet who, "destined at an early age for the Military Profession," gets a commission with the East India Company and is subsequently sent to India. Unlike Welsh's account, however, this work is more cautionary in tone, reminding the reader that the "nature of the society into which a youth falls on first embarking in life, is a matter of more consequence than is generally supposed" (*Twelve Years'*: 18). Unlike Trelawny's hero, who single-handedly shapes his own future, the cadet in *Twelve Years' Military Adventure* seems particularly vulnerable to the moral dangers posed by the world around him—by the "libertine," "hoary sensualist," and "unprincipled gamester." The threat of "contagion" (ibid.: 19) had a singularly powerful ideological function: it laid down a normative standard by delineating the threshold of any transgressive social behavior that might potentially be present within the imagined heroic life in the colonies.

This is clearly brought out in *The Cadet*, a poetic narrative about a young man who leaves the country "full of vague expectations, occasioned by specious stories which he constantly hears of the luxurious pleasures of an Oriental clime" (*Cadet*: xi). Affected by the grand illusion, this "misguided" youth (ibid.: 65) commences a "career of voluptuous pleasure and blind dissipation" (ibid.: xii) whose horror and pain the author conveys in these words:

What are the genuine comforts India brings?
Brutes it begets, and reptiles armed with stings.
(ibid.: 17)

At one point in the poem, the life of the cadet is compared to that of "African slaves":

Still, tho' the keenest woes your lives assail,
Such as no earthly joys can countervail,
. . . Your labour sure is lightsome, when compared
To his whose Freedom's noblest joys has shar'd.
(ibid.: 54)

Never explicit in its description of the "countless horrors of an Indian shore" (ibid.: 143), the poem nevertheless conveys a strong sense of moral outrage at the effects of such a career on youth, often appealing to the ideals of "freedom" and "liberty" sanctioned in the metropolis to highlight the gulf between desire and reality and to dramatize the vulnerable status of the young Briton in India. It is worth pointing out that these nationally ordained values of freedom and liberty normalize social desire at the very moment when they appear to be most vulnerable to "excess."

The fear of "contagion" that these works often evoke also pervades another anonymous work, *The Life and Adventures of Shigram-Po, Cadet in the Service of the Hon'ble East India Company on the Bengal Establishment* (1821). The narrative is modeled on the familiar theme—that of a young boy, "born in a poor family," with no means to "feed or educate so many on a small estate" (*Life*: 2), who, as a mere boy, shows signs of military skills:

This Shigram when he was a boy,
Preferred the Drum to any Toy
. . . Learn to handle sword and gun
And show how Empires would be won.
(ibid.: 4)

Since the boy displays all of the characteristic traits of valor and adventure, he is taken by his father at an early age to meet the director of the East India Company, who assures the latter that

his son would be
Most proud to serve the Company;
Whose grand and princely speculation,
Was worthy of the British nation;
Embracing trade of all degrees,
From Silk and Cloth, to Ham and Cheese.
(ibid.: 37)

The adventures of Shigram-Po in India are, however, narrated with words of caution. Along with "Barristers, Attorneys, parsons, Surgeons" (ibid.: 102), the new cadets find themselves in the company of undesirable "free traders," who

> . . . are fully bent
> To sell their ventures, cent per cent,
> Expecting, they shall nicely fleece us,
> And go back, just as Croesus.
>
>   (ibid.: 103)

Although campaigns of the East India Company were often conducted with the expedient measures involving cunning and intrigue, such expedience was sanctioned by appealing to the nature of military warfare, while the free trader, with his desire to make money, was perceived as a threat to the norms of civility and fair play. A note attached to the poem, however, is ambivalent about who actually profits from the situation in the colonies:

> It is not an uncommon opinion in England, that in the East Indies, Rupees absolutely grow in profusion on the trees. *Some people*, not always very chaste in their ideas as to *the mode in which wealth is there accumulated*, suppose as a 'sine qua non' that a few atrocities must be committed, before a man can retire with real satisfaction to his native country, although themselves, are by no means unwilling to participate in such ill accumulated wealth.
>
>   (ibid.: 103; emphasis added)

The author's moral opinion opposing the dominant feeling that the atrocities committed in India could be justified by the present exigencies throws into relief the problem of differentiating between the legitimate and illegitimate aspects of the desire for profit and power driving young Britons. Scott's Oriental tale highlights this problem right from the beginning when Richard Middlemas declares: "Methinks I have a *natural* turn for India, and so I ought" (Scott [1827] 2000: 199; emphasis added). Like the other cadets, who all appear to have possessed some natural affinity for a military career in India, Richard Middlemass has aspirations that seem typical of the times. Furthermore, up to this point, Scott's representation of Richard follows the traditional stereotype of the "wandering Jew," who, according to Frank Felsenstein, always carried with it the sense of a romantic enigma later associated with the wandering Briton popularized by the Romantics, particularly writers such as Byron and Trelawny. But in Scott that image is subsequently—and strategically—transformed into that of a diabolical and rapacious individual without a conscience, a change facilitated no doubt by a theme common in Scott's time—that of a Jewish child brought up in the camp of his hereditary enemies, who betrays weakness when he comes of age by becoming a renegade. In short, Richard becomes the very embodiment of "contagion" that seemed to lurk at the very threshold of the lives of British cadets.

Single-mindedly pursuing his dream, Richard seeks the help of another friend, the disreputable Tom Hillary, the former attorney's clerk, a man who had abandoned his legal profession to become a captain in the service of the East India Company, and who now displayed his new-found colonial wealth and privilege unashamedly in public. In this world of instant wealth, Scott associates his dark protagonist Richard with this adventurist image of the East India Company, whose reputation as a company of adventurers and freebooters went hand in hand with its reputation as the source of eighteenth-century mercantile wealth. At the same time, however, Richard's identity remains anchored to its own Jewishness, bound incontrovertibly to the truth about his "race." That this inescapable alterity begins to dominate Scott's presentation of Richard's progress in the tale is itself reflective of the link between the author's overt manipulation of colonial history in order to uphold the racial ideologies of an "aristocratic" Britain and his deflection of the darker aspects of the material desires of his own class.

The idea of nationhood that emerges in this period is similarly marked by the co-presence of two contrary impulses, revealing the tension between two faces of Britain's early mercantile adventurism. The image of the East India Company that Scott's tale evokes in its early sections is clearly drawn from an iconic imagination that saw "that wonderful company of merchants" as "princes" (Scott [1827] 2000: 201). Military, political, and economic interests were often seen to be part of the same historical impulse, existing without any rift or division. In his *Essay*, John Mitchell describes the history of the British presence in India in terms of a natural and inevitable transition from trade to conquest and governance:

> During the late and preceding century, a company of British merchants, actuated by that spirit of enterprising commerce, which has so long distinguished the inhabitants of this island, sought and obtained trading stations, first on the coast of Coromandel, and then on the banks of the Ganges. Their first object was traffic, not conquest: but circumstances, in the *natural course of things*, soon arose to embroil them with the natives; and the successful issue of these contests, opened their minds to new views of aggrandisement. Still retaining the name and appearance of a commercial company, they became in fact a great council of proprietors, presiding over the affairs of a vast domain, conducting military enterprises on a large scale, and acquiring from time to time, as the result of these new adventures, an immense accession of territory. In the history of no age or nation has it happened, that a range of country so vast, so rich, so populous, became the *private property of a company of merchants*.
> (Mitchell 1805: 5–6; emphasis added)

Mitchell naturalizes the acquisition of private property as being an inherent part of Britain's social destiny, very much in the manner in which he legitimizes its colonial mission. What stands out is the subtlety with which Mitchell's logic subsumes a "natural" right under the rule of private property acquired from the colonies, thereby sanctioning the vested interests of the merchant class. By identifying natural resourcefulness with a "national" identity, Mitchell provides a compellingly powerful fantasy for many among the lower classes whose fortunes seemed limited within Britain. The power of this fantasy lay in the fact that, at a fundamental level, it appealed to those values of British civility that made individual aspiration for property part of a national destiny. In *A Letter to the Proprietors of East India Stock*, the anonymous author defends the vast economic power of the company by contending that

> no arguments drawn from the superabundance of private wealth, *however unworthily or improperly bestowed*, can be adduced by applying such possessions to the use of the public. . . . The slightest attempt of this kind, like a spark thrown into a magazine of powder, must necessarily tear asunder the strongest bonds by which society is held together.
>
> (*Letter*: 3; emphasis added)

These "bonds" are the inviolable law of private property—the "first inexplicable high flown principles of sovereignty" (ibid.: 5)—which, the author says, is in "no way incompatible with the well-being of the community" (ibid.: 4).

In another anonymous tract, entitled *Examination of the Principles and Policy of the Government of British India*, similar sentiments defending the law of private property are echoed by the author:

> I assume as a position which cannot be controverted, that the British Government is determined to maintain the supremacy of India as long as it can maintain it. It has expended its blood and its treasure in the conquest; and its right of domination is thus established, according to the usual notions of mankind . . . So long as the profit derived by the British Government and nation from India is assured by the sword . . . , any system of Government [that] may be devised for the nations of that empire by their conquerors will, for a long period, perhaps, be accepted by them. They have no alternative.
>
> (*Examination*: 2–3)

If the well-being of the nation was unthinkable without the guaranteed status of the principles of private property and profit, the existence of Britain's power was also inconceivable without the sanction of its methods of colonial conquest and governance, no matter how brutal they seemed to be. As Homi Bhabha comments, as "father and oppressor; just and unjust; moderate and rapacious, vigorous and despotic," the image of authority "must be read between the lines, within the interdictory borders of civility itself" (Bhabha 1985: 75). This disciplinary function of the colonial state in regulating its own desire is nowhere more apparent than in this regulative logic. If cadets were required to provide the ground troops for military conquest, their social aspirations had to be linked to the economic fate of the larger imperial nation. At the same time, these social aspirations needed a system of checks and balances in order to promote the primacy of the existing social order, thus legitimizing the dominant class hierarchies. In *Examination of the Principles*, one sees the way in which the logic behind the primacy of private property is extended simultaneously to include subject races as the property of the

British nation and to justify the interests of the wealthy. Just as there was no "alternative" to the law of private property, subject nations had no choice but to submit to the rule of the conquering British.

Placed in the second decade of the nineteenth century, Scott's *The Surgeon's Daughter* retrospectively invents Britain's mercantile initiatives as an expression of a providential history:

> It was about the *middle of the 18th century*, and the directors in Leadenhall street were silently laying the foundations of that immense empire which afterwards rose like an exaltation, and *now* astonishes Europe, as well as Asia, with its formidable extent and stupendous strength.
>
> (Scott [1827] 2000: 201; emphasis added)

The reference made here is to Robert Clive's acquisition of Bengal after the defeat of the province's powerful ruler, Siraj-ud-Dualah, in 1757. As the word "exaltation" suggests, the period of mercantile expansion and political consolidation is imagined as a manifestation of the magical power of English imperialism. Couched in a symbolic language of economic initiative (instead of violent militarism), the word conveys the force of mercantilism in regulating the nation's aspirations for wealth, knowledge, and social mobility:

> Britain had now begun to lend a wondering ear to the account of the battles fought and the cities won in the East; and was surprised by the return of individuals who had left their native country as adventurers, but now reappeared there surrounded by Oriental wealth and Oriental luxury, which dimmed even the splendor of the most wealthy of the British nobility.
>
> (ibid.)

However, the acquisition of oriental wealth and luxury was fraught with a certain sense of unease. The threat of a foreign "contagion" and its infusion into the established order seems to hover right behind this expression of Britain's imperial glory. Discussing the "influence of the East on British character," John Mitchell observes that in people returning from the colonies one sees the "original traits conspicuously retained," except for the "eastern nabob," who "not infrequently brings back with him a certain squeamishness of taste, and sickly sensibility of feeling . . . a dislike of home, and ennui of life, which are essentially different from the great lines of British temper" (Mitchell 1805: 88). According to Mitchell, the lingering potential of a disruptive transformation in British character, occasioned by the proximity of the Briton to the native subjects, has significant moral and racial consequences:

> This fact shews, that there is a danger lest the bold and somewhat rugged elements of our national spirit should, instead of assimilating the Hindoo character to itself, be melted down into the softness of the country: lest the voluptuousness of Hindostan should prove more fatal than its wisdom or its

valour; and like the luxurious ease of Capua, prepare visitors for being at length subdued by those whom they have vanquished.

(ibid.: 88–9)

Similarly, Scott utilizes the Indian setting to produce and magnify Richard's alterity by associating him with a range of other aberrant figures—from the petty social climber, Tom Hillary, to the monstrous woman adventurer, Madame Montreville. Such a move allows Scott to affirm the legitimacy of a national masculine model of Anglo-Saxon identity, distinguishing its normalcy from the perceived disfigurement of social desire manifested in these aberrant figures.

All of the heraldic imagery associated with the colonial enterprise vibrates with the vision of Britain's collective social destiny found in this tale. Exploiting the popular myths about the empire, Scott's narrator draws a close parallel between the sight of the company ships and the new heraldic imagery that linked the fate of the nation with its economic interests in the colonies. For many in Britain, free trade was the magic word that had enabled Britain to achieve this glory by ensuring domestic peace and prosperity, as well as that of India, the subject nation. *The Letter to the Author of a View of the Present State and Future Prospects of Free Trade and Colonization of India* unambiguously states: "Free trade—that is, mutual commerce, full, unrestricted, and plenteous as you can make it—must doubtless prove of advantage to a country like British India" (Desh-u-Lubun Ocharik 1830: 6).[10] Among the proponents of free trade were those who felt that the losses caused by the diminished demands for goods in the domestic sphere could be recuperated through "increased export to India" (Jackson 1829: 6), since a "free and un-restricted trade to the East" would create a foreign demand for British-made goods, such as lace, hosiery, and cotton yarn. Additionally mercantilism opened up the world of India stocks and bonds. As the historian P. J. Marshall has noted, their lure had significant consequences: they ensured that people who possessed them not only made money but secured powerful patrons in the top echelons of the company (Marshall 1968: 28). India stocks and bonds were also very profitable for the emerging middle classes in Britain: for example, there was an unprecedented rise in India stock with the news of Robert Clive's acquisition of the Dewani of Bengal in the late 1750s.

In Scott's tale, the close alliance between the mercantile wealth drawn from India and the social status promised by colonial appointments is embodied in the figure of Tom Hillary, Richard's colonial connection. Although interested in buying property in the Scottish moorlands, Tom eventually decides not to cash in his India stocks. Apart from his own mercenary and social interests, Tom Hillary's company connection points to the dark underside of mercantile colonialism—the recruiting of impoverished young men by promising them commissions in the East India Company and then forcing them to enlist as petty soldiers in the company's military force. This ploy had been quite widespread among the military wing of the company, which routinely hired agents to lure the poor. In Scott's tale, the primary agent of such activity is, predictably, Tom, the petty social climber, and it is not surprising that Scott uses a member of the desperate lower classes to represent the worst impulses of colonial mercantilism. Although Tom's motives were inextricably bound up with, and fueled by, the opportunities for wealth that the imperial company offered, he remains little more than a petty manipulator, whose only function is to seduce the morally feeble Richard Middlemas, who confuses his own social aspirations with the delusion of instant wealth. On the other hand, Robert Clive, the man reputed to have accumulated great wealth through his military campaigns in India, became the nation's hero (in fact, the "cult" of Clive continued to thrive well into the late Victorian age, with stories about his exploits reiterated in innumerable military hagiographies and bio-graphies, including Thomas Babington Macaulay's *Essay on Clive*). As William Barber points out, Britons were only too eager to cast Clive as the new aristocratic colonial hero, overlooking the often questionable methods he had employed to gain his personal fortunes. Supporters of military action and mercantile expansion in India also conceded that, although the flow of wealth into the country from India could be a "great detriment," any attempt to curb the power of the company and its officers and merchants would be to "check the progress of wealth": "When the machine is put in motion, I am afraid we cannot stop its progress, by throwing unnatural impediments in its way, without crushing or overturning it" (*A Letter to the Proprietors*: 9). Again, the acquisition of personal wealth is justified in the name of the nation and its imperial destiny, one that is figured as part of a machine-like process.

Although Benedict Anderson has argued that "dreams of racism have their origin in the ideologies of class, rather than in those of the nation" (Anderson 1983: 136), it is clear that in this case national identity is produced through the imbrication of class and race, where class differences are negotiated through the creation of the racial other. This is clearly visible in the manner in which Scott organizes the relations between Tom Hillary and Richard, the Jew. After robbing Richard of his thousand pounds and leaving him in a military hospital meant for common desperadoes enlisted in the company, Tom disappears from Scott's tale. His role, then, is limited by the larger demands of Scott's moral allegory: it is the half-Jewish Richard Middlemas, the dreamer seduced by Tom's power of persua-sion, who becomes the focus of the novel, and it is around him that the moral mechanism of the story begins to revolve. As stated earlier, although Richard's desire for social mobility was not unique or even unnatural, its darker aspects are subtly linked to his Jewishness—to his position as an outsider within British society. As Sander Gilman has pointed out, this form of identification produces the Jew who, while representing "the goals and values of a broader society," is made more vulnerable to the "power of such an image" (Gilman 1991: 3). The image is open to all of the subtle and not too subtle mechanisms of projection and demonization by the dominant group. Thus, Richard's dark side, initially concealed behind the image of Scottish respectability, manifests itself in a systematic manner as the story progresses, revealing its true essence after he arrives in India and gets involved in the dubious political machinations of Madame Montreville.

In the early sections of the tale, Richard is portrayed as a romantic young man given to sudden outbursts of passion. He is an attractive figure but, unlike that of

his Anglo-Saxon companion, Adam Hartley, the medical apprentice working under Dr. Grey, Richard's behavior is marked by a irrepressible inconsistency, as he sways between extremes of warmth and understanding and of rage, avarice, and despair. His single-minded obsession with acquiring wealth and improving his social standing is increasingly emphasized in the tale to the extent that this obsession becomes the sole defining trait of his personality. For instance, upon discovering the circumstances of his unfortunate birth and the subsequent rejection by his own rich Jewish family, Richard is filled with a deep sense of social shame, but, rather than listen to his peers, he hardens in his resolve to chart out his destiny independently of their advice. Scoffing at his guardian, Dr. Grey, he proclaims that he is "a true-born Englishman" (Scott [1827] 2000: 182). The inescapably ironic resonance in his claim to being "English" alerts the reader immediately to Richard's place in the national social order of an Anglo-Saxon Britain. Similarly, his assertion that he had a "natural" turn for India (ibid.: 199) serves as a prefiguration of what is, in the future, unveiled as his own radical otherness.

A comparison of Richard with Trelawny's hero in *Adventures of a Younger Son* highlights and amplifies the narrative mechanisms Scott employs in his tale to distinguish between the Briton and the Jew. The ideological function of these narrative mechanisms is evident in the way in which the Briton and the Jew reflect and deflect the nationally ordained ideals of liberty, freedom, and desire for social mobility. As Michael McKeon has observed, the figure of the younger son introduced, within domestic fiction, an ideological tension between progressive and conservative principles, one in which laws of primogeniture, inheritance, and merit are worked out in specific ways (McKeon 1987: 218–19). Trelawny describes the rebelliousness of his renegade hero as a manifestation of "energy, the unshaken resolution and the fierce obstinacy" (Trelawny [1831] 1974: 4), traits clearly characteristic of all young Britons. The reader is told that he "hated all that thwarted [him], parsons, pastors, and masters" (ibid.), and he "never tried half measures, but proceeded to extremities, without stop or pause" (ibid.: 6). His conflict with his despotic and cruel father, evoked starkly in his killing of the father's pet raven, is interpreted as a sign of his fierce love for liberty. Trelawny's hero sees himself as an "utter outcast," but it is precisely this that makes him into a Romantic hero. Drafted in a frigate sailing for the East Indies, he points to the poignancy of his isolation: "Imagine me torn from my native country, destined to cross the wide ocean, to a wild region, cut off from every tie, or the possibility of communication, transported like a felon as it were, for life for, at that period, few ships returned under seven or more years" (ibid.: 34), but it is this isolation that enables him to assert his freedom. Although he supplants his own tyrannical father with that of his mentor, De Ruyter, a European whose "disposition, or restlessness, caused his to be a life of adventure, and consequently of peril," Trelawny's hero can still claim to be part of the "same stock" (ibid.: 87) as his mentor. In short, despite his disregard for the sanctity of familial ties, his new allegiance to De Ruyter ensures his place within a legitimate Anglo-Saxon moral order. Furthermore, although he learns to value his mentor's dictum to "reason justly and tolerantly" (ibid.: 54), he preserves his passionate self throughout the story, retaining his idealism to fight against "tyrants and oppressors" (ibid.: 76), but also keenly aware of his own self-interest: "Now I like spice and tea too; and their [The East India Company's] system of exclusive right not suiting with my ideas of things, I began to open trade for myself" (ibid.: 89). His subsequent questioning of the company's monopoly over trade is shown to be an expression of a robust love for personal liberty and resourcefulness, instead of mere hatred of an unjust social system. As he says, "I am no hungry dog, to stand patiently by, in the hope of picking a bone, which these lordly merchants, in general, pretty successfully blanch before they leave it" (ibid.: 93). Although compassionate and a supporter of the underdog, he fiercely and violently defends himself against those he considers his enemies, even when they include natives defending themselves from colonial intruders. Although he regards himself as having no nation, since "national prejudices are washed and rubbed off by the elements" (ibid.: 134), Trelawny's hero is assured a heroic status in the national imaginary because he can successfully negotiate the contradictions inherent to the norms of civility guiding social behavior, thereby being capable of warding off the "contagion" feared by many in Britain.

To what extent Richard's claim to an "English" identity was acceptable to British readers in the early nineteenth century can perhaps best be fathomed by reviewing the historical events leading to Jewish emancipation.[11] While the National Assembly in France had declared the emancipation of Jews in 1790–91, allowing them rights of full citizenship, Britain, in the first two decades of the nineteenth century, continued in slow pace towards resolving the Jewish issue. Todd Endelman points out that, although medieval views about Jews had lessened, anti-Semitism assumed a new guise in this era:

> During the early years of the parliamentary campaign for Jewish emancipation, Tory MPs voiced their objections in largely secular terms. They did not stress, as did their predecessors, that the Jews were blasphemers and deicides, but emphasized that they were a distinct people and thus could not be considered part of the English nation.
>
> (Endelman 1979: 93)

Explaining the larger ramifications of this change in attitude, Endelman notes: "In a functional sense, there was no shift in the role the Jews played in the fantasy life of the Christians; the latent content of the fantasy remained the same—only the manifest content had changed its shape" (ibid.: 96). Early in the novel, when Dr. Grey's wife expresses her surprise that Mr. Moncada, Richard's Jewish maternal grandfather, who had arrived to claim his runaway daughter, did not look or act like a Jew, saying, "But I thought Jews had aye had lang beards, and yon man's face is *just like one of our ain folks*" (Scott [1827] 2000: 175; emphasis added), Dr. Grey, the very embodiment of liberalism and fair play, is quick to point out to her:

> But the Jews are often very respectable people, Mrs. Grey—they have no territorial property, because the law is against them there, but they have a

good hank in the money-market—plenty of stocks in the funds, Mrs. Grey. . . .
The Jews are well attached to government; they hate the Pope, the Devil, and
the Pretender as much as ony honest man among ourselves.

(ibid.)

Dr. Grey's clarifications are significant in that they point to the ways in which
the question of Jewish identity lingered as a gray area within the nationalist politics
of Hanoverian Britain. On the one hand, wealthy immigrant Jews like Mr.
Moncada had gained a measure of social acceptance by virtue of their power and
influence in society. On the other, perceptions about the Jew as a cruel despot
persisted, which is mirrored in Scott's depiction of Mr. Moncada and his
tyrannical treatment of his helpless daughter, Zilia, who is significantly cast as the
mysterious figure of the Orient, with her face concealed behind a veil.

As Endelman points out, despite their partial acculturation into British society,
most Jews were looked upon with suspicion, as evident in a work such as C. M.
Westmacott's *The English Spy* as well as in many of the satirical odes and political
essays written in verse during this time. Westmacott's work, whose title describes
it as providing the "portraits of the illustrious, eccentric, and notorious," contains
this telling scene at the stockbrokers:

> I will introduce you, *entre nous*, to a few characters who thrive by the destruc-
> tion of a thousand of their fellow creatures. The bashaw in black yonder,
> who rests his elephantine trunk against a pillar of the Exchange, with his
> hands thrust into his breeches pockets, is the Hebrew star—the Jewish
> luminary, a very *Shiloh* among the peoples of his own persuasion. . . . The
> fellow's insolence is intolerable, and his vulgarity and ignorance quite
> unbearable.
>
> (Westmacott 1825: 143–4)

Westmacott describes the manner in which this Jewish figure had risen from
"vending trinkets and spectacle-cases in the streets" to enter the stock exchange,
adding that "the more respectable members of the Stock Exchange, perceiving the
thralldom in which the public funds of the country were held by the tricks and
manoeuvres of the Jew party, determined to make a stand against them" (ibid.:
144–5). In this age of "projectors," when

> *bulls, bears, jews,* and *jobbers* all quit Chapel-court
> To become speculators and join the sport
>
> (ibid.: 134)

the threat of economic competition is pictured as originating from

> these debt-bred reptiles, hungry vermin
> Fed from the mass corrupt of which I spoke,
> Usurp your place. A jew, a dirty German,

Who has grown rich by many a lucky stroke,
    Shall rule the Minister, and all determined
To treat your bitter sufferings as a joke.
                                    (ibid.: 146)

Similarly, in John Wolcot's *More Lyric Odes to the Royal Academicians by Peter Pindar*,
Ode VI opens with:

"Find me Sodom out," exclaimed the Lord
"Ten *Gentlemen*, the place shan't be un*town'd*—
That is, I will not burn it ev'ry board":
The dev'l a gentleman was to be found!

The anonymous author of *The Voluntary Exile: A Political Essay in Verse* says:

But vain the task, O Albion, to expose
Thy faithless friends conceal'd, and open foes.
Pierce the dark scenes of fraud-concealing night,
And drag their actions to the test of light,
Then should that traitor, J—, be shewn
In all the Devil's blackness and his own.
                                    (pp. 12–13)

Fixed by his immutable racial identity, the Jew is thus produced in relation to the structural conditions constituting social desire within the colonial domain. As the figure who cunningly conceals his identity within the continuum of British social desire, he had to be made visible. It is this effort that marks Scott's narrative, as he continues to establish Richard's Jewish connection. Although unacknowledged as the legitimate heir to his father's and grandfather's fortunes, Richard Middlemas still remains attached, in Scott's imagination, to this iniquitous legacy of Jewishness—the "Devil's blackness." In fact, his mother's and grandfather's Jewishness is as much a part of him as his father's scheming and traitorous Jacobite personality. Secondly, Scott constantly points to Richard's physical features that make him inescapably Jewish. Both of these markers of alterity are emphasized to show how Richard's extreme personality cannot be redeemed through socialization—by the nurturing influence of Dr. Grey's Anglo-Saxon family. Whatever feelings he may have had for his surrogate family are often overcome by Richard's irrational yearnings for wealth and social status.

Richard's otherness, as signaled in a series of seemingly innocuous hints about his physical appearance, becomes the means of fixing him in his inescapable Jewishness. Although he is described as a handsome young man, with an appealing sensibility, his "dark eyes" (Scott [1827] 2000: 181) do not escape the notice of people around him. When Richard learns the true story of his Jewish parentage, his "dark eyes flashed fire" (ibid.). His companion and friend, the Anglo-Saxon Adam Hartley, provides the sharpest contrast to Richard's dark image. Both

Richard and Adam train under Dr. Grey as medical apprentices. While Adam is described as being of "full middle-size, stout, and well limbed; and an open English countenance of the genuine *Saxon* mold," Richard, "on the contrary, was dark, like his father and mother, with high features, beautifully formed, but exhibiting something of a foreign character" (ibid.: 188). Deciphering the hidden Jew from what might appear to be typically Anglo-Saxon physical characteristics provides the very thrust that the tale requires to sustain its movement of defining the racially marked core of an Anglo-Saxon identity. Richard's physical differences are also shown to be emblematic of the deeper moral differences between Richard and Adam. Despite their friendship, Adam acts as Richard's moral guide, constantly confronting him with his darker side: "Richard . . . that pride of yours, if you do not check it, will render you both ungrateful and miserable" (ibid.: 198). As a moral foil to Richard Middlemas, Adam Hartley is presented as being secure in his own Anglo-Saxon identity. Richard, on the other hand, constantly searches for that elusive identity that will render him whole, although it is clear by now that he can never be successful in that pursuit.

Thus Richard's attempts to recuperate himself from social ignominy, drama-tized throughout the first nine chapters of the tale, are represented as being motivated by a singular impulse: that of social ambition bordering on uncontrolled avarice. Scott maintains the uneasy balance between the two in a tantalizing manner throughout these chapters. He portrays Richard as being so caught up in his dreams that he is unable to distinguish between reality and illusion, which becomes a defining feature of his personality and his emotional and intellectual make-up. Deceived by the fantastic images of the splendors of this "new-found El Dorado" (Scott [1827] 2000: 201) evoked in his mind by Tom Hillary, the "recruiting captain" (ibid.: 203), Richard finds himself assailed by the grotesque images of India as he lies in a state of stupor and delirium at the hospital after being abandoned and sold by Tom to the master of the brig:

> The effect of the liquor displayed itself, as usual, in a hundred wild dreams of parched deserts, and of serpents whose bite inflicted the most intolerable thirst—of the suffering of the Indian on the death-stake—and the torments of the infernal regions themselves.
>
> (ibid.: 212)

Here Richard's romantic yearnings, earlier referred to as "'Temple and tower,' a hundred flattering edifices of Richard's imagination" (ibid.: 181), are rendered in their adult form. Transformed into images of phantasmagoria, they reflect the potentially dark underside of Richard's psyche, identifying him with those notions of Indian alterity that John Barrell claims formed part of the "barbaresque" imagery of popular Orientalism, and which were often used to "represent 'unimaginable horrors'" (Barrell 1991: 6–7).

These horrors become real as Richard's identity as the Jew takes on a complex signifying dimension soon after he arrives in India. Scott continues to affirm the contrast between Richard and Adam across an entire range of sexual and political

differences, which are deployed to secure the value of the "good" colonial–representing "reason"–pitted against the "bad"–representing all that seemed irrational.
This allows the darker elements of colonial desire (and the dark underside of
colonial history) to be identified with Richard and his compatriot, Madame
Montreville. Absconding from the military regiment in Madras after accidentally
killing a colonel, Richard goes into hiding, and later reappears as the black female
servant of the infamous Madame Montreville, who promises him shelter and
anonymity until the whole affair should be forgotten by the colonial judicial
authorities. Richard's active, masculine, almost Faustian passion, earlier derided
by Adam Hartley as a sign of unchecked ambition, is here transformed into passive
feminine role-playing. By agreeing to play the part of a "woman," Richard is
shown to be only too eager to subordinate himself to a woman like Madame
Montreville who behaves like a man.[12] Such a rendition of the Jew's slavery to
material gain wasn't Scott invention; in *The Voluntary Exile*, the Jew is described as

> he who knows no shame no vice will shun.
> A being he, of such a heart deprav'd,
> That e'en for slav'ry's sake he'd be enslaved.
>
> (p. 13)

Therefore, by ceasing to be a man, Richard relinquishes whatever vestige of
"Englishness" he had earlier claimed. By contrast, Adam Hartley, his childhood
friend, remains faithful to the ideals of chivalric masculinity by retaining his
Anglo-Saxon sense of independence and resourcefulness.

Entering the services of the East India Company as a doctor, Adam Hartley not
only caters to the needs of the regiment, but also establishes a reputation of being a
reliable doctor among the natives. Like Richard's, Adam's aspirations are also
geared towards making wealth in the services of the company, but his wishes are
channeled in what Scott constructs as a morally and professionally acceptable
direction. Adam's professionalism is underscored by the fact that, like the
eighteenth-century orientalist scholar, he learns the languages of the Orient in
order to communicate better with the natives in whose services he hopes to make
his wealth. He, however, does not romanticize the Orient. His marked utilitarian
attitude departs from those of the eighteenth-century orientalists, who were
perceived by many in the nineteenth century (including the historian James Mill)
as being too misty-eyed to comprehend the real tasks of Britain's imperial burden
in India. Adam's guarded and somewhat cynical attitude towards Indians and their
way of life is revealed in his ability to play the part of a judge as well as a learned
Orientalist. He is not only adept at discerning the many deceptions in the Indian
courts but is also able to master them to beguile the natives. Furthermore, Adam
takes the moral initiative to plan the rescue of Menie Grey, who had earlier been
kidnapped by Madame Montreville and Richard Middlemas in order to be sold to
the tyrannical Indian prince Tippoo. Politically then, Adam is savvy in the affairs
of colonial administration, aware of the numerous back alleys of that system; he
approaches the natives with the right balance of understanding and caution, fully

aware that the Briton's responsibility in India was to outdo the natives at their own games. Although he is not strictly an insider, Adam displays all the characteristic qualities of an imperial administrator who knows the cracks and crevices of the colonial system. His powers of inductive reasoning, displayed in his shrewd observations about oriental "character," conjoined with his moral sensibility and rectitude, make him into a prototype administrator that was being engineered in early nineteenth-century Britain by Whig utilitarian reformers. Thus, Adam combines in measured harmony all those characteristics that allowed men in Britain to fantasize entering India and yet not be corrupted by its "contagion." Clearly maintaining and asserting his sense of a national self-identity through duty (towards the company as well as Menie Grey), reasonableness, and intelligence, Adam continues to provide the story with its fantasy of moral stability and aristocratic responsibility in the aftermath of colonial war, intrigue, and plunder.

On the other hand, Richard's alliance with Madame Montreville, the European-turned-native, bears all the shades of moral confusion associated with eighteenth-century mercantilism. Since during this time trade and military exploits were often linked to politically exigent policies, numerous personal and political alliances had been forged between the imperial and the local native powers. But these alliances also created a sense of a loss of British moral authority; in fact, Europeans who had made themselves powerful through these alliances were cast as the ones most vulnerable to the worst influences of colonialism. It is therefore not surprising that Madame Montreville becomes the tale's most powerful emblem of this corruption. Like her husband, who "went into the interior" to set up his private army after the French defeat and was subsequently killed by Mysore's Hyder Ali, Madame Montreville, this "daughter of a Scotch emigrant" (Scott [1827] 2000: 252), seemed to be the figure who had crossed all the social, racial, national, and sexual boundaries that British colonial authorities had so tenuously held on to. But her special status, which had helped her to maintain her power as a fiercely independent adventurer, had been partly derived from the British colonial authorities. Realizing her important function as a mediator in preserving the delicate balance of power between the British, the French, and the native powers during the period of military expansion in colonial India, British authorities had sanctioned her presence in areas under British rule. Scott's tale, however, circumvents the politically expedient nature of such policies adopted by the British, and instead makes Madame Montreville into another Oriental despot whose ambiguous sexuality (ibid.: 252–3) and grotesque masculinity are reiterated in the language used to describe her: "Zenobia" (ibid.: 250), "the Queen of Sheba" (ibid.: 256), "Boadicea" (ibid.: 252), "Amazon" (ibid.: 253), "this unsexed woman, who can no longer be termed a European" (ibid.: 259), "the tyrannical Begum" (ibid.: 266), and "female tyrant" (ibid.: 263).

If the eighteenth-century British "nabob" is a playful caricature of the excesses of mercantile colonialism, Madame Montreville is its sinister counterpart. Unlike the nabob, who always returned to his domestic settings in order to be redeemed, Madame Montreville was a "woman" gone "native." From her spacious house in the "Black Town," away from the Europeans, she conducts numerous intrigues on behalf of her ever-changing political benefactors. In his eighteenth-century *Narrative*, for example, Edward Moor, a popular late eighteenth-century colonial travel writer, gave voice to a similar anxiety about female adventurers, who he claimed were the counterparts of those "European officers" who rendered military service to the "native armies" out of "dissatisfaction, pecuniary distresses, caprice possibly" (Moor 1794: 120). Modeled after the real historical figure Begum Sumroo, who had challenged the military authority of the British colonial authorities, Madame Montreville belongs to the company of those women adventure-seekers whose stories often circulated in Britain. But, more significantly, the female adventurer symbolically represented a "horror" that had its source in a complex cultural reflex system.[13] First, to the masculine colonial imagination, the usurpation by a woman of a masculine role presented an aberration to the scheme of "nature"; at the same time, however, as someone inhabiting the very borders of masculine desire, she was necessary for deflecting the horror associated with the dark underside of mercantile colonialism. Embodying a disruptive womanhood trafficking in a colonial masculinity, she is what Herbert Sussman calls the "violent Other" (Sussman 1995: 21). In order to preserve the stability of the dominant sexual order imperiled by figures such as Richard and Madame Montreville, Scott deploys his "maiden in rescue" theme in the closing sections of the tale. Menie Gray, the very embodiment of femininity in peril, has to be rescued from the clutches of the demonic man-woman. It is Adam Hartley who is entrusted with the task of providing the paternal surveillance rejected by women like Madame Montreville, and it is through his intervention that the sexual hierarchies can be restored.

But before this can be achieved, Scott continues to depict the progressive disfigurement of British masculine desire. Because Richard is now wholly associated with the "other," the narrative can unproblematically work towards eliminating him from its scenes of action, thereby restoring the fantasized image of pure masculine desire unhampered by its links to this dark mercantile history. The conclusion to *The Surgeon's Daughter* is therefore predictably centered on regulating the primacy of an order of sexual and racial distinctions crucial to the maintenance of such desire. The theme of a rescue fantasy helps transform the anxieties attending the narrative into pure theatrical spectacle. The spectacle, with its pictorial and panoramic quality, is cast ritualistically in the form of a tableau of events unfolding in a progressive manner—the details of the Indian landscape and the court of Tipoo Sultan are combined with scenes of native heraldry in preparation for the final rescue scene that will involve Adam Hartley, Richard Middlemas, Madame Montreville, and Menie Grey. During the ceremonial meeting when Menie Gray is being presented to the tyrant Tippoo, Richard is displayed "in a dress as magnificent in itself as it was remote from all European costume, being that of a banka, or Indian courtier . . . His mustachios were turned and curled, and his eyelids stained with antimony" (Scott [1827] 2000: 280). He is shown sitting by the side of Madame Montreville, who seems magically transformed into a regal woman—"begum Mottee Mohul"—the very embodiment of Oriental femininity. Their transformation into what they really are—"Indians"—

is so complete that all vestiges of Europeanness are completely eliminated from their identities. All moral ambiguities are banished from these scenes of the final transformation, and all the accompanying anxieties finally distanced and displaced.

This distancing is further advanced by the narrative denouement to this moral drama. The description of the ritual execution of Richard Middlemas at the hands of the Indian Hyder Ali is itself drawn from popular accounts of ritual punishment inflicted by Indian despots on criminals.[14] Richard's death at the hands of an Indian monarch clears the British moral conscience from any direct responsibility for having to rid itself of its own darkest desires (after all, Richard is still referred to as a "European" as he is being mauled by the elephant). Scott reminds the reader of "how dreadfully the Nawaub kept his promise, and how he and his son afterwards *sunk before the discipline and bravery of the Europeans*" (Scott [1827] 2000: 285; emphasis added), strategically averting any sense of Indian moral victory that might be implied in the resolution of this drama. Britain's political might and victory stand out as singular manifestations of a providential history, celebrating the moral power and ethos of the empire. As in other moments in the novel, Scott has recourse to a historical hindsight to reinforce the idea that British interests in India were morally justified, and that, in the struggle for supremacy over India, history and providence had validated her emergence as the sole legitimate power.

In this chapter I have demonstrated how the disciplining of social desire in the early nineteenth century is accomplished by simultaneously projecting the image of the traitorous Jew in "all his Devil's blackness" and that of the sedate Menie Grey, whose portrait adorns the walls of the Whig gentry. Their co-existence within the same discursive continuum symptomizes the manner in which the dynamic trajectories of national, racial, gender, and class identities had been mobilized to define and give moral force to the norms of civility that guided imperial Britain. The intersection of class and race—both essential to the formation of civility—articulates a powerful ideology that establishes their simultaneity. Reinforcing the belief that Britain's greatness could be assured through its faith in an imagined aristocratic Anglo-Saxon order, that ideology not only maintained, through its hegemonic influence, the lines between sanctioned civility and its deviant forms but also forged new ways in which this deviancy could be harnessed to justify social desire. The works considered in this chapter also articulate a historical voice that reflects the need among British subjects to project the fantasy of their aristocratic destiny in the face of the new uncertainties of the times. The dominant classes were not only forced to confront the new social realities but they also successfully reimagined their roles as national subjects by recuperating the very contradictions within the nationalist–colonialist reflex system that had been threatened by change.

2 Writing the liberal self

Colonial civility and disciplinary regime

The nineteenth-century British nation-state organized itself around a disciplinary regime that was guided by the ideologies of metropolitan liberalism and its reigning political economy. Civility played a regulative normative function within that regime by constituting a form of "governmentality" through its politics of subjectivity. Under this function, the self is always subject to surveillance–to a form of self-monitoring that produced boundaries determining an "interiority" for the liberal self. Coterminous with the formation of this interiority is the need to define and situate the colonial other, a need that manifests itself in the public domain in the imperial articulations of governance. This interlinking of governance, subjectivity, nation, and colony is the focus of this chapter on civility. By centering my arguments around John Stuart Mill's *Autobiography*–an exemplary narrative about the process of writing the "liberal self"–and his colonial writings I wish to excavate two underlying histories, histories that mark the terrain between the disciplinary tasks of colonial governance and the constitution of liberalism's normalizing discourses. I trace these two histories as they appear embedded in the life and political career of Mill, and then in the life that he captures in his retrospective autobiographical narrative.

From 1823 to 1858, John Stuart Mill not only developed his philosophy of liberalism through his political writings but also served as an examiner in the Office of Correspondence with the East India Company, where he deployed his liberal philosophy for shaping his ideas on the administrative policies of the Indian empire. In addition to authoring such key works as *System of Logic* (1843), *The Principles of Political Economy* (1848), *On Liberty* (1859), and *Considerations on Representative Government* (1861), he contributed numerous essays on ethics, religion, history, law, and education to major Victorian periodicals during this period of his life. It is clear that the formulation of the key concepts of liberalism in Mill took place within a discursive environment charged with questions about colonial governance. The story of his own life that Mill recounted in the *Autobiography* was published posthumously in 1873. The account of his political career as a colonial bureaucrat can be gleaned from Mill's numerous handwritten "Indian dispatches" published as official East India Company documents; from his essays in the *London and Westminister Review*, *Parliamentary Review*, *Sessional Papers of the House of the Lords*, and *Fortnightly Review*; and from key petitions he wrote as an East India Company

official. The last includes the evidence he provided about the company's administration in India to the Select Committee of the House of Lords (1852), and the
Memorandum of the Improvements in the Administration of India and *Petition of the East-India
Company to Parliament* (1858) written on the eve of the transfer of power to the
crown. In assessing his political and professional career as a colonial bureaucrat,
historians have been struck by the fact that, despite his interest in India and his
intimate links to the administrative set-up of a colonial company, Mill dismissed
his Indian experience in a few short paragraphs in his monumental *Autobiography*.
The first section of this chapter is an investigation of this "silence"—an attempt to
read it as a particular symptom of a colonialist epistemological stance that was
intrinsic to Mill's liberal outlook. This colonialist stance can be discerned throughout the *Autobiography* as a position from which he produces a particular politics of
metropolitan subjectivity by retrospectively utilizing his own life as a paradigm
for defining that subjectivity. A closer examination of the *Autobiography* reveals
that underlying that politics is a discourse of "interiority," a discourse that, like
Foucault's notion of liberalism's "polymorphousness," functioned as a normalizing
mechanism. By initially differentiating the "self" into two essential spheres—the
private and the public—Mill subsequently regulates the relational function between
the two in a strategic manner. Within this regulative logic, the "private" presents
the site of individual self-fashioning and of resistance to the outer world, while the
"public" represents the sphere of action realized within a progressive historical
temporality and national culture. As the narrative of the *Autobiography* shows, this
difference between the "private" and the "public" is worked out in a manner that
allows self-presence to be simultaneously preserved and linked to the ethos of a
"national culture." It is within this dialectic that Mill identifies a more public
"national character" that is seen to serve as the source as well as the *telos* of metropolitan subjectivity, and also as the justification for colonial governance based on
notions of colonial difference. Foucault claimed that liberal "government"
constructs itself in the form of an "excess" to "society," which helps structure and
activate its own normalizing power. The metropolitan self in Mill is subject to a
similar normalizing mechanism: the authority of the "public" is constituted in a
manner that allows it to resonate with the demands of individual self-fashioning.
Since this discursive interrelationship between the private and the public is
mirrored throughout in his writings, I read the link between Mill's narrative about
his self, his own silence about India in his *Autobiography*, and his articulations about
colonial India in his public writings as a specific historical expression of the
disciplinary regime of the modern liberal state.

   The chapter is divided into two main sections. The first section concentrates on
specific sections of the *Autobiography* by situating them within the wider context of
his public writings on colonialism in general, and India in particular. My argument
in this section rests on the claim that the liberal notions of the "self" across which
Mill defined his own autobiographical impulse depended on positing a particular
"nature" to the metropolitan historical subject. That "nature," envisioned as
necessarily historical, is also posited as an entity defined by certain distinctive
mental faculties of judgment and discriminative feeling, and by its evolution within

a dialectic of continuity and change belonging exclusively to the metropolitan European order. As I will attempt to clarify, Mill's writing of this "self" in the *Autobiography* also necessitates a technique of "management" that is aimed at resolving any possible rupture within this dialectic of continuity and change. This strategy of management has significant implications for our understanding of Mill's justification of the liberal political arrangements in India and of the conception of civility that underlies his ideas about non-white colonized subjects.

The second section moves the focus of discussion to another locus within this liberal legacy: it directs attention to an obscure and anonymous poetic work by a young civilian in India, and on the public writings of Robert Rickards, who had served as a collector in the Indian Civil Services and who later became a member of parliament. As a parliamentarian, Rickards opposed the efforts of the East India Company to have its charter renewed in 1813. Both the anonymous poet and Rickards question the principles upon which Mill was to justify colonial rule by directing attention to the exploitative mechanisms and expedient measures adopted by the very policies of the colonial government that were claimed to have been directed by liberal principles. I wish to explore the extent to which their critiques reflect what Foucault has argued about liberalism's "polymorphism"– that it exists in "simultaneous forms as a regulative scheme of government practice and as the theme of sometimes-radical opposition" (Foucault 1997: 75). Furthermore, I wish to examine to what extent these oppositional discourses bring out a very different understanding of the limits of civility defined by the notion of "enlightened despotism" sanctioned by Mill's liberalism, and the effects of the political, economic, and social fallout precipitated by it on Britain's civil character.

NARRATING CIVILITY: THE PRIVATE AND THE PUBLIC SPHERES

In his *Autobiography*, Mill tells the story of his life from the position of a public intellectual; in his public writings he tells the story of India from the position of a witness to the larger historical changes in Indian administration during the 1830s, 1840s, and 1850s that were facilitated by the political initiatives of the company which he served. Underlining both of these stories is an epistemological stance which I argue was central to the liberal politics that he espoused; it was a stance that strategically regulated how the field of relations between the knowing subject and the knowable object could be deployed across two different spaces and two different, although interlinked, histories–those of metropolitan England and colonial India. In the *Autobiography* Mill presents himself simultaneously as a subject authorizing a story that gathers its identity through its telling, and as that omniscient entity located outside that story who can fix his gaze on it and "read" its evolving patterns of meaning. The pattern of self-understanding inscribed in this mode of "reading" is based on a retrospective stance which, as Mary Corbett has suggested, enabled Mill to "sum up a life as it draws to a close" (Corbett 1992: 10). Corbett argues that, unlike Wordsworth or Carlyle, for whom the autobiography constituted identities yet to be enacted, Mill's enterprise draws its epistemological power from this sustained retrospective stance. However, the uniformity of narrative, guaranteed by this stance, is counterpoised at one stage in the *Autobiography* by a sense of dislocation that is signaled by a disruption in its continuity. This occurs when Mill describes, in painstaking detail, the story of his own "mental crisis." Reading this dislocation from a rhetorical perspective, I argue that, far from disrupting the narrative, the story of crisis constitutes the very dynamics of self-fashioning that is fundamental to Mill's liberalism. Although caught between the forces of historical determinism and its own creative liberty, this tactical break produces a narrative of self that casts itself as an inwardly mobile and organic entity possessing a unique interiority, one that aligns it simultaneously with the "nation" and its own particularity.

The "rupture" is therefore a necessary condition for suspending the deterministic logic of linear growth, thereby allowing the self to assert its own sovereignty as an agent of change in a world dictated by outside forces. This story—well known for its evocative delineation of his encounter with the poetry of William Wordsworth—becomes a moment of transformation, providing Mill with an alternative affective terrain for defining the task of "writing" the liberal self. The political implications of Mill's reading of Wordsworth implicit in this process of "writing" the self become increasingly clear as Mill subsequently devotes himself to the task of defining his public role as a professional bureaucrat. What also becomes evident is that the disciplinary regime embedded in the production of this double identity functions as a form of discursive engagement with the legitimizing discourses for civility and civil governance. In other words, the rupture itself serves as a mechanism for connecting the *telos* of his own evolving self to the public role he assumed as a philosopher and imperial bureaucrat. In turning to his public writings, it becomes apparent that it is India as the subject nation which serves as the "object" of knowledge for Mill: he reads India while speculating about its political and social nature and about its history, which was being shaped by the mechanisms of colonial law and administration in whose formulation he played a key role. Such an epistemological arrangement between the knower and the known allowed Mill to track India's entry into the imagination of Victorian liberalism and to carve out a place for it in the order mandated by liberal political institutions. Correspondingly, such an arrangement enabled him to create initially a separate, transcendental site for locating the power of the metropolitan knowing subject. It is my view that such an arrangement should be understood not in terms of an ahistorical normativity—that is, epistemology as transhistorical condition of knowing—but in terms of the interested nature of the institutional effects set in place by the liberal politics of Victorian colonialism, which involved the tasks of negotiating land and property relations in the colonies, and of regulating policies on law, education, and administration in a realm that lay far beyond the traditional *habitus* of the metropolitan subject.

A few preliminary remarks are necessary for clarifying how colonial institutions during Mill's era functioned as enabling structures within the system of "dual" government adopted in India. Broadly imitating a metropolitan "democratic" system outside the borders of the metropolis, these institutions were represented by two bodies in India: (1) the Board of Control, which was in charge of supervising the company and (2) the Court of Directors, responsible for colonial administration and serving as the executive part of the company, elected by the larger shareholders and its main sectional interests (Mill 1990: ix). The Office of the Examiner of Indian Correspondence that Mill headed for a significant number of years occupied a key position within this dual form of government, assisting the court and its committees in drafting the dispatches to satisfy the scrutiny of the Board of Control, and formulating authoritative statements of policy and principles for the guidance of the governing bodies in India. In 1852, while responding to questions about the efficacy of the company's government, Mill had defended this dual system by stating:

> I think the fact that all Indian proceedings are reviewed by two separate bodies, independent of one another, is a much greater security for *good government* than would exist under any system by which those two bodies were merged into one. The double revision by persons of a different class, in a different position, and probably with different prepossessions, tends greatly to promote a close and rigid examination.
>
> (ibid.: 42; emphasis added)

Here Mill appears to espouse the cause of "difference" and "plurality"—the very cause he believed advanced the values of the liberal belief in representative government. However, the reality was that the governance of India did not rest on a representative system; in fact, the process of checks and balances in place for reviewing Indian proceedings relied on the judgment of individuals from the metropolitan middle classes whom Mill described unambiguously as "the classes unconnected with politics, or with the two Houses of Parliament" (ibid.: 38). By incarnating the system of checks and balances of a metropolitan government, these two bodies, Mill claimed, promoted the interests of the people of India who did not have direct representation in the parliament. As Francis Hutchins notes, Mill "misjudged the nature of both Parliamentary politics and the middleclass rulers of India" by making "a virtue of the Company's remoteness from politics [and] by presuming that political activity could never serve Indian interests" (Hutchins 1967: 91).[1] It is clear then that "Indian interests" could be defined only through this political disinterestedness, imagined at another level to be a manifestation of a legitimate rational order of checks and balances maintained outside the realm of the political.

It is through such strategic justification of "difference" and "interest" that Mill later engaged in defining the divergent economic, political, and social interests that were being served by colonial rule, out of which he forged the rationality of a political order that guaranteed "good government." This political rationality required Mill to locate India within an epistemological field that would enable a steady differential to be maintained between the colonial subject authorized *to know* and act on its behalf and the subject nation that would be illuminated by the colonialist's scopic power. In raising the question of such an epistemology, one is necessarily forced to reconsider the ways in which Mill positioned himself as someone who, through a dispassionate understanding of "interest," could successfully reconcile the divergent colonial interests–those belonging to the British nation ruled by its parliamentary representative system, those of the company run by investors and directors whose interests he directly represented, and those of India whose governance was the charge entrusted upon the company. At a general level, the philosophical rationalization that lay behind such a conceptualization of "interest" was founded on Mill's liberal skeptical world-view, with its own disciplinary regime. As a liberal philosopher, Mill believed that all claims to "truth" were provisional and that "we may rely on having attained such approach to truth, as is possible in *our own day*" (Mill 1993: 26; emphasis added). Mill further asserted that "this is the amount of certainty attainable by a fallible being" (ibid.), thus mobilizing a form of disciplinary government based on a *realpolitik* that attempted to marry the idealist strains of liberal thinking with its realist strain. To the extent to which this *realpolitik* is itself produced out of the critique of government, which Foucault asserts is intrinsic to liberalism, both the rhetoric of "interest" and the question of whose interest was at stake in any colonial governmental system were discursively bound to a range of colonial practices that had been naturalized and validated by the epistemologies of liberal, humanist thought. Such a strategic position on "interest" undergirded Mill's thinking about representative governments in enlightened European societies and about the economic rationales for a company-run empire, but what stands out about these colonial practices is that they were aimed not so much at instituting change as a way to ensure better governance as at managing the diversity and–at times–the incommensurability of divergent "interests" in the name of "good government." Liberal colonial practices can therefore be described as disciplinary in function since they did not simply "create" difference but operated through a normalizing discourse where diversity and difference could be co-opted for the purposes of rationalizing government.

The function of this normalizing discourse can also be observed in the way in which Mill often deployed a systematically flexible conceptual machinery to regulate notions of "national subjectivity" and "history." Within it, national subjectivity was conceived in terms of an inherently progressive view of a self-determining society and its power to establish and maintain those political institutions that served its own political interests. As Uday Singh Mehta has pointed out, this subjectivity, understood as "human nature," was premised on the "critical capacity for making a choice," identified by Mill in *On Liberty* as "a distinctive endowment of a human being." This capacity, linked to "the human faculties of perception, judgement, discriminative feeling, mental activity and even moral preference" (Mehta 1999: 72), is the domain of the "private." On the "public" front, "history" provided the necessary foundation for the social and political life of metropolitan subjects by furnishing a sense of continuum through change for the realization of these faculties. Furthermore, it was "history" that allowed these traits to emerge within the national psyche, making metropolitan subjects aware of their own interests and their own powers of dis/interested judgment and discrimination. In the colonial context, this interrelationship between the private and the public had significant ideological ramifications—it allowed a liberal philosopher such as Mill to uphold those structures of power that allowed the interests of the British nation and the privately owned East India Company to be identified through the common and shared good—that of ruling India under the guise of offering "good government," as well as allowing it to be guided by Victorian paternalism.

By stressing this commonality of interest, Mill was also able to differentiate the national subjectivity of the people of his own country from those of the newly educated Indians who he felt were "constantly becoming fit for higher situations" of office, although not "*yet fit* for the highest appointments" (Mill 1990: 63; emphasis added). In the *Autobiography* this disciplinary discourse of "interest" is crucial to supporting the ideological structure of its humanist *Bildungsroman*. It enabled the liberal philosophy of individualism—which Mill described as "the inward domain of consciousness" (Mill 1993: 15)—to be anchored in a fundamentally colonialist epistemology. In other words, the *Autobiography* functions as a literary counterpart to his philosophical theorizations about human liberty upon which his entire reasoning on the nature of the relations between self and society had been fashioned.[2] Significantly, the dual and inter-animating disciplinary relationship—of influence and interaction—between society and the individual—society acts upon the individual so that the individual can differentiate itself in its liberty—found in the *Autobiography* formed the very basis on which Mill rationalized the entire enterprise of colonialism as being a form of benevolent despotism in which the colonial nation needed the disciplinary tutelage exercised by an enlightened parent in order to realize itself.[3]

Given this relationship, Mill cannot imagine the possibility of India ever asserting its own political aspirations, his argument being that "the public of India afford no assistance in their own government. They are not ripe for doing so by means of representative government" and that "the great security for good government—public discussion—does not exist for India" (Mill 1990: 49). In his conceptualization of "public discourse," Mill provides what Homi Bhabha calls a "a colonial substitute for democratic 'public discussion,'" which meant that "events experienced and inscribed in India are to be read *otherwise*, transformed into the acts of governments and the discourses of authority in *another place*, at *another time*" (Bhabha 1985: 73). This form of "deferral" is clearly founded on Mill's own conception of a "possible" national subjectivity for the subject peoples of India. That subjectivity is perceived as being always possible but incomplete because its *telos* is regulated by forces outside itself, forces over which it has no direct access. Based on this reasoning, Mill argues in *On Liberty* that "despotism is a legitimate mode of government in dealing with barbarians ... Liberty, as a principle, has no application to any state of things *anterior to* [the] *time when mankind has become capable of being improved by free and equal discussion*" (Mill 1993: 13; emphasis added). In a parallel, albeit extreme, form, these sentiments are echoed in the defence of the East India Company by the arch-colonialist Thomas Campbell Robertson, in which he explicitly states that "the natives of India are *better servants than subjects*; and it is in the former capacity alone that we can ever expect to com-mand their co-operation in any emergency" (Robertson 1829: 80; emphasis added). Although it is unclear if Mill perceived Indians to be mere "barbarians," while replying to questions raised about the employment of natives to administra-tive office during the debate for the renewal of the East India Company's charter in 1832, he circumvents the possibility raised by his questioners that the employment of Indians might jeopardize the "dependence of India" upon England by stating, "I think it might, by *judicious management*, be made to continue till *the time rises* when the natives shall be qualified to carry on the same system of government without our assistance" (Mill 1990: 65; emphasis added). The deferral of a national subjectivity—here worded as "character"—communicated in "till the time rises"—through "judicious management"—gained its valence from an understanding of progressive history whose rationality is discerned in the *Autobiography*. Here "time" takes the side of the metropolitan individual, providing the very conditions needed for constructing the freedom and inwardness of the metropolitan "self," while excluding the colonial subject from the possibility of attaining its freedom. As I have commented in the Introduction, the debates about the education of natives are of crucial significance in the light of such reasoning that originated in the metropolis, and which was articulated so persistently by a figure such as Macaulay, the pioneer of Western education in India.

In his *Autobiography*, Mill states that there were three reasons behind his desire to "leave behind [him] such a memorial of so uneventful a life": first, to offer a description of his "unusual and remarkable" education in the hope that it would provide an instructive model for educating children; second, to present to his readers a model of a mind evolving through successive phases in an "age of transition in opinions" [in both the external and the internal worlds]; and, third, to acknowledge "the debts which [his] intellectual and moral development owes to other persons" (Mill 1981: 5). Mill's justifications for writing about his own life combine a metropolitan belief in the Romantic notion of self as intrinsically driven by an "inward nature"—including the belief in the dynamism of individual self-creation—with rational utilitarian ideals of the exemplary life that formed "character," which he had derived from his father, James Mill. Worth remember-ing is the fact that it was utilitarian thinking that inspired much of the educational policies in colonial India in the 1840s and 1850s. It might be worthwhile to gloss the point that John Stuart Mill had himself been subjected to this utilitarian program in the form of an experimental education based on his father's rational and utilitarian views on home education. Also, it is this very rational and utilitarian education that Mill rejects in his *Autobiography* as he attempts to carve out a space for the child who becomes the repository of sentiment, which in turn is attributed to Wordsworth's "culture of feelings." On the other side of the colonial divide, the Indian children of Macaulay tutored by Western education were demanding recognition to which imperial culture reacted by creating the *baboo*.

The autobiographical subject in Mill learns to inscribe itself simultaneously as a self that is aware of history—whose inwardness is produced by the changes that history fosters in the "age of transition"—and as a self that is able to transcend its own historical finiteness and know itself as an "autonomous" entity. Repeatedly, this epistemological certainty recuperates for Mill what he had philosophically perceived to be the limits inherent in any form of understanding in a "fallible" being–whether it was the understanding of the self or the understanding of history. This recuperative strategy is fundamental to the division between the "private" and the "public," indicated before. It materializes in the subsequent chapters of the *Autobiography*, where the story of the self is cast as a history of a struggle–between the forces of determinism and freedom, which Mill dramatizes in his description of the conflict between a seemingly despotic father (James Mill) and himself, the rebellious son. I will return to this theme later in the chapter. Here I wish to emphasize the point that the process of self-individuation, seen in these chapters of the *Autobiography*, is produced out of the very conflict between the two forces. Simultaneous with the act of individuation is the identification of the metropolitan self with the British nation and the company: both are bound together by a shared historical destiny. Just as the nation/company had realized its own interests in relation to the colonial society, the individual realizes its own liberty in the process of defining, regulating, and limiting the world that acts upon it and from which it acquires its own significance. When Bhikhu Parekh, in his essay "Liberalism and Colonialism," wonders how liberalism that had offered "one of the most inspiring statements of human equality" could justify "colonialism with a clear conscience" (Parekh 1994: 81), he fails to see that the terms in which Mill's liberalism articulated a vision of "human equality" were coterminous with the justifications for colonial rule.[4] Because Mill's justifications were often defined in terms of a flexible notion of "interest," which was fundamental to liberal colonialist politics, the contradiction that Parekh notes within liberalism should be read, not in terms of a great rupture between theory and praxis, but as a strategic one, constitutive of the very possibility of a liberal colonialist epistemology and its politics.

Imbricated in this epistemology is a vision of the temporality of history. By this vision I mean the perception of history's steady movement through finiteness and change, allowing it to reach its own *telos* in the subject. This is the sense of temporality that underwrites Mill's autobiographical impulse. However, for Mill, as stated earlier, the temporality across which the colonial nation moves towards its own *telos* can only exist as a deferred temporality, producing an incomplete subject. In Mill's argument, it is national "character" that simultaneously is formed out of history and moves history; in the case of India, the move towards self-realization is always retarded by a lack. He repeats that the natives of India cannot be responsible enough to govern themselves "until [they] are very much improved in character." This understanding of history as a character/nation-shaping force secures the colonialist's power to continue to act upon its object through "judicious management," a power that is also secured by maintaining the necessary distance between the metropolitan "self" and the colonial "other," an idea reinforced by Mill's observations about the Indian "character":

> India is a peculiar country; the state of civilization, the character and habits of the people, and the private and public rights established among them, are

totally different from those which are known or recognized in this country; in fact the study of India must be as much a profession in itself as law or medicine.

(Mill 1990: 49)

Mill's call for a professional approach to "studying" India as an object sanctions the role of the East India Company, particularly those professional company bureaucrats engaged in Indian affairs and with the most direct "interest" in India. In the *Report to Court of Proprietors on India Bills* in 1858, he describes them as individuals who had "passed a considerable portion of their lives in India, or who feel that habitual interest in its affairs which is *naturally* acquired by having aided in administering them" (ibid.: 166; emphasis added). He morally justifies the "interest" of these ruling classes of career bureaucrats paradoxically by seeing them as "disinterested" individuals: "Those who possess the influence, exercise it under a sufficiently strong sense of responsibility to the public" (ibid.: 46–7). This implicit equation between "power," "natural disposition," "responsibility," and the "natural" acquisition of knowledge by men with colonial administrative experience reflects Mill's conflation of interest with the dispassionate claims of knowledge. The close identification between "local knowledge" of administrators with the "general principles of law making" (ibid.: 21)—something that he admired in the work of the framers of the New Penal Code of 1838—was for Mill a sign that the government of the East India Company was serious about protecting the natives of India from "serious oppression and denial of justice" (ibid.: 20). It provided the moral basis for governance, and, as he reminds his readers in "the Minutes of the Black Act," that, if the conviction in the reputation of our "character of being more just and more disinterested than the native rulers" was to erode in any way, it would only result in the final dissolution of "our empire in India" (ibid.: 15).

The colonialist epistemology underwriting Mill's political thinking is also reflected in his preoccupation with historical temporality and the evolution of a metropolitan moral conscience. Writing about India in 1861, in his review of Henry Sumner Maine's *Ancient Law: Its Connection with Early History of Society, and its Relation to Modern Ideas*, twelve years after he had left the services of the East India Company, he evaluates Maine's legal discussion of early Teutonic agricultural customs. As a legal historian, Maine (1822–88) had based his study of European customs by comparing them to the practices among contemporary Indian rural communities. Because of the persistence of customary common property relations in agricultural land-usage and ownership, India provided, Maine argued, "the great repository of verifiable phenomena of ancient usage and ancient juridical thought" (quoted in Mill 1990: 216). In assessing the merit of such an approach to history, Mill praised Maine for "pointing out' the historical origin not only of institutions, but also of ideas, which many believe to be essential elements of the conception of social order" (ibid.: 215). Mill stated that, since the "historical origin" of modern-day European institutions and ideas was no longer available to the modern European consciousness, having been superseded, and therefore rendered invisible, by the historical transformations taking place within Europe, that lost origin could be located elsewhere—in this case, India and within its museum-like space of indigenous village communities seemingly untouched by history. Mill therefore endorses Maine's historical approach by advancing a Victorian anthropological perspective: his support of Maine's view of India, confirming that the colonial power to "deduce practical inferences from facts" (ibid.: 221) went hand in hand with the anthropological view of the "other." In this anthropological view, India was an entity that could be known by virtue of its location outside the geographical and historical boundaries of the metropolis. Furthermore, the colonial "time-lag" allowed the metropolitan subject the access to an appropriate object for reclaiming its own past.

That this sense of colonial belatedness was a significant feature of a colonialist epistemology is nowhere more apparent than in Mill's precarious balancing of his own critique of the administrative failures in India with his condoning of the alleged insularity of the metropolitan consciousness:

> We have done, and are still doing irreparable mischief, by blindly introducing the English idea of absolute property in land into a country where it did not exist and never had existed. . . . This injustice has been done by the English rulers of India, for the most part *innocently*, from sheer *inability to understand* institutions and customs almost identical with those which prevailed in their own country a few centuries ago.
>
> (Mill 1990: 222; emphasis added)

In this moment of historical hindsight triggered by the fallout of the 1857 war, Mill bemoans the fact that imposing English ideas on India had created "irreparable mischief." Although he is willing to point to its "injustice," he also contends that no bad motive could be attributed to this mischief, since it stemmed from the rulers' inability to comprehend the links between India's institutions and customs and "those which prevailed in their own country a few centuries ago." What seems pivotal to Mill's argument is that both the "time-lag" in India's history and its alien exteriority provide a suitable rationale for Mill's defense of company administration.

In his public writings on India, Mill constantly deploys a discourse of metropolitan historical consciousness by utilizing the power of a colonialist epistemology. A few years before his essay on Maine, Mill had argued in support of company officials, who were in his view more closely associated with "Indian interests" (and therefore to be regarded as being more knowledgeable about India). Based on this logic, Mill had argued that these officials were better suited to carry out the tasks of governing India than British parliamentarians, who could rule only under the principles they comprehended within the narrow compass of their own interests as a nation. The strategy to use history as a way to justify the empire appears to be of greater significance than his support of the interests of the company to which he had remained loyal for nearly twenty-five years of his professional career. It is clear that, even when he recognizes the faults of the system that he had supported all along, he utilizes the rationale of the "time-lag" to let the system off the hook.

Mill's deployment of a discourse of historical consciousness is therefore under-written by the tacit authority of a metropolitan epistemology. That epistemology remains fundamental to this thinking, even when it performs what Foucault would call an "auto-critique." Echoing much of nineteenth-century histories about India, including his father's *The History of British India*, Mill here circumscribes India within a timeless zone. India's present belonged to Europe's past, which the process of history in the metropolis had pushed out of its bounds of knowledge and discarded as new institutions for representing the people came into existence in progressive Europe.

Taking my cue from Dipesh Chakrabarty's important essay "Postcoloniality and the Artifice of History," I suggest that Chakrabarty's theory of colonial "difference" has to be read across the ideological ramifications of a colonialist epistemology as that epistemology locates different temporalities and utilizes them to define the range of "interest" within the national and colonial orders.[5] Indeed, the difference between the self-creating metropolitan individual whose personal history forms the basis of the *Autobiography* and the subject nation whose history remains locked within the gaze of the colonialist lies in this differential relationship with historical temporality. If there is a larger dialectical process that guides the formation of these histories, that process is always marked by a belatedness that allows the metropolitan subject to command the colonial "other"—the entity that lies outside its own site and remains in a state of subjection, forever eluded by the incompleteness of its "character." The truth of a necessarily historical humanity in Mill therefore required that India be outside properly historical and political life. Liberal philosophy reinforced this sense of difference when it took into account the history that it perceived as having materialized within the metropolis: unlike the people of Britain, who could see their interests mirrored in the national imaginary of a representative parliament or in the expanding world of global colonial markets, the people of India possessed no such self-reflecting surfaces. Instead, they were their own great antagonists: it was colonial governance that provided them with the institutions to begin the task of defining themselves.[6]

Like other utilitarian reformers, such as Bentham and James Fitzjames Stephen, Mill viewed the formation of a legal code in India as a guarantee against judicial discretion. In his review of the Penal Code of 1838, Mill writes:

> Alone of all known countries, that British Colony [colonial Ceylon] now actually enjoys a judicial system constructed on the best conceptions of philosophic jurists—a system in which, without any servile deference for the authority of Bentham, the principal improvements made in the theory of the subject by that great man have been, with due consideration of local circum-stances, adopted and carried into practice. The system is understood to have worked admirably during the few years it has been in operation ... The operations of the Indian Law Commission are adding a second instance in support of a prediction once made, that the foreign dependencies of the empire will enjoy the benefits of many reforms.
>
> (Mill 1990: 21)

Much of this early optimism regarding the efficacy of a code for ensuring judicial reform in India was soon to be tempered by Mill's growing belief in the value of "instructed leadership" of select individuals. This faith in charismatic leadership was also dependent on the notion of an ideal of disinterested liberal English character. In his essay on Ireland, for example, he sets the attitudes of "liberal Englishmen" apart from those who thought that the Irish disaffection was the result of a "special taint or infirmity *in* the Irish character" (Mill 1982: 507; emphasis added). Liberal Englishmen were capable of a degree of self-reflection unavailable to others since they possessed an understanding of the history of "unredressed wrongs" (ibid.) that had resulted from England imposing its own system of absolute property on the Irish nation, which, like India, was "very differently circumstanced" (ibid.: 517). Stressing the point repeatedly that "the difficulty of governing Ireland lies entirely *in our own minds*; it is an incapability of understanding. When able to understand what justice requires, liberal Englishmen do not refuse to do it" (ibid.: 529–30; emphasis added), Mill reminds his readers of the inherent good will and judgment of these leaders. Liberalism's fallibility becomes the very source of its virtue—it transforms an epistemological limitation into moral strength. It is not surprising, then, that it is British liberalism's experience of governing India that Mill provides to his readers for pointing out the example Britain might follow in administering Ireland:

> Persons who know both countries, have remarked many points of resemblance between the Irish and Hindoo character; there certainly are many between the agricultural economy of Ireland and that of India.
>
> (ibid.: 519)

Fortunately, British liberalism's colonial responsibilities, Mill claimed, had coincided with the development of a national "conscience," a "character-trait," if you will, that had enabled liberals to slough off their "insular prejudices" and "the reckless savagery of the middle ages," and to "govern another country according to its wants" (ibid.). Furthermore, as Mill emphasized, this remarkable ability to comprehend and master difference was reflected in the government of India, with its empathetic understanding of the interests of its people who were also, like the Irish, so "differently circumstanced." He goes on to state that those "Englishmen who know something of India, are even now those who understand Ireland best" and that "what has been done for India has now to be done for Ireland; and as we should have deserved to be turned out of the one, had we not proved equal to the need, so shall we lose the other" (ibid.). Traversing the entire essay is Mill's abiding faith in the power of the metropolitan liberal state to intervene in the existing social and economic arrangements—between landlord and tenant, and between state and landlord, in order to serve as the "hand of the reformer" (ibid.: 531), and to remedy those ills that had resulted from England's "incapability to understand" (ibid.: 529). It is clear that this kind of historical-analogical reasoning—deployed to work out a stable rationale for the continuance of colonial rule in two different geographical locales—is ultimately founded on the centrality of a metropolitan colonialist epistemology, one that is repeated in order systematically to produce the knowledge of the "other" within the interiority of liberalism's critical consciousness and its metropolitan subjectivity.

"Wheel in the machine"

Mill's *Autobiography* provides a site where we can begin to tease out the ideological ramifications of this form of the liberal metropolitan consciousness. The work also allows us to locate the ideological links between the concept of history and historical belatedness, discussed earlier. Following his intended purpose, Mill begins his *Autobiography* by presenting an extensive account of his education in the principles of utilitarianism, established by Bentham, of which his father, James Mill, had been an active proponent. The first four chapters trace the many stages of that influence by offering details about Mill's personal education at the hands of his father, and his subsequent involvement in the movement initiated by the philosophical radicals, including his work for the *Westminister Review* and his role in the founding of the utilitarian society and of the London Debating Society. Acknowledging that his practical education had prepared him to join the Examiner's Office of the East India Company, Mill proceeds to clarify how that education interacted with the practicalities of dealing with the colonial administrative system that he had inherited from his father:

> I am disposed to agree with what has been surmised by others, that the opportunity which my official position gave me of learning by personal observation the necessary conditions of the practical conduct of public affairs, has been of considerable value to me as a theoretical reformer of the opinions and institutions of my time. Not, indeed, that public business transacted on paper, to take *effect on the other side of the globe*, was of itself calculated to give much *practical knowledge of life*. But the occupation accustomed me to see and hear the difficulties of every course, and the means of obviating them, stated and discussed deliberately, with a view to execution; it gave me opportunities of perceiving when public measures, and other political facts, did not produce the effects which had been expected of them, and from what causes; above all it was valuable to me by making me, in this portion of my activity, *merely one wheel in a machine, the whole of which had to work together*.
>
> (Mill 1981: 87; emphasis added)

The passage is noteworthy for two reasons: one, perhaps the most obvious, is Mill's acknowledgment of his role as an imperial administrator; the other, perhaps more significant, is the implicit analogy between the sense of the *telos* of his own life and his functionary role as a "wheel in the machine." How does one read this Pascalian image of the machine within the discursive limits of the *Autobiography*? On the one hand, the image could be seen to represent the relentlessly organized enforcement of an order to which the individual is attached, as a functioning wheel is to the totality of the machine, but which the individual can still perceive from the outside. The image itself assumes the draconian vision of the great utilitarian rational order that recurs throughout the nineteenth century. On the other hand, the image could also signify a global system authorizing Mill to define his own public role as a reformer of the "opinions and institutions" of his time. In other words, the very image that serves to evoke the brutal order of a cold utilitarian world-view is now normalized to signify a global system operating under the principles of liberal imperialism. This role, Mill contends, did not offer him any "practical knowledge of life," which reinforces the idea that, even while implicated in a public role as the holder of these principles of liberal imperialism, the liberal self maintains its freedom from the practicalities of the "imperial" order. Homi Bhabha has noted that "this slippage between the Western sign and its colonial significance . . . emerges as a map of misreading" (Bhabha 1985: 73). I see this slippage in terms of the metaphorical construction of the system as a "machine": the Pascalian stance allows Mill strategically to recuperate the immediacy of the personal from the purely public by erasing the threat created by the uneasy distance between the metropolitan knowing subject and the colonial object who is subjected to metropolitan laws. The metaphor simultaneously reinforces the ability and the need, on the part of the liberal individual, to distance himself from any "organized" system, much in the manner in which Mill removes himself from the closed rationality of his father's utilitarianism in order to deal with his own mental crisis. Furthermore, it helps sustain the apolitical vision of the liberal self as a self-creating and self-differentiating entity. Therefore, the machine can be seen in a sense to embody the multiply textured logic of the *Autobiography*–as that principle that negotiates the structure of continuity and change across which the project of writing a history of the self can be realized in the *Autobiography*. The co-presence of continuity and change, each producing the other dialectically, provides the strategic flexibility that enables Mill to order, master, and deploy the "difference" that lies at the core of a self fashioned out of history.

At one level, then, the process of self-individuation dramatized in the *Autobiography* requires the self to be extricated from this machine, which Mill traces by rupturing the very deterministic order and continuum that the mechanical machine mandates. This is conveyed in a passage from Mill's narration of his mental and spiritual breakdown in the chapter entitled "The Crisis in my Mental History," which I will quote in detail:

> It was in the autumn of 1826. I was in a dull state of nerves, such as everybody is occasionally liable to; unsusceptible to enjoyment or pleasurable excitement; one of those moods when what is pleasure at other times, becomes insipid or indifferent . . . In this frame of mind it occurred to me to put the question directly to *myself*, "Suppose that all your objects in life were realized; that all the changes in institutions and opinions which you are looking forward to, could be completely effected at this very instant: would this be a great joy and happiness to *you*?" And the irrepressible self-consciousness distinctly answered, "No!" At this my heart sank within me: the whole foundation on which my life was constructed fell down. All my happiness was

to have been found in the continual pursuit of this end. The *end* had ceased to charm, and how could there ever again be any interest in the *means?* I seemed to have nothing left to live for . . . At first I hoped that the cloud would pass away; but it did not.

(Mill 1981: 137–9; emphasis added)

Suffused with a pervasive sense of discontinuity and personal displacement, this passage marks a break in the narrative whose significance becomes apparent when one considers how the "irrepressible self-consciousness" forces itself out of the stasis presented by the crisis and begins to speak. As the self asserts its voice in the powerful enunciation of "No!" a new division is created between the "private" and the "public." While he had earlier claimed to be a "reformer of the opinions and institutions of [his] time who "act[ed] on public business" that "took effect on the other side of the globe" (ibid.: 87), that public end is seen to be no longer adequate in sustaining the *telos* that Mill's narrative of the self demands. The paternal continuum from which the self–as son–had hitherto acquired its own identity had to be disinherited, which is achieved by shifting the focus on to the father, James Mill:

> My father, to whom it would have been natural to me to have recourse in any practical difficulties, was the last person to whom, in such a case as this, I looked for help. Everything convinced me that he had no knowledge of any such mental state as I was suffering from, and that even if he could be made to understand it, he was not the physician who would heal it.
>
> (ibid.: 39)

Through this dramatic displacement of the father's authority Mill suggests the failure of a regimented and rational paternal education in dealing with the complexities of individual growth and the formation of individual self-consciousness.[7] The failure of that paternal legacy in securing personal happiness signifies not only the limitations inherent in the utilitarian thinking represented by James Mill, but also the limitations imposed on the process of self-individuation by the weight of one's immediate history, as well as by the excessive pressures of enforced authority. For the self to continue speaking, it had to overcome this impasse. As Mill elaborates on this condition, it becomes apparent that the break is strategic to, and indeed constitutive of, the entire *telos* of this nineteenth-century autobiographical work. That break is eventually explained, accounted for, and ascribed a place within the evolving totality of Mill's own life. The transformation resulting from the rupture, then, begins to signify a *new* stage in the overall continuity of the self-maturing process. However, it is a continuity that is clearly subsumed under the dialectic of change, and can therefore recuperate the very rupture that is introduced into its continuum, which is disclosed in the very linearity of the title of the chapter: "A Crisis in my Mental History: One Stage Forward." Read as an attempt, on Mill's part, to stabilize and harmonize what could potentially have been disruptive of the entire moral *telos* of the work, this linear pattern is carefully orchestrated and the moral utility of disruption and dislocation managed by a new rationality of self-governance.

This rationality reconstitutes the private–public opposition in terms of an epistemology that has significant political implications, and becomes visible in the manner in which Mill narrates his discovery of Wordsworth during this period of mental crisis. The return to Wordsworth's poetic world, he says, "proved to be the precise thing for my mental wants at that particular juncture":

> In the first place, these poems addressed themselves powerfully to one of the strongest of my pleasurable susceptibilities, *the love of rural objects and natural scenery*; . . . What made Wordsworth's poems a medicine for my state of mind, was that they expressed, not mere outward beauty, but states of feeling, and of thought coloured by feeling, under the excitement of beauty. They seemed to me to be the *very culture of the feelings*, which I was in quest of. In them I seemed to draw from the source of *inward joy*, of sympathetic and imaginative pleasure, which could be shared in *by all human beings; which had no connection with struggle or imperfection*, but would be *made richer by every improvement in the physical or social condition of mankind*. . . . I needed to be made *to feel* that there was a real, permanent happiness in tranquil contemplation. Wordsworth taught me this, not only without turning away from, but with greatly increased interest in, *the common feelings and common destiny of human beings*. And the delight which these poems gave me, proved that with culture of this sort, there was *nothing to dread from the most confirmed habit of analysis*.
>
> (Mill 1981: 151, 153; emphasis added)

Suffused with Wordsworthian sentiments, this passage expresses the division of the public and private in terms of a new opposition between "mere outward beauty" and inner "states of feeling," only to subsume that opposition under the all-encompassing notion of the self ("me"). The affective power of this self is realized in its capacity to experience an "inward joy" that allows it to overcome the trauma created by the opposing pull of the public–private dichotomy, and to identify itself with "the common feelings and common destiny of human beings."

My reading of this moment of reconcilement in the *Autobiography* suggests that it reflects a colonialist epistemology that aided Mill to justify colonial rule. Indeed, the consciousness that this joy could be shared by all human beings, irrespective of time and location, is the very consciousness that secures this privileged metropolitan epistemology outside the public–private domain. This exteriority also guaranteed that colonial difference could be read, comprehended, and validated at the site of a general "culture of feelings," without actually being implicated in the history of the "other." In other words, the seeming impersonality of the consciousness attuned to this culture appears to place the thinking/feeling self beyond the realm of difference, and thus makes it the ground from which all historical difference can be disinterestedly comprehended. At the same time, it is clear then that, by identifying itself with such a notion of culture, the self acts out its own *telos* that empowers it to transcend its own finiteness. It is also worthwhile recalling here that, as a philosopher, Mill had acknowledged this very finiteness to provide the condition of human fallibility under which liberty could be imagined in enlightened societies. By transcending that finiteness, Mill reinforces the moral superiority of the metropolitan subject and its epistemological authority.

Some historians have felt that this adoption of a Wordsworthian sensibility on the part of Mill is a reflection of the philosopher's turn to a more "organic" conception of the world, to a realm in which the power to "feel" conquers the cold and hard rationality of utilitarian "analysis." Lynn Zastoupil, for example, tracks that change in this significant moment of Mill's discovery of Wordsworth, claiming that "there exists an obvious chronological parallel between the 'weaving anew' of his intellectual framework that J. S. Mill described in the *Autobiography* and his evolving administrative views" (Zastoupil 1988: 49). Zastoupil suggests that Mill's growing concern for the vitality of rural life mirrored his own engagement with questions about the value of preserving India's indigenous social and political order, which Benthamite utilitarian reformers had disregarded in their zeal for providing an efficient, metropolitan-organized governing system in India. Furthermore, Zastoupil implies that, by "transport[ing] himself into the minds of the people [of India], as the Romantics recommended, in order to understand the unity of their thoughts and sentiments" (ibid.: 53), Mill was radically questioning the authority of Benthamite reform in India. Similarly, Wendy Donner states that, as "a revisionary or rebel utilitarian and liberal," Mill can be regarded as "a transitional figure who made the breakthrough in the movement from classical to contemporary utilitarian and liberal theories" (Donner 1991: 2). While it is indisputable that Mill's evolution as a thinker was inextricably linked to his political thinking about the colonies, Zastoupil's interpretation of this "radical" change in Mill's outlook needs to be interrogated. My reading of this change confirms that the ethically driven negative capability that Mill claims for himself is little more than a strategy for consolidating the privileged space for a colonial epistemology that reveals its foundations on narrow nationalist assumptions about an idealized "English" character, rural life, and nature. It served to mask his *realpolitik*, as well as the inequality in power relations across which colonial difference was posited and enforced within the political institutions of the British empire.

It is not hard to discern the recurrence of this ideological recuperation throughout Mill's writings about India. Uday Mehta has rightly pointed out that Mill's commitment to "character-development" and his embracing of the "Germano-Coleridgian doctrine" combine "to vitiate any competence of universalism" (Mehta 1999: 66). Mill valued India's tradition-sanctified systems of administration so long as they signified that nation's repository of old loyalties and feelings unhampered by time or history. In playing up the opposition between the "rural"–which becomes the repository of "feeling," "allegiance," "loyalty," and "tradition"–and the principles of "reason," "progress," and "change" upheld by Benthamite utilitarianism, Mill appears to rehearse another version of the private–public dichotomy he deployed in writing about his self. This, in turn, becomes the means through which he justifies the continuance of governance by the representatives of the company who he had argued were closest to the heart of India, as well as resolving questions about maintaining the status quo in a system of unequal power relations in India. This becomes evident in his dispatches from the Chief Examiner's Office located in London, in which he argued that, in Kathiawad, a western province in the Indian subcontinent, the British authorities should leave the local institutions of governance intact because the loyalty that such ancient institutions elicited from the people could be secured in the future by the colonial powers themselves. His recognition of India's traditional and indigenous culture, based on a Romantic pastoral world-view, therefore, translated into support for those existing power structures in India which were most beneficial for extending and reinforcing the interests of the East India Company.

Furthermore, what Eric Stokes has called Mill's "new eclecticism" (Stokes 1959: 242) was produced at a time when Mill the philosopher, dissatisfied with Benthamite programs, looked for a more syncretic approach to colonial governance by accommodating Bentham's radicalism to the belief in the efficacy of "instructed leadership" (Moir 1990: xix). Derived in part from Macaulay and St. Simonianism, this trust in the opinions and knowledge of people specially trained to lead reflects Mill's support of the class of "enlightened" bureaucrats entrusted with the job to govern the colonies. Given the fact that Benthamite programs initiated in the first half of the century were being challenged at home, Mill's eclecticism can be interpreted as a tactical move on the part of the philosopher bureaucrat to restore confidence in the authority of the company officials who could claim to be enlightened bureaucrats.[8] We can therefore conclude that, tied to Mill's concern and respect for India's indigenous traditions, there was the desire to ensure that the bonds of feeling for, and loyalty to, tradition among Indians were retained and their ideological power exploited when required to ensure maximum support for the continuing presence and authority of the company's government in India.

Therefore, when it came to diagnosing the dangerous state of affairs in Ireland, Mill repeats the same tactical move that he later employed in "England and Ireland," published in 1868:

> What harm to Ireland does England intend, or knowingly inflict? What good, that she knows how to give her, would she not willingly bestow? Unhappily, her offense is precisely that she *does not know*, and is so well contented with not knowing, that Irishmen who are not hostile to her are coming to believe that she will and cannot learn.
>
> (Mill 1982: 509)

As opposed to his detached stance on Britain's failure to know history as stated in his comments on India, Mill here appears to be issuing a warning that, given the rise in popular "nationalist" opposition in Ireland to continuing colonial oppression, Britain could no longer afford to be "content with not knowing" the consequences of its policies. The "rebellion for an idea—the idea of nationality" (ibid.), fired by Fenianism, had brought the disaffection "to our own homes, scattering death among us who have given no provocation but that of being English-born" (ibid.: 508). That immediate threat had its source in the hatred that

Mill reminds his readers "will run all risks merely to do us harm, with little or no prospect of any consequent good to itself" (ibid.). Therefore, Mill's understanding of the moral basis for the outrages committed against the landlord in Ireland leads him to propose that "revolutionary measures are the thing now required." I believe that Mill's study of the colonial situation in Ireland provides a vital counterpoint to his thinking about India, highlighting the ways in which questions about national character and history were heavily implicated in the authorization of colonial knowledge, and underlining the shifting nature of the ideologies that guided the production of that knowledge.

Given the fact that Mill invested so much time and energy in contemplating and arguing about Indian affairs, how are we to interpret his silence about India in his *Autobiography*? In his "Introduction" to John Stuart Mill's *Writings on India*, Martin Moir asks:

> How could someone so deeply committed to the understanding and better-ment of human society apparently fail to appreciate the importance and interest of his own central position in the formulation and review of the East India's Company's policies in South Asia? Was he really comparatively detached from his official duties, as his *Autobiography* suggests, or was he more committed than he chose to admit?
>
> (Moir 1990: viii)

Moir then suggests that "any exploration of the problem of Mill's East India Company role leads imperceptibly to the more basic and, to the postcolonial sensibility, more puzzling issues of how to connect Mill the administrator with Mill the political philosopher" (ibid.: viii). It has been my effort to reopen this line of inquiry by rethinking Mill's colonial epistemology and by situating it within the realm of "difference" based on notions of "national subjectivity" and "history," and by revealing its basis on the idea that "Europe works as a silent referent in historical knowledge" (Chakrabarty 2000a: 28).

Interestingly, the historian R. J. Moore has read Mill's silence about India in his *Autobiography* as a fair representation of what he considers to be an understandable gap between the mechanistic demands of a colonial career, spent in an office writing and editing dispatches, and the more dynamic and challenging engage-ment with the world of intellectual ideas. However, it has been widely recognized that, as a professional bureaucrat with the East India Company's Office of Indian Correspondences, Mill was intimately connected with the complex machinery of an expanding colonial administrative system, an involvement that required more than the detached rigor of everyday profession. Having started his career at the young age of seventeen in 1823, when he served as an unpaid clerk in the office, he rose to the ranks of the chief examiner, ultimately retiring in 1858 in the wake of the transfer of power from the hands of the East India Company to the crown. As Trevor Lloyd has demonstrated, Mill's function as an administrator was an important one, encompassing an entire range of responsibilities—from taking care of important colonial correspondence, especially that concerning the affairs of

Indian princes, to writing important dispatches on education such as on Lord Bentinck's education policies in India in 1836, to giving evidence of the company's administration of India during the 1853 renewal of the charter, as well as vindicating the company's performance to parliament in 1858. As pointed out earlier, he routinely discussed India and Indians in his reviews on Macaulay's draft Penal Code, and in *On Liberty* and *Considerations on Representative Government*. If he preferred to characterize his profession, in the *Autobiography*, as no more than a job that was "sufficiently intellectual not to be distasteful drudgery" and "not a strain on my mental powers" (Mill 1981: 85), that attitude reflects an unwillingness on his part to acknowledge the full implications of his complicity with the colonial machinery. It is clear that for Mill the professional experience of managing the Indian empire could not be easily subsumed under the narrative of the self-growth and evolution that had provided the overarching rationale for his *Autobiography*. Although he had stated that one of his primary purposes in writing his autobiography was to acknowledge his intellectual and moral debts, he was not willing to grant his "India experience" the kind of significance that would make it worthy of such consideration. More importantly, I think, the elision confirms the ideological separation of intellectual labor from professional duty, an elision that allowed a philosopher such as Mill to recognize and affirm his identity as a European (metropolitan) thinker and molder of opinions. While he is able to envision, in his *Autobiography*, his own mind's potentiality in terms of its ability to evolve in relation to the dynamic personal and national traditions of "Europe," that mind remains securely founded on its given, or assumed, providentiality and colonial sovereignty in relation to India. That sense of colonial mastery was founded on the tacit perception of the metropolitan self's unquestioned ability to exercise authority over the "object"–rural, pastoral, dehistoricized–in this case, India–while precluding any possibility of being determined by it.

THE GLOOMY DREAM OF CIVILITY

In 1834, an anonymous writer who called himself "a Young Civilian of Bengal" published a long poem entitled *India: A Poem in Three Cantos*. Containing the reflections of a young man who had joined the civil service as an officer, the poem is structured as a personal rite of passage as well as described by the anonymous writer himself as a "poet's reverie" and a "gloomy dream" (ibid.: 69). Horrified by what he witnessed–the brutal exploitation of the people of India under the colonial government–the poet announces at one stage: "Think not the awful accents are my own; / They are the echoes of a nation's groan" (ibid.: 27). The status of such a work as a political critique can perhaps best be understood in terms of its place within the anti-slavery discourse.[9] In contrasting the idealism and insularity of the newly initiated officer in India–"in virtue armed and impregnably secure"–with the reality that he encounters there: "He comes–he sees–the naked truth is there; / And pride, joy, virtue, what are they, and where?" (ibid.: 37), the poem begins to unmask colonialism's ideological ruse.[10] In the "Preface," the poet targets those "numerous and valuable works on the Politics and Statistics of India" for having "utterly failed in their attempt to direct attention against the sins and abuses of the Indian Governments," asserting that a poetic appeal might better aid in arousing the "passions of mankind . . . for the exercise of the national will" (ibid.: i–ii). This solicitation of a "national will" through poetic passion signifies the poet's belief in a national moral order that supersedes the interests of political order served by the colonial government; it is a moral order held by "the simple honesty of freemen" (ibid.: iii) that rises above expedient interests in order steadfastly to oppose anything that "represses the latent principles of national and individual improvement and defeats the great end of man's creation upon earth," irrespective of "whatever precedents" are utilized to support these "iniquitous" (ibid.) deeds. It is significant that the term "national" here evokes a kind of universalism that is unqualified by the sorts of distinctions made by Mill between the inherent natures of Europeans and the subject races. In fact, as I will demonstrate later, this ideal of a universal claim to humanity is resolutely based on the poet's understanding of the operations of political economy under colonialism. Throughout the poem is an abiding sense of the ways in which the political, social, and economic policies of colonial rule had deformed the basic freedoms that the subject races had originally enjoyed. This is most clearly articulated in the "Preface" in the poet's rendition of the condition of India in which he engages in an unremitting attack on the "corruption of that unlimited power" which lead to "the general annihilation of landed property . . . the insecurity of chattel interests, and the entire disregard of personal immunities" (ibid.). In the poem, the "enlightened despotism" of Mill loses its liberal rationale, becoming yet another manifestation of the government's own despotic power in India. Unlike Mill, the poet sees this despotism as having deep consequences not only for the people of India but also for Britons at home: if despotism could have an unchallenged sway abroad, what would prevent it from being exercised at home?

It is true that the historical vision of India undergirding the understanding of the political economy of colonialism in this work is reminiscent of eighteenth-century orientalists who had idealized India's ancient (pre-Islamic) past.[11] To that extent, it seems limited by that idealization. However, it is worth pointing out, that in reverting back to it, the poem challenges the reigning historical understanding of Indian history and character as developed by post-orientalist liberal utilitarian historians such as James Mill and Macaulay. Such a challenge is embodied in the poem's strategic focus on the "present," particularly on the palpable effects of utilitarian programs on India, thereby contesting its claims to universal improvement and fair play. This is achieved ironically by imagining India's pre-colonial past in idealistic terms—as being marked by

> A happy people [who] tilled a fertile land:
> O'er its wide plains continuous extent
> Man lived in peace, and laboured in content;
> No needy slaves of indigence were there,
> But every son of Menu had its share.
>
> (*India*: 3)

Projected back to India's pre-Islamic past when "there was no power above the people's voice, / And none could stand but on the people's choice" (ibid.: 6), this image of an egalitarian and democratic society mirrors the condition of modern Britons, and becomes a way to let Britons identify with its subject people. Distinctions of caste are explained in terms of the division of labor that incarnated an "organic" interrelationship between people and their place in society. According to the poet, such harmony had been disrupted by the Islamic invasion that is presented as ushering in the era of despotism through unfair taxation, "oppression's curse" (ibid.: 9), which the poet alleges becomes part of the expedient policies of the present colonial government. What is revealed is the level of hypocrisy informing the imperial mission, underscored by the fact that Britain called itself "a wise nation," marked by "calm, deliberate design" in order to distinguish itself from the Muslim invaders who merely acted "on wild impulse" and "caprice" (ibid.: 17). That "calm, deliberate design," "fixed to systems never known to cease" (ibid.), reveals its demonic and aggressive underside—the subtle and calculating efforts of British despotism: "It's a dark tale, the deed was done of late, / And trust me, 'tis oppression's crowing weight"(ibid.: 43). While Britons had imagined the colonial mission as an effort to "Roll o'er the country like the orb of day, / And drive the darkness of Islam away" (ibid.: 14), colonial intervention had presented a different reality:

> How were these hopes fulfilled? Blush! Britain blush!
> Time stands aghast amid his awful rush
> . . . The more thy sons have won, the more they sought
> Give to the winds and waves—'tis nought—'tis nought—.
> (ibid.: 16)

Calling Britain's effort a "weight of shame," the poet asserts: "You injure more than those you overthrew, / And Britain, what were they, and what are you?" (ibid.: 17).

The poem thus constructs history as a way to unmask the story of British despotism. Contrary to the claim made by utilitarian reformers, this story that the poem charts is the "tale of tyranny, the tale of shame" (ibid.: 27), and reveals that "the only pestilence is power" (ibid.: 38). By replacing "enlightened despotism" with "tyranny," the poem plots the way in which tyranny "proceeds, / Building fresh horrors on its past misdeeds" (ibid.: 44). It questions the fundamental principles of civil, political, and economic laws, including the bureaucratic system in place, by unmasking the expedient policies of the government in India. Countering the belief that the "law restrains irregularities," it exposes the ways in which laws furthered the economic exploitation of poor Indians:

> Yes! All is law, and what a law it is!
> Cruel you are, though politicized your mood,
> And boast your justice, whilst denying food;
> Strict punishers of thefts, your own produce,

Whilst plundering millions, you denounce abuse;
The subjects rights you settle and secure,
And then imprison him for being poor.

(ibid.: 17)

The poem further says:

this is the system that your law prolongs,
That law an insult to its wrongs:
A gaudy fillet flutt'ring on the beast
You lead to sacrifice, and make your feast.

(ibid.: 18)

The effects of the extractive policies of the government on the "mind and body" of
the people, as well as the vulnerability of the poor subjected to these policies, are
constantly highlighted:

Was it for you . . .
To tear away man's earliest, dearest right,
From honest hands that worked but could not fight,
To make their schemes the basis for your own,
To wear the country's bosom to the bone,
To exact the growing tribute as it ends.

(ibid.: 18)

Very clearly the poem burrows into the utilitarian value on collective happiness by
showing not only how the extractive policies ran counter to its own principles but
also how its economic policies ensured that the working poor were left in a
perennial state of penury and degradation:

As if man's happiness were a pretence,
man's worth, an estimate of pounds and pence?
And when men fainted with the load they bore,
And vexed earth would yield her stores no more,
Was it for you to call arrears a debt,
To sell goods, houses, all that you could get,
To strike amazement thro' the heart of home,
And drive the starving wretches forth to roam
Thro' winter's rain or summer's blazing day,
Because they cannot pay what they cannot pay?

(ibid.: 19)

The image to convey this is indeed striking: "The sponge is dry, and yet you
squeeze it still; / Fools! Is it squeezing that will make it fill?" (ibid.: 21).

The entire civil, bureaucratic order is described as being modeled on a tyrannical structure that systematically reproduces the inequities of colonial economic policies through its insular and sometimes blatant disregard for the common weal as well as its distribution of privilege to the influential few. Earning a salary of "three thousand pounds a year," the "Magistrate" is described as acting as a "sole monarch" whose only job seems to be to impose fines on insolvent debtors. The collector's chief function seems to be to exact as much tax from the poor as is needed to support the company's own defense expenditures: "But 'tis their right, the only just pretence / For taxing is, that we afford defence!" (*India*: 42). The colonial system of combining the duties of a "publican and judge" is also questioned: "Why join employments in themselves distinct– / Where one must yield, and never doubtful which?" (ibid.: 43). In the face of stiff opposition to reform the system by the very collectors enjoined to serve the people, the government is described as beginning "to chafe, / God's death! Take care the revenue is safe" (ibid.: 44). The subordinates serving the system are described as being "mazed and cowed,"–" A contradiction in its aim and end, / One hand must injure and one hand defend" (ibid.: 45). As a young subordinate himself, the poet depicts the predicament of many like him who, despite their good will, are confused about their own role within a system designed for exploitation and extraction. The different levels of social hierarchy and patronage under the colonial system—which Mill saw as a manifestation of instructed (and enlightened) leadership—reflect the competitive and aggressive posturings of civil servants intent on moving up the social ladder:

> Young boobies thus on older boobies rise,
> While burning merit stands below and sighs;
> New mischief springs afresh from mischief past,
> And both combine improvement's aim to blast.
>
> (ibid.: 65)

Here is the counter-image of that ideal of "instructed leadership" which John Stuart Mill had upheld as being the basis for the East India Company's great achievements in governing India.

Perhaps the most damning charge aimed at the colonial system comes when the poet describes the relations of labor and production under colonial government. Agreeing with the mainstream thinking among liberal thinkers that "true labour is the origin of wealth" (*India*: 22), the poet casts the colonial economic policies as little more than extortion:

> True, property's a pleasant thing to take,
> But who acquires it for another's sake?
> How will men labour when they may not reap?
> How fabricate the stores they may not keep?
>
> (ibid.)

The poem also contains a description of a scene at the court to demonstrate how, in the face of successive crop failures and impending droughts, a poor peasant is trapped in mounting debts that eventually lead him to prison. Unable ever to pay his arrears because of the way in which the government takes control over his meager property, the poet asks in amazement:

> Sold? Aye! For ten rupees: he's paid that sum,
> The debt was thousands: whence are they to come?
> Then how and whence does he obtain discharge?
> According as the sum is small or large.
>
> (ibid.: 49)

The comparison of poor Indians with African slaves makes colonial rule out to be just another face of a practice that had only very recently been abolished in Britain.[12] The effects of British civil rule are delineated not in terms of the power to produce the docile bodies of educated Indians (as Mill does), but in terms of the disaffection created among the poor that goes unnoticed:

> Full half a century has passed away,
> And never, never, in one Indian soul
> Of all the millions crushed by thy control
> Hath love, hath gratitude for aught that's dear,
> Stirr'd towards thee, or any thought but fear.
> We live among them like a walking blight,
> Our very name the watchword for right;
> No sympathy, no pity, no remorse,
> Our end is profit, and our means are force.
>
> (ibid.: 79)

The rhetoric of *India* is also reminiscent of those parliamentary discourses that emerged during the debates initiated by Robert Rickards, a member of parliament who spoke in the House in 1813 against the motion to renew the East India Company's charter. Rickards was a political figure who had a twenty-three-year colonial career as a collector behind him, and his speeches, published later in 1829 as *India, or, Facts Submitted to Illustrate the Character and Condition of the Native Inhabitants*, often provoked a powerful response from the opposition, particularly from Thomas Campbell Robertson, also a civil servant in charge of judicial and political departments of the Bengal Civil Service. Rickards's visibility and prominence as a political figure contrasts sharply with the anonymity of the writer of *India*, a work that might have appeared to many as little more than the poetic outpourings of a frustrated young civilian. It is possible, however, that, since he withheld his name, the poet had feared that his work would be considered incendiary. Like the anonymous poet, Rickards focuses on the effects of British despotism on the character of the people of India. Opposing the dominant views of Indian character, espoused by utilitarians such as James Mill, Rickards contends:

I believe them capable of all the qualities that can adorn the human mind; and though I allow many of their imputed faults, (where is the individual or the nation without them?) I must still ascribe those faults more to the rigour of the despotisms under which they have long groaned, and which unhappily we have but slenderly alleviated, than to the natural depravity of disposition, or to any institutions peculiar to themselves.

(Rickards 1829: 3)

He counters the stereotype of the "Hindoo" character in Britain by reminding his readers that the manner in which Indians had been vilified and exoticized made it seem as if "they were not composed of flesh and blood, nor had passions and desires, as the rest of the human species" (Rickards 1814: 50). The "imputed faults" of Indians are the result of erroneous European perceptions of the "natural depravity" of the people, which Rickards imputes to James Mill. He argues that Mill had made broad and simplistic assumptions about Indian character based on his limited knowledge of India's immense diversity (Rickards 1829: 2). Rickards attributes the "overwhelming pressure of arbitrary power" (Rickards 1814: 244) to be the source of poverty in India. He contends that, when Mill blamed India's religions for having barred all "progress of improvement" by binding the people "as slaves to the observance of minute ceremonies," he failed to acknowledge the effects of Britain's own "despotic power" in warping the minds of the colonized people. Drawing attention to the propensity for misapprehension, he says that "there is no greater error—perhaps no greater presumption—than to ascribe factitious effects to the hand of nature. . . . that what they now appear to be is not their nature, but what the caprices and severities of their rulers have made them" (ibid.: 245).

Like the anonymous poet of *India*, Rickards provides a romantic view of India's pre-Islamic past, crediting the Muslim invaders for carrying on with the policy of "fire and sword" (Rickards 1814: 279), and emphasizes the present responsibility of Britain in continuing to oppress the colonized subjects. He observes that, far from introducing a government based on equity and justice, British colonial rule had simply preserved and continued the legacies of despotism it had replaced. He finds support for his claim in the works of liberal historians whose works Rickards claims show how "new forms of government, and domination, have risen and set, as the most powerful prevailed; but these revolutions brought no relief to subjects suffering from grinding extraction of their successive masters; who, however unlike in some features, were the image of each other in their rapaciousness" (ibid.). Focusing on the economic policies adopted by the British colonizers, he reiterates:

One of the most oppressive systems of revenue ever known, continues to be enforced within the limits of our India empire. It perpetuates that extreme poverty and wretchedness into which the people were for ages plunged by their Mahomedan conquerors; in consequence of our adopting from the latter the financial principles, and rate of taxation, which they imposed, as the price of blood, on vanquished Pagans.

(ibid.)

Rickards provides an account of the taxation system imposed on India by its Muslim rulers, which he called "the origin of this detestable extraction" (ibid.: 280), and which led to the "complete degradation of one of the most important classes of society—the landed proprietors" (ibid.: 283). He alleges that the power of the Indian government rested solely on the exercise of economic might that was no more than just another manifestation of this brutally extractive and unjust power over the material lives of the people:

> From the impure foundation of [Muslim] financial systems did we, to our shame, claim the inheritance of a right to seize upon half the gross produce of the land as a tax; and wherever our arms have since triumphed, we have invariably proclaimed this savage right; coupling it, at the same time, with the senseless doctrine of the propriety right to these lands being also vested in the sovereign, in virtue of the right of conquest.
>
> (ibid.: 285)

The ironic resonance of the word "civilized" is amplified when he discloses how the government's own narrow interests had dictated its rationale to promote the prosperity of the country by "assert[ing] the same financial rights merely because they had been promoted by their predecessors" (ibid.: 286–7). Rickards is referring to the dewani of Bengal, Bihar, and Orissa, which had been granted to the company by the Moghul emperor Shah Alam in 1765. He calls the Permanent Settlement of Lord Cornwallis "lamentably defective" (ibid.: 364), since it had been made with a powerful few—the zemindars—"whose ignorance, rapacity, oppressions, collusions, and abuses of all kinds, are so uniformly attested in the public records that nothing, one would think, could be wanting to prove their entire unfitness for the trust" (ibid.: 385). In his view, the true principles of liberalism had simply been sacrificed to the expedient demands of finance.

It is worth noting that, despite his attacks, Rickards's materialist understanding of "human nature" and the "nature of things" (Rickards 1814: 46) is securely premised on the liberal principle of "industry." He believes that despotism runs counter to this principle. Quoting from Doctor Blair that "industry is the law of our being; it is the demand of nature, of reason, and of God," he continues, "Without industry, there can be no change in the circumstances of man. His lot is that of never-varying poverty and ignorance; the corner stones of despotic power in every region of the earth" (Rickards 1829: 277). Appealing to a metropolitan faith in the power of "industry," he reminds his interlocutors of the basic principles upon which the country had rested its hopes and aspirations for wealth, security, and justice. He represents his own faith in liberal doctrines by pointing out that the "means wanting to the happiness of the people of India" are "moderation in the rates and collection of land tax, and freedom of trade" (Rickards 1814: 2). He calls "free trade" the "natural course of commercial freedom," which, when opposed to secure the interests of a few, leads to "ruinous losses," distracting the attention of the government "from greater objects, it is now their duty, as much as it is their interest to pursue" (ibid.: 44). Like a true liberal, he conflates "duty" and "interest," and shows why monopoly fails to achieve the harmony between the two:

> Every merchant is a monopolist at heart; but when every merchant is on an equal footing, the same principle pervading every beast neutralizes by its natural operation the prejudicial influence of a love of gain, and produces through the mass of society common benefits. But when a merchant is raised by exclusive power above his equals, that power is sure to be abused; it cannot, in the nature of things, be otherwise; and this, as far as my experience goes, has invariably been the consequence of the Company's interference in the trade of India. Where the market is exclusively in their own hands, prices are arbitrarily kept down, to the prejudice of production. Where the market is open, their agents enter it as competitors, who must, at all events, be served, and prices are raised, to the prejudice of consumption.
>
> (ibid.: 45–6)

It is true that Rickards's contention, that the "natural operations" of freedom counter "the love of gain" in order to maintain the imperatives of a common weal, reflects an abiding belief in the governing principles of liberalism, as does his faith in the basic fairness of free trade. I have emphasized elsewhere the need to differentiate between "government" and "governmentality." As an administrative function governance can take distinct forms, but the notion of "governmentality" circumscribed by liberalism, as Foucault has pointed out, offers a wider normalizing and disciplinary regime that consolidates specific notions of metropolitan subjectivity in relation to national principles. Although, unlike Mill, Rickards opposes the actions of the government of the East India Company, his arguments presuppose an ideal of "governmentality" that is itself founded on the principles of liberalism as espoused by Mill. Part of my general argument in this chapter is that the company for which Mill served as a spokesperson had cast itself as a specific "government," taking on the authority of "governmentality"–as defined by the liberal metropolitan state–in order to work on behalf of the society of the colonized. This was possible *because* colonial "government" could not be envisioned in its relation to colonial "society" through the same rationale that the liberal state had established for its own governance of "British society." What Mill's writings–his *Autobiography* and his essays and speeches–demonstrate is the efficacy of this larger normalizing discourse of "governmentality" forged by liberal doctrines for managing that difference as a way to consolidate its historical and geopolitical authority. The oppositional stances, advanced by the anonymous poet and Rickards, stem from a critique of those liberal doctrines, although their underlying presuppositions about civility, responsibility, and fair play remain firmly anchored within liberalism and its normalizing discourse. In other words, the interlinking of subjectivity, nation, and colony–out of which the discourse of civility is shaped and deployed–continues to circumscribe liberal imperial politics and to energize the polymorphousness that remained crucial to its ideological functions.

3 Policing the boundaries

Civility and gender in the Anglo-Indian
romances, 1880–1900

A woman is a foreign land
Of which, though there he settle young
A man will ne'er quite understand
The customs, politics, and tongue.
B. M. Croker, *Angel* (1901)

Although gender represents an abiding structure of difference within colonial discourse, its metaphorical role in defining the provenance of imperial masculine power has always been a tenuous one. In the above epigraph, taken from the popular Anglo-Indian romance *Angel: A Sketch in Indian Ink*, the conjoining of gender and colonialism appears, on the surface, to rehearse a familiar metaphorical theme—that men were providentially entitled to settle in or govern foreign lands in the same way in which they had access to the passive bodies of women. In fact, the ideological valence of this metaphor rested on the past achievements of colonialism—of conquering and bringing under civil rule alien lands. Mirroring the ruling tenets of male civility that dictated nineteenth-century Britain's national and domestic order, the metaphor also links the disciplinary modalities of control and governance to the imperial enterprise of "settling" in a "foreign land." Yet, that powerful metaphor also appears to be infected with a sense of uncertainty: because both women and the colonized world possessed an intransigent—and, indeed, irreducible—"foreignness," the imperial masculine task turns out to be at best a vulnerable enterprise. In fact, it is often ridden with the problem of unreadability and incomprehension, and with the attendant anxieties of being eluded by the very object that had appeared to be so immediately accessible.

I am concerned here with the ways in which this problem reverberated in the popular stories about the Indian empire that were narrated in the Anglo-Indian romances of the late nineteenth century, of which Croker's *Angel: A Sketch in Indian Ink* is a fitting example. These stories often speak of a crisis in civility, a crisis that is linked to the very definition of power and masculinity. Historically that crisis had been propelled by key shifts in the larger domain of gender and class relations within colonial Britain, changes that necessitated a reworking of masculinity in the cultural imagination of the public in order to restore faith in the colonial enterprise and in its underlying patriarchal arrangements. This process of reworking masculinity also entailed a renegotiation of those norms of civility that had formed the ideological basis of colonial culture in the late nineteenth century. Instead of being caught up in the contradictions created by the material changes within colonialism, the disciplinary modalities circumscribed by civility helped create new thresholds for testing the limits of masculinity and class identity, and for recuperating their authority whenever their defining norms were challenged. The political institutions of the disciplinary state themselves offered new sites for regulating civility, simultaneously offering fixed standards for marking its normativity while allowing it to move into those arenas where those standards were perceived to be in peril.

Although the Anglo-Indian romances had broad appeal in late Victorian England, they have often been regarded as no more than mere Victorian curiosities, and therefore received little scholarly attention.[1] *Angel: A Sketch in Indian Ink* is only one of four now-forgotten Anglo-Indian romances authored by Bithia Mary Croker. Set against the backdrop of the Indian empire, these romances employed familiar love plots that revolved mainly around the relations between imperial Englishmen, Englishwomen, and native Indian or Eurasian women. Despite the conventionality of plot, these romances portrayed Englishwomen as independent and aggressive individuals, presenting a different picture of womanhood than those found in the popular fiction of the day. Indian women often appeared in the form of exotic and tantalizing "nautch girls"—both powerful and threatening, simultaneously necessitating distance from and control by the ruling masculine order. By metonymically linking the impossibility of "reading" such powerful women and comprehending their "nature" to the monumental tasks of governance faced by imperialists in the colonies, the epigraph to Croker's novel opens up a new space for critical inquiry of these romances. It is with this general purpose in mind that I wish to focus attention on these romances, and examine the ways in which the question of civility punctuates their narratives by helping untangle the complex ideological fabric that held them together as products of popular culture in late nineteenth-century Britain.

The extent of the popularity of these romances can perhaps best be gauged by the fact that in 1892 Rudyard Kipling co-authored, with Wolcott Balestier, *The Naulahka*, a colorful romance set in India. As a work that proved far more profitable than his first published novel *The Light That Failed* (1890), *The Naulahka* deals with the adventures of the dare-devil American hero Nick Tarvin as he pursues his lady love, Kate, who comes to India to work for the welfare of "oppressed" Indian women. Filled with local details and color as well as the more familiar exotic ingredients of imperial fantasy, *The Naulahka* marks a rising trend in fiction writing that attracted, in the 1880s, the 1890s, and even the early 1900s, a host of writers of novels costing 1*s.* 6*d* and 6*d.* The true progenitor of these romances is the historical romance, a genre popularized by Philip Meadows Taylor in the 1860s and 1870s.

Taylor claimed, in the introduction to his romance *Seeta*, that his objective was to offer "a general impression of the time which of all others in the history of India, is the most absorbing and interesting to the English reader" (Taylor 1872: vii). Now almost forgotten, a host of writers followed on the heels of Taylor–F. E. Penny, Bithia Mary Croker, Eliza Pollard, Morley Roberts, May Edwood, Alice Perrin, Maud Diver, Hume Nisbet, Victoria Crosse, Sara Duncan, Nina Stevens, Braunston W. Jones, F. W. Bamford, Robert Edward Forrest, and Charles E. Pearce (the last two were popular writers of the mutiny novels), who produced in a span of about thirty years the most spectacular variety of fiction set in India.[2] These works encompassed a wide range of subjects, such as the question of inter-racial romance and marriage and of inheritance and social mobility in a colonial society, as well as delineating the "tasks" of the empire and revisiting the topical "woman" question, a subject that had come to the very fore of Victorian society in the 1880s and 1890s. In so doing, the Anglo-Indian romances seized on an entire variety of popular subgenres of the romance–melodramatic tales of conspiracies and plots hatched in the zenana, sensational "gothic" tales involving serpents, cults, and mysteries, and mystical autobiographies–to cast their fictional worlds.

As items of mass consumption in an age of rapid expansion of the market for popular fiction, the Anglo-Indian romances became part of the prodigious production of an imperial imaginary that included, among other things, juvenile adventure stories for boys and girls, histories of imperial heroes, poetry of the East, accounts of social life at British stations in India, and almanacs and manuals of the empire, as well as picture postcards, cigarette cards, and board games. Even as early as 1870 the *Calcutta Review* commented that there was a "fair field for a good Anglo-Indian romance" ("Anglo-Indian Romance," *CR* 1870: 182). Acutely conscious that the novel was a "marketable commodity" (Crawford 1893: 9), F. Marion Crawford, the author of the popular *Mr. Isaacs: A Tale of Modern India*, argued in *The Novel: What It Is* that the system of "supply and demand" made the novels of the time "subject to the same laws, statutory and traditional, as other articles of manufacture" (ibid.: 12). This marked awareness of the market isn't surprising: in an age that had witnessed such a dramatic increase in the production and consumption of popular fiction, tales about the empire were items that easily fueled and satisfied the spectacular fantasies of the middle-class public in Britain. Such consumption also dictated the kind of appeal these romances possessed for their readers in late Victorian colonial Britain. Embedded in what Martin Green has called "the energizing myth of English imperialism" (Green 1991: 32), they possessed an unquestionably masculine appeal that allowed them to perform the cultural work of representing for the public the tasks of the empire. To this extent, they shared their imperial themes and plots with colonial adventure stories and ripping yarns that had been popularized by writers such as Rider Haggard, G. A. Henty, R. M. Ballantyne, and the lesser known Bertram Mitford, the author of *The Fire Trumpet: A Romance of the Cape Frontier* and *Through the Zulu Country*. However, unlike these standard colonial adventure tales–works Elaine Showalter has called a "boys' fiction primer of Empire" (Showalter 1990: 80)–the Anglo-Indian romances were authored by an increasing number of women writers. Furthermore, they were aimed at an adult readership, and often depicted–with a mixture of humor, irony, and seriousness–the changing roles of, and relations between, the sexes, set against the backdrop of the Indian empire. Articulating powerful pathologies of power that had their source in the changing ideologies guiding imperial Britain in the late nineteenth century, these romances provide a new perspective to the modern reader on the multiple genealogies of imperial fiction as we know it today.[3]

As the many forms of popular imperialism proliferated in the last two decades of the nineteenth century, these romances found immediate popularity among the reading public looking for new sources to feed its curiosity. The reader's familiarity with the "sensational novels" of the 1860s had helped generate and sustain an interest in these romances. As products of a rapidly expanding commodity culture in the 1860s and 1870s, the "sensation" novels of Mary Elizabeth Braddon and Wilkie Collins had exploited the demand for an immensely marketable sensationalism to produce stories about women who had transgressed the norms of Victorian Britain's social and moral order. In their day, these novelists had been attacked by many Victorian critics as "preach[ing] to the nerves" (quoted in Cvetkovich 1992: 20)—an allegation that, in some significant way, symptomizes the anxious reactions of the Victorian public, who felt that the reader's sensibilities had been somehow feminized by the sudden exposure to the aggressive new "market" for sensational fiction. The Anglo-Indian romances continued on the track that had already been laid out by the sensation novels of the 1860s. By establishing British India as the new site for dramatizing the fantasies of a colonial culture, they articulated questions of power, racial identity, and sexuality that had been taboo for mainstream metropolitan Victorian culture.

Although the sensational novel can be considered to be a significant precursor to these romances, the latter belong, in an important sense, to a hybrid category. They went beyond the simple didacticism of the colonial adventure stories: no longer dealing exclusively with narratives of adventure and quest that depended on adolescent assertions of colonial supremacy, their morality took on a more complex ideological profile. For example, in the more traditional colonial adventure stories of Henty, Ballantyne, and Haggard, the colonial landscape is symbolically endowed with an entire range of masculine "affect" that helped reinforce the heroic ideologies of masculinity within imperialism. As Joseph Bristow has suggested, "each story [made] empire into an adventure" (Bristow 1991: 147). Furthermore, Robert Dixon has noted that the revival of the adventure romance in this period can be seen as "a men's literary revolution intended to reclaim the kingdom of the English novel for male writers" (Dixon 1995: 4). This reclaiming of a literary tradition signified a reinvention of adventure, and making it dependent exclusively on ideas of masculine aggressiveness derived from the culture of colonialism.[4] Such reinvention was closely linked to a didactic function, which, as Gail Clark notes, was to "teach history and inculcate moral character" (Clark 1985: 49), so that the claims of "morality" could be yoked to masculine ideals. History—especially colonial history evoked for example by Meadows Taylor—provided a terrain of action for inspiring young middle-class men in Britain to contemplate careers in the far-flung areas of the empire.[5] Although closely aligned to the form of the colonial adventure story, the Anglo-Indian romances concentrated more on love plots that are often reminiscent of conventional Victorian tales "devoted to the knightly virtues of honor, valor, and the protection of women" (Sharpe 1993: 99). However, these new tales about Victorian honor had a more complicated ideological task—that is, they had to recuperate, through the deployment of specific narrative forms, the power that had been seriously threatened by the growing rivalries between European nations for control of the colonial world by the rising tide of the women's movement within Britain. By so doing, they utilized the empire to provide new scenarios for the enactment of love, power, and imperial mastery, which explains, in part, their more complex ideological profile.

The threat posed by the women's movement is clearly visible in the debates around sexual surveillance initiated within both the metropolis and the colony and triggered by the introduction and the eventual repeal of the Contagious Diseases Act of the 1860s. Given this history, these romances used the female body to mark their disciplinary function: by imagining and, thus, forging new links between the sexes, the love plots produced a complex discursive circuitry of gender and empire, subjecting notions of English masculinity to the changing ideologies of English femininity, and continually testing the limits of that masculinity as a way ultimately to consolidate and manage the contested gender roles.[6] As Joanna De Groot has pointed out, in this period "women's situation as women . . . evolved not in isolation but as part of the material and cultural history both of feminine and masculine genders, and the development of boundaries and/or interactions between them" (De Groot 1989: 90). Graham Dawson has argued that "the modern tradition of British adventure has furnished idealized, wish-fulfilling forms of masculinity to counter anxieties generated in a social world that [was] deeply divided along the fracture-lines of ethnicity and nation, gender and class" (Dawson 1994: 282). It is true that, like the popular adventure stories, these romances were written for a middle-class reading public who felt the need to identify with heroic figures as a way to "fix one's own place within the social world, to feel oneself to be coherent and powerful rather than fragmented and contradictory" (ibid.). Through what Cora Kaplan has called "the linguistic strategies and processes of the text" (Kaplan 1986: 162), these romances inscribed a form of subjectivity for their mass readers that enabled them to justify and reinstate the nationally ordained norms of imperial power while continuing to stretch and test the existing thresholds of civility. In other words, since the conventional norms had themselves been subjected to questioning as a consequence of the social and political developments in the late nineteenth century, the narrative processes of "fixing" a coherent place within the social world entailed recasting the imaginative boundaries of class and gender relations. As a result, questions about class affiliation and class privilege, which had been consolidated earlier in the century, entered this discursive setting in a manner that resulted in the simultaneous questioning of the powerful status quo arrangements within imperial society and the renegotiating of the existing alignments of class and gender relations. In the face of working out and reinventing these relations, the Anglo-Indian romances deployed narratives that, although highly contradictory, were ultimately syncretic in function. They utilized tactical means to secure and recast simultaneously the stability of a middle-class imperial patriarchy and the collective fantasy of a nation enthralled by the force and power of change. Through the process of manipulating its readers into entering these fantasies, the romances engage them in working out the crises and resolutions of the love plots in multiple ways, opening up a densely arranged discursive space. This space, therefore, makes visible the sometimes incommensurable and conflicting forces that were shaping the ideologies of this renegotiated imperial identity, as well as the dissenting voices that were begin to emerge at that time. As Michael Ryan has reminded us:

> Cultural representation designates a materiality of need and desire which cannot be fully shaped to suit the prerequisites of domination. There is a necessary misalignment between the idealizing representation ideology imposes and the material need or desire the representation addresses, and progressive political possibilities reside in this aporia. If ideology consists of the shaping of potentially counter-hegemonic needs and desires in ways conducive to maintenance of domination, then that undecidable difference of force is likely to be enacted as difference of rhetorical modes.
>
> (Ryan 1989: 115–16)

The Anglo-Indian romances often embody this enactment of difference through reworking dominant rhetorical modes in order to negotiate with what Ryan has called "undecidable difference of force." Historically speaking, the tensions between the emerging middle class and the established colonial governing class—or the Victorian colonial "nobility"—in this era had led the former to question the dominant imperial ethos held in place by the entrenched colonial hierarchy. If the empire had earlier promised social mobility for many middle-class men in Britain, it had also become evident that name, stature, and links to this colonial nobility provided the only means of securing a stable career in the empire. This circle of privilege, protected zealously by upper-class imperial men, therefore resulted in a growing sense of resentment among the rest, many of whom attributed the military and political failures of the 1880s to the continuing power and presence of this circle. During such a moment, women and romance provided alternative routes to recapture the lost glory and the fantasy of the empire. However, as Laurie Langbauer has argued, "subordinating women . . . grant[ed] those ranked above them at best local (although effective and destructive) power, for total control resides in the system of construction and representation in which all terms are determined" (Langbauer 1990: 5). In late Victorian England, that system had been held in place by the entire network of social relations within imperial society, including those claimed by the emerging middle classes, who were equally invested in the fate of the British empire. The epigraph to Croker's *Angel* points to that crisis of authority; however, as I will clarify in the course of my analysis, a wide range of strategies are deployed in these romances to contain that crisis and to secure the primacy of a middle-class male order in order to continue providing a necessary unifying "national" fantasy. In this chapter I have chosen to discuss four of these Anglo-Indian romances that best represent the dramatization of, and recuperation from, this crisis: Rudyard Kipling and Balestier's *The Naulahka* (1892;

henceforth cited as TN), *A Son of Empire* by Morley Roberts (1899; henceforth cited as SE), F. E. Penny's *The Romance of the Nautch Girl* (1898; henceforth cited as RNG), and Charles Johnston's *Kela Bai: An Anglo-Indian Idyll* (1900; henceforth cited as KB). I explore the manner in which these works of popular fiction codified their fictive enclosures by reordering those contested sites that were being actively produced by the shifting class and gender relations in late Victorian colonial England; how this very codification was rife with the tensions and contradictions between traditional ideologies that were being challenged and the newly emerging ones that needed, in the face of this conflict, to retain their ties to the former; and how these contradictions were often managed through the deployment of specific rhetorical and figural modes. But first, brief summaries of the romances I consider in the essay.

Rudyard Kipling's Indian romance, co-authored with Wolcott Balestier, *The Naulahka* concerns the adventures of a young American from Topaz, Wyoming, Nick Tarvin. Nick goes to India in pursuit of two interconnected goals: to win back his beloved, Kate, who had earlier refused to marry him, preferring to go to India to work for the benefit of Indian women; and to bring back the precious diamond, "the naulahka," from the hands of an Indian prince as a lure for the wife of the chief of the railway company responsible for bringing the railways to the western boom town where Nick has political ambitions.[7] After a series of adventures involving the local Indian maharajah and the wicked rival queen and former court dancer, Sitabai, Nick finally wins the favor of his beloved, who sees the error of her ways in choosing to come to India. Kipling's hero procures the diamond by carefully manipulating the political and domestic systems in place, but ultimately gives it up in the familiar Kiplingesque gesture of imperial sacrifice, believing that gaining Kate's approval was more valuable to him than bringing back the priceless diamond.

Morley Roberts's *A Son of Empire* is about a headstrong and independent-minded young British girl, Madge, who falls in love with an imperial soldier, Richard Blundell, while vacationing in the Swiss Alps. As a worshipper of heroes and conquerors, Madge is infatuated by the man's reputation as a worthy son of empire. She also learns from him that, despite his reputation as a skilled fighter, Richard had been relegated to the position of a civil magistrate in a remote part of India because of an old rivalry with his senior commander over a woman. Outraged by this injustice, Madge promises to use her family influence to have him released from his civil duties and sent to lead the military campaigns on the frontier. However, unable to persuade her friend's influential father to grant her this request, she steals his private telegraph cipher, forges his signature, and sends orders, unbeknown to the man, to the commander-in-chief in Simla, to send Richard to the frontier. Somewhat puzzled by the sudden change in his fortunes, Richard joins the campaign, where he proves himself a worthy fighter and leader, and after successfully suppressing the insurgents on the borders of the Indian empire returns as a hero. However, the forgery is soon discovered and Richard returns to England to clear his name. Madge confesses her crime and is forgiven, but her lover is sent away to Africa on a dangerous mission. Chastened, Madge waits for his return for two years, and the novel ends with her visiting him, as he lies injured in a hospital, in Brindisi.

F. E. Penny's *The Romance of the Nautch Girl* is set in a colonial civil outpost in southern India, where William Manning, the younger brother of the resident civil surgeon, Felix Manning, goes missing the day after the conclusion of the local "devil dance" held outside the native temple. Suspicion falls on the local *dasi*–or nautch girl–Meenachi, with whom the young man had been romantically linked, although the Anglo-Indian community had earlier assumed that he was pursuing the hand of the local engineer's daughter, Beryl. Although both Beryl and the nautch girl Minachee are in love with Felix, the latter seems too busy in his medical duties to take notice of this fact. Minachee becomes a loyal follower of the doctor, helping him in the clinic and offering her services as a nurse. Although initially impressed by Minachee's dedication and personal charms, Felix is later appalled when he realizes that he is the object of her desire. The mystery of the missing brother is eventually solved when his body is found in a shallow grave. The small Anglo-Indian community learns with horror that William Manning had been sacrificed by the local worshippers after being caught spying on their sacred rituals. The romance ends with the disappearance of Minachee and Beryl's acceptance of Felix's proposal of marriage.

Charles Johnston's *Kela Bai: An Anglo-Indian Idyll* is cast as a spiritual "rite of passage" autobiographical narrative of a district collector posted in a remote part of Bengal. The beautiful town prostitute, Kela Bai, appeals to the collector for his assistance after being wrongfully accused of attacking the local Indian sub-inspector. The inspector brings this case to the collector to avenge himself for being slighted by the woman. Sure of her innocence, the collector dismisses the case and reprimands the native police official, but, infatuated by Kela Bai's beauty, finds himself torn between his desire for her and his sense of moral responsibility as a colonial magistrate. Gradually that temptation evolves into a spiritual journey: as the man begins to see himself and the woman in a new light, his sexual desire is transmuted, and Kela Bai gives up her sinful life and departs on a religious pilgrimage.[8]

The sensational empire

As products of the 1880s and 1890s, the Anglo-Indian romances may be seen as the typical products of imperial propaganda constituting what Mackenzie has called a "self-generating ethos reinforcement, a constant repetition of the central ideas and concerns of the age" (Mackenzie 1986: 3). Their flamboyance is indeed reminiscent of the forms of chivalry mobilized in nineteenth-century adventure stories, and they often have recourse to the forms of identification with imperial power that had been established in these stories of the heroes of daring. Following Ann Cvetkovich's line of inquiry in her examination of Victorian sensationalist fiction, I suggest that the affective responses generated by these romances are to be seen not only "in a conservative way as a means of naturalizing ideology" (Cvetkovich 1992: 24) but also as a denaturalizing process that forces our attention to the discursive apparatus deployed for establishing the primacy of British civility.

In the nineteenth century, gender identity had been linked to civility by producing a set of oppositions between the "outer" from the "inner" sphere, and the "public" from the "private." On the one hand, modern warfare, with its accompanying system of spying and surveillance based on policies of civil administration, determined this "outer" sphere as a "masculine" one, offering a sweeping range of fictional scenarios for the enactment of male desire and power. Within this terrain, the fighter and spy (Richard Blundell), the colonial entrepreneur, adventurer, and strategist (Nick Tarvin), the civil surgeon (Felix Manning), and the civil servant (Johnston's narrator) authorize themselves as actors and agents of the empire. At the same time, for the British "new woman," the imperative to walk the streets of London, to travel unescorted on the railway, to ride, bike, and exercise, and to reject the time-honored norms of marriage and domesticity created new conditions for asserting womanhood (Calder 1976: 163), which were then transposed on to the colonial scene. Madge in Roberts's *A Son of Empire* flouts maternal authority by traveling unchaperoned up to the hills to meet the man she loves; that same rebellious power is later evoked in her determination to infiltrate what seemed to be an invulnerable and impenetrable male colonial system. By going against her father's wishes and training as a nurse in distant New York, the simple Western girl, Kate, in Kipling's *The Naulahka* seeks to define herself in a way that effortlessly translates into a missionary philanthropic zeal: "But India wants me more—or not me, but what I can do, and what women like me can do" (TN 56).[9]

At this time, for most (middle-class) Englishmen the need to reassert mastery in the face of the new demands placed on their masculinity by such women seeking a space outside the conventions of the Victorian sexual and moral order often intersected with the increasing competition they experienced in their own public lives. The Anglo-Indian romances attempt to negotiate this crisis by strategically reconstructing the power of men threatened by such developments: they are depicted as being impelled by the need to be motivated by powerful women, whose energies are then reharnessed to consolidate their own masculinity. But these reconstructions are often complex, given the multiple ways in which ideologies of gender, race, and nationality interacted with each other and mutually reinforced or displaced the given hierarchies within their dominant orders. For example, in the political climate of the suffrage movement, Englishwomen had begun to negotiate their new power in relation to existing colonial patriarchal structures, which paradoxically required them to access the ideological authority of a masculinist empire while securing their own place in the rising liberal post-Enlightenment, Darwinist political and moral order. The narrator of Roberts's romance describes Madge as "construct[ing] empires and mak[ing] each Englishman, each Briton, an emperor" (SE 6). This is the same woman who conspires against what she perceives to be an effete colonial system in order to restore power to men like Richard Blundell. Madge's "power" then rests on an ideology that simultaneously challenges the existing patriarchal authority based on class privilege while ultimately upholding its essentially masculine ethos. Similarly, middle-class imperial men had to define the challenges presented to them in a manner that allowed them to uphold the patriarchal order while continuing to oppose a social system of power and influence that had excluded them from the privileges of that order. In both cases, the boundaries of civility authorized by the dominant order are simultaneously challenged and preserved.

By imagining new relations of dependence between the "free" Englishwomen and their "oppressed" counterparts in India, the Anglo-Indian romances furthered the imperialist ideology of colonialism as a "rescue mission." As the figure of Kate in Kipling's romance illustrates, the perceived oppression of Indian women helped justify and further the moral cause of white women, who were led to assert their newly found power to affect and transform their own lives by acting on behalf of their oppressed colonial sisters. As Kate says, "I'm called. I can't get away from it. I can't help listening. I can't help going" (TN 9). Able to step in and out of the circumscribed spaces of the zenana in which many Indian women were thought to be imprisoned, Kate earns the undying loyalty of the queen of Rhatore as well as the native gypsy woman. Both the queen and the local gypsy woman can imagine their own freedom only by aligning themselves with their emancipated imperial sister. Similarly, Indian women, such as the "wily" Sitabai in *The Naulahka*, the mysteriously seductive Minachee in *The Romance of the Nautch Girl*, and Kela Bai in Johnston's work, serve as the medium through which imperial men re-envisioned their authority and consolidated the very power that was perceived to be threatened by the rise of the aggressive "new woman." Predictably, then, these fallen women had to wait for their imperial masters in order to be rescued from the tyranny of their own men.

Of particular significance is the figure of the "nautch girl" in so many of these romances: although representing that pervasive threat to the established racial and sexual codes, she remains as the tantalizing object of male scrutiny, and as a source of incitement and challenge for men. In both cases, the objectification of women along gender and racial planes is enabled by the discourse on female "agency" that had been prompted by the rising women's movement.[10] It meant situating Englishmen and Englishwomen in particular relationships to Indian women, relationships that helped test the boundaries of male power and female agency. However, it is important to remember that this sense of female agency—and with it the possibility for asserting a sexual and political identity outside the patriarchal order—is often inseparable from the mechanisms of male fantasy around which the narratives operate in these romances. These mechanisms manipulate female agency in order to serve the ends of a colonial patriarchy. As Anne Stoler has suggested in another context, it is these "new forms of scrutiny" (Stoler 1995: 212) underlying the objectification that are key to regulating the thoughts and actions of the new woman, ensuring that they are assigned a specific place within the established gender and racial differential. A critical look at these processes makes it amply clear that these forms of scrutiny lie embedded in the complex circuits of identification and differentiation fixed in these romances. It is along these circuits that the romances stage their gender politics, helping direct and mold the subjectivity of their nineteenth-century male and female readers. Simultaneously expressing and deflecting the anxieties of middle-class Englishmen, these circuits become repositories of fractured and sometimes irregular histories of imperial identity in the age of high imperialism. Simultaneously displaying and disavowing the anxieties of middle-class men, the conflictual economy of the narratives provides significant traces of these histories.

Any analysis of these romances, therefore, entails complicating the tendency to see high imperialism—the period when these romances were written—as a simple and programmatic consolidation of men's power in relation to the empire. One has to reconceptualize this era in historically variable terms—as an era suffused with an internally contradictory sense of identity, marked by the class anxieties and tensions of a nation faced with an increasing erosion of the belief in a monolithic empire governed by a unitary center. It is worth remembering that this belief in the solidity of the imperial system had validated the centrality of middle-class civility—particularly that of the traditionally held "gentlemanly" notions of European territoriality that had hitherto assured the sense of colonial ownership. In the 1870s, for example, Disraeli's empire policy had re-energized the strong public opinion concerning the value of the colonies to Britain, which extended to the 1880s and 1890s, when popular expressions of imperial majesty reached their height. As Robert MacDonald has shown, the display of imperial images in the popular press—from pull-out maps of the Imperial Federation to illustrations of Britannia served by its female attendants—held the attention of the public through the circulation and dissemination of popular fantasies about the empire. MacDonald further explains, "The Queen and the army were moved to the center of the imperial stage, a cult of heroes and heroic national history was celebrated in popular literature and infiltrated school textbooks, and the music halls exploited patriotic sentiment in songs and tableaux. Imperial ideas reached a mass audience" (MacDonald 1994: 2). However, behind these celebratory outbursts of nationalist fervor lay the realities of the late Victorian colonial order that had affected middle-class male consciousness in significant ways.

Writing in 1858, Sir Edward Sullivan had commented that "The upper middling classes founded and cemented our Indian Empire . . . India is the *safety valve* for the *escapement* of the surplus energy of the upper middling classes" (Sullivan 1858: 214; emphasis added). By the 1880s, a different mood had begun to appear. While the British empire had hitherto served as the fairly secure ground for the exertion of middle-class men's economic and political initiatives (so pointedly described as the "escapement of surplus energy" by Edward Sullivan), the changed political scenarios within Europe and the current state of the colonies had severely stymied these opportunities. Underlying the wondrous "red on the map" was the awareness that the British empire "represented in truth at best only a dominion of opinion and a grand anomaly, and at worst a temptation to illusions of grandeur" (Hyam 1992: 1). What appeared to be a monolithic power held up by a centrally controlled invulnerable imperial body of administrative, economic, military, and legislative systems was in fact riddled with conflicts and contradictions that often confused and frustrated middle-class perceptions of colonial mastery. This often resulted in attacks on the power of the colonial nobility who were held responsible for the current state of affairs, and on the entrenched nepotism and incompetence that had come to be identified with the latter's mode of functioning.

Popular poetry written by colonial officials in India continued to satirize the power of this colonial nobility. Aliph Cheem's narrative poem "Tempora mutantur," for example, tells the story of a mediocre army man, Cecil Mole, who successfully moves up the social and professional ladder with the aid of his social connections: "A most unmistakably common-place soul / Intended by nature to play a dull role," married "early in life / Quite a gem of a wife, / Who when he got in, pulled him out, of a hole." The poem ends with:

> Interest, interest—that was the key,
> Opening locks, sir, on both sides the sea!
> Merit? bah—interest, influence, birth,
> He who had these, you might wager, had worth.
>   (Cheem 1871)

The ideology of individual "worth" clashed with the "dim officialdom"–the "endless passages" of the War Office described in *A Son of Empire*, where "beyond the door lurked Influence, behind that sat Red Tape," signifying "the crookedness of things" (SE 210). It is not surprising that middle-class organizations such as the Primrose League and the Imperial Federation League, supported by figures such as Benjamin Kidd and Karl Pearson, pressed for the replacement of incompetent persons at the helm of colonial administration and army by "individuals selected exclusively according to their ability and independently of social status" (Baumgart 1982: 167). These societies imagined a possible rejuvenation of the empire by rearming the middle classes that had been left out of the entrenched hierarchies within the colonial aristocracy. A new nationalist rhetoric imagined these classes asserting themselves from outside of the social boundaries of inherited class privilege to secure the authority that was clearly slipping from existing colonial hands.

But the general failures ascribed to the colonial aristocracy had their roots in the larger political, economic, and military developments in Europe at this time. Eric Hobsbawm has pointed out that the rapidly industrializing nations of Europe in search of new markets "hoped to carve out for themselves territories which, by virtue of ownership, would give national business a monopoly position" (Hobsbawm 1987: 66–7). Such aggressive economic attitudes had led to a series of intense territorial rivalries among the emerging imperial powers of Europe, resulting in a number of conflicts–the Anglo-French war in West Africa, Anglo-German rivalry in East Africa and Samoa in 1885, the Anglo-Portuguese scuffle in the Congo, and other conflicts in parts of Morocco and China that had been triggered as early as the 1870s. It had become evident to a beleaguered middle-class English society that the traditional policies of "informal supremacy, moral suasion, confederation panaceas, and gentlemanly agreements between leading European powers to avoid elbowing each other on the periphery of the empire had begun to fail" (Elridge 1973: 245). As Phillip Darby has noted, the sense of an imagined European community unified by a common purpose had begun "to splinter in the face of new and aggressive nationalisms" growing in Europe, leading to the emergence of the four great imperial powers–Germany, France,

Austria-Hungary, and Russia—in direct conflict with Britain (Darby 1987: 13–14). After the 1870s, British interests in India, for example, were threatened by the growing power of the Russian empire, resulting in a radical shift in global power relations. The direct consequence of such a shift was that no power could act unilaterally without disturbing the equilibrium hitherto guaranteed by the politics of status quo. So the very equilibrium that had worked in favor of English imperialists gave way to an uneasy and sometimes precarious scenario marked by the formation of unexpected "power vacuums" that had to be countered to "forestall the intervention of a rival" (Elridge 1973: 247).

The threat of imminent rivalry is articulated in Alfred Lyall's famous historical account of the empire, *The Rise and Expansion of British Dominion in India*, published in 1894. In this work, Lyall—the eminent apologist for the British empire—asserted that "the situation of our Indian Empire is . . . in many respects unique" and that "the annals of modern sovereignties show no parallel," but also admitted that "continual expansion seems to have become part of our national habits and modes of growth" (Lyall 1894: 344). Seeing England's imperial mission in Darwinian terms as the "unending struggle out of which the settlement of the political world is resolved," Lyall linked that struggle to the violence of "the material world shaped out of the jarring forces of Nature" (ibid.: 346). Although the same Darwinian vision is deployed to uphold what he called the vigor of "adventurous pioneering" (ibid.) among the imperialists, the sense of exhaustion and depleting energy becomes an abiding theme in his writings. Lyall's poem "Siva," for instance, concludes with the following lines: "Far as the Western spirit may range / It finds but the travail of endless change" (Lyall 1907: 105). As the expression of the threat of change that had been created by the political conditions in Europe, Lyall's assertion in *The Rise and Expansion* that "Henceforward the struggle will be, not between the Eastern and Western races, but between the great commercial and conquering nations of the West for predominance in Asia" (Lyall 1894: 347) assumes special significance. Transposing the conventional Manichean opposition between "civilized" Europe and the "barbaric" East to the conflict and rivalry *within* Europe, Lyall's words symptomize the shifting political relations within the Western metropolis in the late nineteenth century.[11] Politically exigent maneuvers, often relying on half-comprehended decisions, and triggered by unpredictable military developments on rival sides, led Britain to enter a period of military intervention and expansion in the 1870s and 1880s. The northwest frontiers of the Indian empire, situated far from the seat of imperial governance and considered vulnerable, became flashpoints of dispute and intense rivalry, needing constant military surveillance. In contrast to the relative stability that the imperial government had imposed on the semi-autonomous princely states within the Indian empire, the frontiers seemed vulnerable to foreign infiltration whenever European political alignments shifted. It seemed that the line separating the governance and the protection of the empire from policies of expansion and annexation were only tenuous. For example, threatened by Russia, Britain had to secure India as well as safeguard her routes of communication, which initiated the border wars in Afghanistan in 1885.[12]

In imaginative terms, then, geographical "borders" became symbolic of the imminent threat to colonial suzerainty. Such a threat could only be met through the decisive actions of a select group of individuals—mainly outside the existing colonial nobility—who could lead the military campaigns armed with a new frontier sensibility. The Anglo-Indian romances often reinvent this frontier sensibility, but, unlike the adventure stories where the frontier had always been rendered as an actual geographical setting, the setting in these romances is often rendered as a symbolic space. For example, in Kipling's *The Naulahka*, the conjunction of an "American" frontier sensibility with the spirit of British imperialism signifies a reimagined global British empire that could reunite an Anglo-Saxon United States with the aspirations of a beleaguered imperial nation.[13] Although the kingdom of Rhatore is imagined as a remote outpost of the Indian empire, it is Nick's American frontier sensibility that is constantly emphasized in the romance. In Roberts's *A Son of Empire* that frontier is set on the northwestern peripheries of the Indian empire, where Richard Blundell, a man unconnected with privileged order and rank, fights against the marauding tribes in the battle for the Afghan succession. "Never shooting anything more savage than a quail or a snipe" (SE 137) while serving as a magistrate, Blundell strikes "terror" (SE 144) in the hearts of the tribesmen, vanquishes them, and emerges as the new hero. In Richard Blundell's case, the frontier is cast as a form of "sensibility" that is intrinsic to the hero's potential power. As a romantic hero, he is honorable and maintains his civility with that rare balance of masculinity and tenderness that his beloved finds irresistible; as a soldier, his ruthlessness only matches the force with which he restrains himself from directly opposing his own imperial peers (that responsibility falls on his girl, Madge). In Johnston's *Kela Bai* and Penny's *The Romance of the Nautch Girl*, the frontier is symbolically reconstituted within the empire and located at the more mundane site of civil governance, where it marks the fragile border between civility, moral righteousness, and sexual desire. It is at the site of this remote civil station in Bengal that Johnston's narrator, the English collector—another incarnation of the son of empire—uses his civil and moral authority to "rescue" the local prostitute from the clutches of an Indian official. As a civil surgeon posted in a remote southern province, Felix Manning in Penny's romance becomes an investigator, utilizing his medical skills to interpret the signs that lead to the solving of the mystery of his brother's disappearance. The frontier is here located within the boundaries of civil and medical authority, posing a new challenge for the civil surgeon in his role as investigator, healer, and civilizer.

As the whole fantasy of the Indian empire started to become more brittle, the feeling of an aggressive paramountcy heightened during this era. In fact, the pervasive jingoism of high imperialism might have been propelled by these developments. Even when that jingoism appears muted, the "imperial task" becomes an obsessive topic of discussion and debate. J. R. Seeley, the author of *The Expansion of England* (1885), remarked in "The Indian Question":

> In the present state of the world a dependency held by military force may easily be like a mill-stone round the neck of a nation . . . India, at the same time

that she locks up an army, more than doubles the difficulty of our foreign policy.

(Seeley [1885] 1971: 152)

In an earlier passage he had stated that "our possession of India imposes upon us vast and intolerable responsibilities; this is evident; but it is not at once evident that we reap any benefit from it" (ibid.: 146). Seeley continues:

> But the abandonment of India is an idea which even those who believe that we shall one day be driven to it are not accustomed to contemplate as a practical scheme. There are some deeds which, though they had been better not done, cannot be undone.

(ibid.: 154)

Accompanying this pervasive cynicism and uncertainty about the future was also a sense of dissipation—of the dwindling of those energies that had helped forge the empire in the first place. This sense increasingly came to be seen as part of a national malaise afflicting the middle-class social order. Medical and eugenic discourse dwelt on this issue and repeatedly called for the "preservation of the national stamina" (Davin 1978: 19). As stated earlier, the sense of dissipating energy associated with the daunting tasks of the empire even haunts the poetry of the historian Sir Alfred Lyall. His "The Land of Regrets" can be read as a poem about loss, but at its center are the predicaments of a middle-class imperial man who is portrayed as a vulnerable figure ensnared by the temptress India:

> What far-reaching Nemesis stirred him
> From his home by the cool of the sea?
> When he left the fair country that reared him,
> When he left her, his mother, for thee,
> That restless, disconsolate worker
> Who strains now in vain at thy nets,
> O sultry and sombre Noverca!
> O Land of Regrets!

In this poem, the colonial impulse is projected as an external "voice of the siren," to which the man is described as being a "slave that ... frets / In thy service." Rather than being the source of strength for the middle-class imperial man, the "surplus energy" that Sullivan had earlier valorized only renders the man weak:

> What lured him to life in the tropic?
> Did he venture for fame or for pelf?
> Did he seek a career philanthropic?
> Or simply to better himself?
> But whate'er the temptation that brought him,
> Whether piety, dullness, or debts,

He is thine for a price, thou hast bought him
O Land of Regrets!

> (Lyall 1907: 113)

In what seems like a perfect allegory of the crisis of middle-class masculine aspirations for social mobility and power, India serves as the source of a colonial desire, but it is a desire that is seen to be perverted and caught in the traps of its own making. Compare this with the passage from *A Son of Empire*: "To work for the Empire seemed in the hour of dawn and disillusion striving to augment the vast proportions of a devouring polyp. . . . Chronos and Empire both devoured their children" (SE 332). What is striking about Lyall's poem is that its feminization of India as "Circe," the temptress, disarticulates the metaphor of woman as the "foreign" land to be conquered, and instead endows it with a threatening power that entraps men.

This expression of unease recurs throughout the poetry of the empire that was produced by amateur poets during this time. The Anglo-Indian poet Thomas Frank Bignold writes in "Our Peers":

O Britons, to the rescue!
For the need is sharp and sore,
The rights our sturdy fathers won
Shall be our rights no more!

> (Bignold 1888: 22)

If this is a crisis of continuity interpreted as a crisis of inheritance and privilege, it also signals the deep sense of dissatisfaction with the status quo in affairs of the empire. In fact, the unalienable rights that had been perceived as natural to middle-class men now seemed to be threatened by the anxieties triggered by an ungovernable empire. Reacting to this larger climate of unease, Morley Roberts, who made his career as a popular writer of romances, revived an image of heroism, an image based on men fighting on the frontiers of the empire and on the high seas of Africa, Australia, and the United States, hardy and rugged men without the trappings of privilege or status. In his poems, however, a different mood prevails. In "Greece and England," published in 1891 in a collection significantly entitled *Songs of Energy*, Roberts writes:

Great is our country, but our gods are not
The Passionate beauty that made Greece divine;
We are divided, they were singly wrought
Into one glory, like a summer vine;
We seek all ends, but they, content with one,
Are more immortal with their Sophocles
Than we with all our empires in the sun,
And guarded straits and close forbidden seas.

> (Roberts 1891: 56)

The harking back to a pastoral vision of unity and beauty only heightens the present anxieties, and, as the title of the collection suggests, the sense of paranoia here is intimately connected with an obsessive and unnerving sense of dissipating energies, paradoxically signified by a claustrophobic awareness of the political world. This is again clearly articulated in another of Roberts's poems, "Poppy Seed." As a darker version of Tennyson's "Lotos Eaters," this poem evokes the soporific power of the poppy, from which opium, an important item of colonial trade, was extracted in order to ward off "Ghosts that chatter things of ill / Ghosts that fret but cannot kill." Also strikingly reminiscent of De Quincey's *Confessions of an English Opium Eater*, this poem is suffused with an abiding sense of paranoia stemming from the apprehension of

> Hideous things that bite and creep
> . . . Shivering flesh that crawls
> Horrid hands that ever keep
> Writing jests obscene on walls
> Mixed with minatory scrawls.
> (Roberts 1891: 15)

The writers of these unidentifiable jests and scrawls remain invisible to the colonial eye, eluding the understanding. As I will illustrate later, the paranoia of being watched and monitored, and of being the object of an invisible gaze, recurs in Kipling's *The Naulahka* and Johnston's *Kela Bai*, where that paranoia is carefully reworked and transformed in order to restore the power of imperial mastery. These instances underscore the fact that behind the aggressive assertion of imperial identity often seen in this era of high imperialism lurked a sense of crisis—rendered in personal or public terms—depending on the demands of particular narratives, which surfaces time and again in the expressions of fear, frustration, horror, and disgust.

As noted earlier, the most immediate historical context for the staging of the itinerary of such relations of power was provided by the new women's movement of the 1880s, the source of the most radical challenge to Victorian patriarchy. However, the empowerment of women in Britain largely depended on reinventing their status as middle-class subjects of an imperial nation. The Anglo-Indian romances looked towards the "new woman," and the new relationships between the genders being proposed by the movement as a way to redefine and, at times, consolidate men's authority. As Mrinalini Sinha has demonstrated in *Colonial Masculinity*, serious debates about English masculinity in the nineteenth century, which often coincided with, and stemmed from, the women's movement, took place within the context of the empire. The advent of organized feminist campaigns, beginning in the 1860s, had been accompanied by a proliferation of novels about the "new woman" in the 1880s and 1890s, as well as essays in feminist periodicals such as *Woman's Signal* and *Shafts* (see Caine 1997: 142–5), and in public debates in the national journals, such as the *Westminister Review*, the *Fortnightly Review*, and the *Nineteenth Century*.[14]

Having reached a mass audience quickly, this discourse sensitized middle-class women to the sometimes very contentious issues about the extent and limits of their ability to envision their new power. As Lisa Tickner has noted:

> The development of nineteenth-century feminism took place in a series of political contexts and across a series of reforming campaigns, which often diverged in their particular positions they adopted on the nature of femininity and the proper social role of women.
>
> (Tickner 1988: 3)

Contradictions arose not only between feminist and anti-feminist positions, but also within the emerging forms of feminism itself. The multiplicity of viewpoints expressed within the movement—some of which seemed contradictory—provided fertile ground for the rise of an array of discourse opposing the new cause. Some of these, as Ann Ardis and Sally Ledger have demonstrated, promoted the ideological discourses on the new woman "in order to ridicule and to control renegade women" (Ardis 1990: 65). Others accessed those aspects of the movement that provided the most flexible resource for reinventing the power of men. The Anglo-Indian romances belong to this latter category.

Part of this was facilitated by the fact that the British empire itself had begun to play a key role in English women's definitions of their new power. The ideologies of gender and class inflected each other with a considerable degree of social and moral torque within the discourse of the empire throughout the century. In opposing equal educational opportunities for women, Elizabeth Sewell used the Indian Civil Service exam as an example to prove that women were physically and mentally unable to compete with men. She claimed that, unlike the man who had "been tossed about in the world, left in great measure to his own resources, and been inured to constant physical education," the woman, who has "been guarded from overfatigue," could never be "able to work up the subjects required for an Indian Civil Service examination in which boys do" (quoted in Hollis 1979: 143). At the same time, as Kenneth Ballhatchet has noted, these same civil service examinations were often criticized for allowing only "the bookish, socially inept, and physically inadequate individuals" (Ballhatchet 1980: 8)—Arnold's "crammed men," feminized and thus rendered effete—to enter the services of the empire. In Roberts's romance, Madge is portrayed as avoiding the company of such effete colonials, whom she regards as being a "detestable fat lot" (SE 100). She takes every opportunity to subject such imperial men to her withering sarcasm: "A man is a very rare creature, a real one, that is. Most of them are imitations" (SE 111). In rejecting Sewell's norm of masculine ideal, Madge questions not the overarching patriarchal order of the day, but only those class hierarchies that stood in the way of "real" men like Richard Blundell from achieving their objectives. Similarly, Kate, in *The Naulahka*, asserts her will and independence by offering herself to the cause of the empire's mission, and, as the narrative unfolds, she also becomes the medium through which Nick Tarvin justifies his own quest for power. Towards the end of Kipling's romance, Nick Tarvin muses: "Had he not the Naulahka? She went with it; she was indissolubly connected with it" (TN 294).

To take up imperial service in the name of "Victorian womanhood" seemed to preserve "the ideological assumptions about English women's superior moral strength" (Ledger 1997: 64). This was an ideology that proved powerful enough to be supported by the evangelical and social-Darwinist inspired constituencies within imperial society. For example, Maria Sharpe, the wife of the evolutionist Karl Pearson, claimed that Darwin had "put instruments in our hands by which we may help ourselves. It is . . . my earnest conviction that it is through the right understanding of these laws that women alone will be able to solve the *problem of herself*, her mission and her end" (quoted in Bland 1995: 79; emphasis added). If the challenges to Victorian patriarchy had created a problem for/of women, those challenges could be efficiently met by the power of Darwinist ideals. The ideals of imperial motherhood evoked in late Victorian England found much support in the women's rights campaigns inspired by the newly emerging eugenic sciences, as well as by evangelical politics. Seen as the source of an energized race, emancipated women could find their true mission by fighting for the cause of oppressed Indian women. As evident in the work of Annette Ackroyd in India, this strategy often worked in favor of the imperialists, who were able to win the ideological support of Englishwomen in their attempt to thwart native nationalist sentiments (see Vron Ware 1992: 122–6). These newly charted relations between women and empire presented a productive site because they provided new and elastic definitions of femininity across which men's power could be reinvented. "Our national virtue must fall with our domestic virtue, and our national power must decline with both," announced the writer of the anonymous pamphlet *The Eastern Question: The Three Great Perils of England* in 1877. The new woman had irrevocably emerged as a new species of power in the imagination of the masses, a figure that could symbolize the inherent vitality of a race meant for leadership and governance.

The struggle to define "woman's nature" in the midst of a rising politically militant climate in late Victorian society provided a means of reinserting women into a national imaginary that was essentially based on patriarchal norms. For example, opponents of the suffragists argued that anything that threatened to lessen "the national reserve" of the "moral forces" of "sympathy and disinterestedness" with which women were naturally endowed should be condemned (*An Appeal Against Female Suffrage*, 1889; quoted in Hollis 1979: 323–4). Once women were defined as part of the "natural and national resource," the resultant conflation of "nature" and "nation" prized open the space for reconstituting the very ground on which men asserted their being as natural holders of a national imperial destiny. As Susan Kent has pointed out, since it was a widely held belief, popularized by social thinkers such as Spencer, Geddes, and Thomson, that women were biologically constituted to reserve or conserve energy (as opposed to men who were responsible for its dissipation and expenditure), the former could serve as the repository of those reserves of biologically directed impulses that could be shored up against what was perceived as the gradually eroding energies of men engaged in public sphere within the empire (see Kent 1987: 164). Lady Jeune's remarks in her essay in *The Modern Marriage Market* rehearse this belief:

In the history of any Western country the influence which women exercize must largely affect its destinies: where the women are strong and virtuous a country must prosper in just the same proportion as it will decay if they are the reverse.

(Modern 1898: 68–9)

As the contemporary arguments about women and marriage interfaced with the widely prevalent discourse about the decay of a nation's "reserves" of energy– embodied, as for example in Max Nordua's *Degeneration* (trans. 1895), yet another site for the strategic definition of woman's nature emerged. At the same time, the inner sphere for women was emphasized, as in the poem "To a 'New Woman,'" in which the poet addresses the "new woman" in the following manner:

What good is there in knowing much,
If there is little you can do?
. . . New Woman, mend your little ways!
Forget the properties of rocks!
Chuck learning up and take to stays!
And knit some babies' socks.

(Lays: 20)

It was again these contending ideas about women and their sphere that were reflected in the conflict between traditionally held Victorian beliefs regarding the essential and timeless quality of woman's "nature" and the belief held by many Victorians that all human nature could be irretrievably altered by historical change. What might appear as yet another contradiction actually opened up an entire range of possibilities for reinventing the roles of women. In the words of Linda Shires, representations of women could "be used simultaneously to support opposing political frameworks" (Shires 1992: 185), which she sees as a character-istic feature of the late Victorian era. For example, the implicit or explicit acknow-ledgment that women's identities were historically constituted led to varying conceptions of *how* women could be agents and subjects of historical change in the world. Women, for example, could hold the destiny of the empire by acting as conservators of precious national energy; they could, as Madge does, act on their own intuition to redress the imbalances of power and help remasculinize a failing system; or they could, like Kate, take up the role of colonial savior, a role that C. Amy Dawson canonizes in the following manner:

Who are the strong salvation of our land,
Let the deep sorrows of a kindred race,
Sprung with our own from the old Aryan home,
Awaken you to burning thought and speech,
Till the pathetic echo of your tones
Has made the weakest strong, the strongest sad.

(Dawson 1892: 63)

If the romances recuperate strong women as a way to contain their power and agency, and thus retain their subordinate status, the logic of such a process was also found in the popular rhetoric of the day. The language of the Women's Disabilities Bill (*Hansard*, 3 May 1871), for example, represented women not only as lacking in practical experience but also as being emotionally amenable to the power of undesirable male persuasion, and therefore not to be trusted with political power:

> On the question of fitness to govern, was it not true that in all matters connected with the army, the navy, and matters commercial, diplomatic, and legal, women would have to judge on the basis of information obtained second hand, and not from practical experience? The ballot was about to be adopted ... how enormous would be the power of the priest ... Surely it could not be expected that women would give an unbiased vote, the result of political conviction?
>
> (quoted in Hollis 1979: 306)

Although capable of decisive action and being able to match her own inventive-ness with Richard Blundell's power as a master "tactician" (SE 27), Madge has eventually to give up that power to the man. Moreover, her heroic transgressions (she infiltrates the closed bureaucratic circuits of the nation's imperial structure) also signify a real threat to the secrecy of colonial security systems, particularly those of information and transmission. Yet, despite this threat, Madge's deception remains key to activating Blundell's manhood. The recuperative processes of disciplining Madge can therefore take place through sudden reversals or disavowals of women's power, or by repositioning a woman like her to her essential "womanhood" through the use of equivocal language and rhetorical manipulation. Madge's decisive and headstrong behavior, for example, is explained by the narrator of Roberts's romance as being part of her unpredictably emotional nature, which concealed an underlying "cunning inherent in all femininity" (SE 92). While Kate, in *The Naulahka*, forcefully contends at one point that "even for women there is more than one kind of devotion," at the end of the novel, her position is compromised, as the narrator describes her condition in these words:

> The first breath of a cold-weather night made Kate wrap her rugs about more closely. Tarvin was sitting at the back of the cart, swinging his legs and staring at Rhatore before the bends of the road should hide it. The realization of defeat, remorse, and the torture of an over well-trained conscience were yet to come to Kate. In that hour, luxuriously disposed upon many cushions, she realized nothing more than a woman's complete contentment with the fact *that there was a man in the world to do things for her*, although she had yet not learned to lose her interest in how they were done.
>
> (TN 376; emphasis added)

Here it is the narrative turn of events that forces Kate back into a man's world, revealing that, when men fantasized their own power and self-independence but felt threatened by the uncertainties of the new political order, they could guard against them by subjecting their women to their essential "natures." Time and again, "woman's nature" becomes a holding place for the co-presence of opposing beliefs, helping to manage and transform the felt contradictions in men's lives into manifestations of a higher, "universal" truth *about* the separation of the two spheres. Opponents of the women's cause simultaneously reclaimed and gave new profiles to the traditionally held binary polarities regarding men's and women's natures and spheres of influence, oppositions that had been central to maintaining the dominant gender politics of Victorian patriarchy. But even such a move lent a powerful discursive thrust to the debate, unwittingly introducing a multivalent rhetoric concerning their nature. This rhetoric is clearly visible in many of the romances I consider in this essay, particularly in the manner in which they give voice to the newly felt power of women even when they are ultimately recuperated by the dominant patriarchal ideologies.

Even as social codes governing gender were constantly strengthened through the discourse of "affect," that discourse found new meanings and purpose in the era of high imperialism. For example, within the Victorian ideology of domesticity, the "world of emotions" to which women were seen to belong allowed them limited agency, but, in the context of the imperial world, that world of emotions was actively intertwined with the "masculine" tasks of the empire. Although the empire builders were cognizant of the fact that physical tasks often claimed the "poetry" of men's nature, leaving women the task of conserving it, it is this poetry that helped sustain faith in the empire and made it viable as a political and economic enterprise. As imperial propaganda proved time and again, the power to evoke emotions through the rhetoric of words, images, and pageants was essentially "feminine," equally significant to, if not more significant than, the job of carrying on with the masculine duties of governance and military expansion. John Ruskin's conservative political belief in separate spheres had significant ramifications for the empire, since his domestic ideology carefully mirrored this traditional ideology of colonialism:

> The man's power is active, progressive, defensive. He is eminently the doer, the creator, the discoverer, the defender. His intellect is for speculation and invention; his energy for adventure, for war, and for conquest, wherever war is just, wherever conquest is necessary . . . *The woman's power is for rule*, not for battle—and her intellect is not for invention or creation, but for *sweet ordering, arrangement, and decision.*
>
> ("Of Queens' Gardens," in *Sesame and Lilies*;
> quoted in Hollis 1979: 16; emphasis added)

But Ruskin's own preference for the "Gothic ornament" was based on what he considered to be the primacy of style, of "arrangement" and the disposition of details, which Christina Crosby has shown to be crucial to his own belief in "truth of the historical age, express[ing] the epoch" (Crosby 1992: 103). While Ruskin's arguments rested on the conventional ideology of gender, they also introduced a play of possibilities which, when translated into the realm of imperial culture, held together, albeit in a somewhat precarious balance, three related points about women: that, contrary to men, whose "intellect is for conquest," women could use their "rule" and their powers of "decision" to establish their own agency; that that power could release those vital energies that men were often incapable of accessing; and that the expression of those energies could enable a resurgent masculine imperialism. Even though the idea of "separate spheres" was constantly revived by opponents of the "woman" cause, the notion that she was potentially a significant player in creating and sustaining the most powerful emotions fueling the empire was never abandoned. Women could stimulate, through their perceived power over rhetorical "affect," those urges that men needed in their call for heroic action. Thus, this two-pronged ideology dictating the reality of a woman's intrinsic sensibility re-excavated, in a sense, a feudal chivalric ideal in which women assumed rhetorical agency only eventually to surrender it to the men.

The heroine of Roberts's *A Son of Empire*, Madge, appears to be an ideal representative of the "new woman" cast along this double discourse. It is the novelty of her mind, her spiritedness, that initially makes Richard Blundell long for her company. Throughout Roberts's romance, however, Madge's aggressive newness is carefully coded so as to reinsert her into an essentially male colonial imaginary: she is "new" because she breaks away from a generation of effete Victorian women (represented by her complacent and constantly complaining mother) and regards effete colonial men with disdain; simultaneously, she is also linked to the timelessness of the nation's racial and national identity—"warriors of the sea and warriors of the land"—that reproduces in her being the glory of imperialism. She also becomes "romance, sole sitting in a waste of convention . . . of such romance empire makers have need" (SE 6); as "a Queen Medea" she is said to have "cut her hero to pieces and really renewed him" (SE 26), and, as "bit of a boy and a gipsy," she combines the traits of a hero-worshipper and an outsider to the established order. She is also made to embody a militaristic spirit that was beginning to be fueled by the call of the frontiers: she stands behind her man who "would help extend the Empire, and would set the Indus on fire" (SE 131). However, the emotional Madge is also depicted as being a conscience-stricken and a self-divided individual, one who painfully weighs the pros and cons of her game of forgery and deception before stealing the cipher. Richard, on the other hand, known for his reputation as a spy—a "master of deception" (SE 10)—is described as being in his natural setting on the frontier, which brings out what he essentially is—a man and an efficient fighter, plain talker, and strategist. His powers of clever and strategic surveillance, in great demand by the military authorities, are key to defining the very gaze Roberts's romance utilizes to regulate the potentially wayward power of independent women like Madge. It is for such a man that Madge gives up her childish hero worship of Napoleon and Wellington: "I want to be ruled," she says, "Oh! beat me, my man, and make me obey" (SE 4).

In Kipling's *The Naulahka*, Kate's allegiance to the ideals of the newly independent woman takes on a more complex dimension. First, there is her dedication to the imperial cause: moved by the account of the plight of Indian women (delivered in the form of a speech to American women) by the Indian woman reformer Pundita Ramabai, Kate experiences "the mantle of the Spirit" descending on her: "She had found herself"(TN 3).[15] Kate's progressive and emancipatory ideals are, however, constantly under surveillance by Nick, who, while identifying Kate with the "liberated" Dora in Ibsen's *A Doll's House*, also reassures himself that Kate does not fully "sympathize" with the "unfaithful" Dora: "Well, then, that's where you are solid *with* the Indian Empire. *The Doll's House* glanced right off this blessed old-timely country" (TN 130; emphasis added). Unable to read the elusive Kate or predict her reactions, Nick seeks comfort in interpreting her seeming disavowal of Dora in terms of what he perceives to be the conservative ideals of the East, thereby forging an imagined alliance between her and the values of marriage and motherhood that she had initially rejected. This is again strengthened by the wise words of the native queen of Rhatore (associated with the aristocratic but effete Indian royalty under the protection of the British) whose admiration for Kate is accompanied by these words of Eastern wisdom: "Thou hast given thy life to the helping of women. Little sister, when wilt *thou also be a woman*? (TN 342; emphasis added). The inherently male gaze through which the narrative operates constantly amplifies Kate's rejection of patriarchal values to a starkly ironic pitch: for example, we are told early in the story that Kate's refusal to marry was based on her inability to give "the whole of herself in marriage," a norm that she could/did not dare to question even when she refuses to abide by it.

During this era the opposition to the women's movement inadvertently opened up the very realm of masculinity by reiterating the definition of "womanliness" through negation. When Eliza Linton described the new woman as someone with "passionate ambition, virile energy, the love of strong excitement, self-assertion, fierceness, and undisciplined temper" (quoted in Hollis 1979: 20–1), or when Malcolm C. Salaman, in his *Woman: Through a Man's Eyeglass*, described the "individual woman" as someone who "believes in herself and has the courage of her individuality" (Salaman 1892: 86), they unwittingly drew attention to the world of imperial "affect" that men wished to claim for themselves. Richard or "Black" Blundell is a fantastical image of that world. Blundell, like Madge, is described as being an outsider to the established colonial order. Like Madge, his unconventionality is the source of his seductive power because it stands in contrast to the all-pervasive effeteness of that order (represented by Bobby, Madge's brother and Maitland, her socially approved suitor). But, on his own, he is powerless: like Aliph Cheem's Cecil Mole, it is only through the intervention/ deception of a woman that his hidden power can be released. Madge, on the other hand, sees her own deceit as "virtuous" (SE 116). She reasons in the following manner: "At the very best it would be a dishonourable act, a petty, mean act. Or, it would have meant that but for the end she had in view. The end made all the difference. Richard's good was the end . . . She was the little mouse, he the black lion in the red tape net" (SE 126). Thus, she dedicates her resourcefulness to the cause of her suitor. Similarly, Nick Tarvin is a self-made man, but the only way he can gain political power in his native Topaz is by wresting it from the hands of the established political gentry, represented by Kate's father. Paralleling Nick's imperial quest for Kate/Naulahka, Kate's own imperial mission for saving Indian women is ultimately subordinated to Nick's quest for social and political power.

Women with "ill-regulated desires"

> Then arose the cadenced stamp of the dancers' feet and the ring of the anklet-bells, as they moved with stealthy, gliding steps, and waved their arms in graceful curves. They turned about and the many-plaited skirt expanded, displaying all its rich embroidery, the silken trousers, and the jewelled feet.
>
> James Blythe Patton, *Bijli the Dancer* (1898)

The Indian women's relationships with Englishmen were instrumental in simultaneously articulating and resolving the tensions that had arisen in class and gender relations within late nineteenth-century metropolitan culture. It is significant that the most powerful representative of the Indian woman in three of these romances is the "nautch girl." Whether it is the wily Sitabai in *The Naulahka*, or Minachee—the "dasi" or temple girl with "the wild ill-regulated desires" (RNG 238)—in F. E. Penny's *The Romance of the Nautch Girl*, or the woman with "the gleaming eyes" in Johnston's *Kela Bai*, her representation in these romances is crucial to dramatizing the power and scope of a resurgent imperial masculinity. References to the nautch girl as "public prostitute" abound in colonial travelogues and political and social commentary, as well as in poetry, painting, and drama of the nineteenth century.[16] Her pervasive presence in such a wide range of discourses can be attributed to the existing political and social conditions under which sexuality was being regulated within the empire as well as in the metropolis during the closing decades of the nineteenth century.

As the primary target of sexual surveillance by the colonial authorities, the nautch girl served to maintain class and racial boundaries crucial to imperial governance.[17] With the increasing number of British soldiers deployed to fight the frontier wars in the 1870s and 1880s, it became imperative for the authorities to ensure the supply of the best fighting men. Even as far back as 1856, a medical manual offering advice to British officers warns that the

> passions of manhood and the penalties entailed upon their gratification are causes of more broken constitutions than all other indiscretions put together. *Lies* everywhere abounds [*sic*] and occupies [*sic*] a large figure in every sick report. This is the Scylla of European life in India; the Charybdis is left-handed alliances with native females; and the "medio tutissimus ibis" is either through the Straits of Continence or of Matrimony.
>
> (McCosh 1856: 70)

However, contrary to the practice of discouraging colonial officials from marrying or having sexual relations with Indian women (abstinence was considered the ideal moral conduct), common soldiers in the army had always been permitted to visit local prostitutes. In fact, female sergeants were often appointed to recruit such prostitutes (Butler 1885: 5). At the same time, there was a rising concern over the spread of sexually transmitted diseases in the cantonments, which led to the setting up of "lock hospitals" to facilitate the processes of registering prostitutes and inspecting their living conditions (Ballhatchet 1980: 36). A memorandum from the commander in chief reads: "In the regiment bazaars it is necessary to have a sufficient number of women, to take care that they are sufficiently attractive, to provide them with proper houses, and above all, to insist upon means of ablution being always available" (Butler 1885: 4). Colonial regulation of prostitution thus went hand in hand with the medicalization of native women, particularly those from the lower classes. Although some of these "lock hospitals" had been set up as early as 1858 after the conclusion of the 1857 Indian Mutiny, the efforts to regularize the administration of civil and criminal justice in military cantonments gathered new force after the introduction of the controversial Indian Contagious Diseases Act in 1868. The concern with "nautch" as a social and moral phenomenon fired a public discourse that brought together a diverse range of issues about the relationship between imperial institutions and men and women's social and sexual roles.

In 1859, colonial authorities were warned that the practice of visiting "dancing girls" was "ruinous to youth," and that the authorities needed to promote marriage among the soldiers so that the wives could serve as effective nurses (*Our Plague Spot*: 2). In some native newspapers, however, the dancing girls were reported as individuals who enjoyed a level of freedom of movement within "native society" denied to "public women in civilized countries" (*Indian Messenger*, quoted in *Nautch Women*: 6). Christian organizations in India such as the Punjab Purity Association and the Christian Literature Society, however, saw this as a threat, and called for a total ban on the practice of "nautch," warning that "the great power of the immodest nautches is found in the strong desire of corrupt human nature to have congenial means to feed its lust and to inflame its passions" (Rev. Thomas Evans in *Opinions on the Nautch Question*: 5). In the context of middle-class Indian society, the banning of *nautch* was seen by many middle-class urban Indian men to facilitate the emancipation of Indian women: "If we lock up our females inside the zenana and keep ourselves aloof from them during our waking ours, is it a wonder that the Bazaar women should be sent for?" asks H. C. Mukherji (ibid.: 17).

The perceived threat of sexually transmitted diseases posed by nautch girls was often met by instituting specific policies that served to guide public behavior. Such policing of behavior was also essential to maintaining the class boundaries between British officials and soldiers. For example, as a professional doctor trained in England, Felix Manning in Penny's novel treats native diseases that were often associated with those appalling physical and moral conditions of native Indian life with which the British soldier was always in close contact. As the temple girl who had spent many years in the local landlord's harem, Minachee might well signify the pervasive threat of sexually transmitted disease. Like Patton's description of Bijli, the constant reiteration of her beauty, suppleness, and cleanliness in Penny's romance only heightens what many in the colonial administration saw as a degrading native lifestyle that needed correction and surveillance by the authorities. The horror expressed by the small Anglo-Indian community at William Manning's sudden disappearance signifies that threat, and the investigation initiated by the community is aimed primarily at getting at the source of that threat—Minachee. This process of demonization takes a familiar route in Penny's romance. In initially emphasizing Minachee's skills as a nurse whose care and dedication draw the attention of the doctor himself, Penny's romance deliberately blurs the line between Felix's appreciation of her labor and her status as a worker and his half-acknowledged attraction for her. Minachee's presence is sanctioned as long as she works towards her own moral redemption by serving the doctor selflessly. However, as soon as the doctor realizes that it was he himself and not his brother who was the object of the dancing girl's desire, he is "lost in the torrid colours of the Oriental passions which blazed before his dazzled vision" (RNG 316). Struggling against those "unfamiliar" passions that he felt were the work of the "devil," he bars the door with "fierce haste and fury" (RNG 317). Early in the narrative, Minachee had redeemed herself by her unselfish dedication to the cause of medical treatment, but once the reader is alerted to the nature of her desire she becomes unpredictable, subject to wildly changing moods and her "ill-regulated desires." In many ways, her personality matches that of the hysteric woman who was being increasingly pathologized by the medical sciences during the period of militant suffragism. It is no coincidence that Felix's turning away from the *nautch* girl coincides with his proposal of marriage to the stable English Beryl Holdsworth and with the final disappearance of Minachee from the narrative. This resolution to the story of a threatened English class respectability is recast in many versions in the Anglo-Indian romances—those of Maud Diver, Nina Stevens (the author of *The Perils of Sympathy*), Alice Perrin (the author of *The Waters of Destruction*), and F. E. Penny (her other work *Caste and Creed* deals with the same theme).

The portrayal of Kela Bai in Johnston's romance at first appears to depart from the conventional narratives demonizing the figure of the public prostitute. However, on closer scrutiny it becomes obvious that the question of Kela Bai's "purity" remains on the edges of the narrative, and is articulated fully in the concluding segments of the romance when, in renouncing her world, she is described as "step[ping] clean out of her old life" (KB 79). Throughout the narrative, Johnston plays with the contrast between different colors, displaying the spontaneity and variety of Kela Bai's world, a world in which each of her movements matches the changing physical environment of the East—the sky, the air, the bazaar. In that world, her "red" saree signifies the physical attraction of Johnson's narrator, but it is an attraction that is also countered by the fact that she had "friends everywhere" (KB 4), alluding to her profession as a public prostitute. As if describing the accouterments of a lover's body, the first-person narrator meticulously delineates Kela Bai's physical attributes: "very alluring she was, and comely; with rounded curves, sleek hair, glossy skin, small hands, and bare feet" (KB 43). It is this physicality that is transformed in the course of the narrative into the bare and colorless "white" of the saree in which she dresses herself before departing on her pilgrimage, emblematizing an emergent consciousness of purity that cleanses her.

This allows the narrator to circumvent his own "oriental" passions that could otherwise easily have undermined his moral and civil authority.

The nautch girl also served as the medium for testing the limits of the social and political aspirations of the beleaguered middle-class Englishman. Acting as both the incitement to and the interdiction of a socially sanctioned norm of mobility and civility for men, her figure is also inextricably linked to the codes of behavior regulated by colonial authorities. In the many studies of social vices within the empire that proliferated in the 1880s and 1890s, "prostitution" in the colonies emerged as a major topic for discussion and analysis (see Hyam 1990: 137–81; Levine 2003). As mentioned earlier, norms of chastity for men were determined on the basis of class: unlike soldiers, colonial officials were encouraged to stay away from concubinage. Prostitutes were classed according to rank and wealth in order to determine who could be allowed to service the fighting men (see Hervey 1912; *Appeal to the Scientific World*). In fact, the profession itself achieved an unusual degree of scrutiny in colonial discourse: for example, in the tract entitled *Appeal to the Scientific World*, the "prostitutionising process" is compared to the "triple one of religionising, moralising and philosophising" (p. 51):

> The highest ambition of the prostitute is to turn everybody that comes before them into an associate and co-worker—with the aggressive end in view of saving the labor of exercise of even the destructive activities of their own by making such people to work for them and act as aggressors for them.
>
> (ibid.: 52)

That the prostitute transmits her aggression on to the social fabric, creating a ripple effect, signified a perversion of what had been regarded as the masculine ideals of professional excellence, aggression, competition, and mobility. In fact, these were the ideals that were highly prized as desirable traits in imperial men of adventure. Since the *nautch* girl represented a perverted form of that social desire, she had to be constantly monitored, a need heightened by the fact that she, unlike the sons of empire, had no allegiance to any institution set in place by the colonial government. In short, a new vocabulary is visible here, one in which female professional "aggression" is seen to provide a counterpoint to the masculine ideals of professional mobility and healthy competition.

Kipling's Sitabai appears to embody this form of aggression: as a former dancing girl in the royal court of Rhatore and a former member of the maharajah's harem, she does not wield direct power but possesses considerable influence within the inner workings of the kingdom. She exercises this power through her innumerable plots and conspiracies. Recognizing the strong kinship between herself and Nick, she says: "I am like yourself–alone" (TN 279). Nick's fascination for Sitabai rests on the fact that he sees in her an image of his own reckless desires and aspirations: "The large and masterly range of her wickedness, and the coolness with which she addressed herself to it, gave her a sort of distinction . . . He almost revered her for it" (TN 275). Initially Nick's personal aspirations (his quest of the priceless diamond of Rhatore) are couched in the familiar language of imperial labor:

it made him tired to see the fixedness, the apathy and lifelessness of this rich and populous world, which should be up and stirring with rights–trading, organizing, inventing, building new towns, making the old ones keep up with the procession, laying new railroads, going in for fresh enterprises, and keeping things.

(TN 121)

Those imperial aspirations are often frustrated by his inability to discern, sort through, and fix the objects that meet his eye in the colonial world.[18] This is most dramatically signified by the many invisible eyes of the royal harem that gaze at him through the dark, or by the traces of the footsteps Nick imagines on the wet and slippery surfaces of the Gau Mukh, both of which he is unable to interpret. Out of this confusing and frustrating multiplicity, and the sense of the uncanny, Sitabai materializes as a "dangerous" woman, offering a distinct shape to Nick's own desires and the challenges he has to confront to achieve them. In short, Sitabai becomes a foil for Nick, whom he has to overcome in order to "win" the priceless diamond.[19]

The gendered overlap between the various discourses about "professions" touches different facets of the colonial order. To Richard Blundell in *A Son of Empire*, the civil duties of a magistrate keep him from the more masculine tasks of fighting, spying for, and defending the empire. Penny describes Felix Manning as being completely dedicated to his medical profession, a commitment that ultimately rescues him from the evil advances of the prostitute. In Johnston's romance, the duties of the collector at first appear to belong to a feminine order– conveyed in part by the romance's meticulous description of Kela Bai's toilette– until Johnston's narrator confronts the task of "rescuing" the helpless woman from the clutches of the Indian man. Such a movement allows the narrator to return to his masculine task as arbitrator of law, which is fully possible only when femininity has been transcoded in the language of masculinity.[20] As a task that involves the white man, the Indian woman, and the native policeman, the narrator's actions in judging Kela Bai set two kinds of masculinities in direct opposition to one another–the colonial and the native. Although the colonial magistrate is easily able to counter the challenge to his authority by the native subordinate by virtue of the social power entrusted to him, he cannot easily extricate himself from his own personal sexual feelings which threaten that very authority. Johnston narrates that tension by describing his narrator as being torn by the contrary pulls of "Don Juan and Saint Anthony" (KB 62) and utilizes it to enact a new masculinity, one that differentiates the narrator's power from the blatant lasciviousness of the native man, protects and affirms his own class and racial superiority, and also endows him with an empathetic eye that both frees and colonizes the colonial subject.

This new masculinity is figured through the specular relationship established between the narrator and Kela Bai:

Through her great dark eyes he was looking into the myriad eyes of the Indian world–eyes that gleamed, full of impenetrable mystery; eyes that glowed with emotions like his own, yet different; eyes that looked on the same green earth and overarching sky, and saw them transformed and haunted; endless myriads of eyes seemed to be looking into his through hers: all full of life, full of recognition and behind them were others, of the dead who yet live, going back generation on generation, for a myriad years, full of the awful light that lightens the heart of man. All life rose before him, from its twilight dawn, glowing before him out of those myriad eyes. And he felt the eternal mystery and might that lay behind them . . . A veil was lifted, and he beheld the vast ocean of the souls of men.

(KB 65–6)

Kela Bai's "return gaze" is rendered in equally significant language:

In her turn, she felt the magnetism of her new friend pouring into her and disquieting. She found herself touching new sides of life, undreamed of before, but palpably present in the stranger, who was yet so clearly akin; who had comforted her so wonderfully in her distress, so easily overruling all the powers that had menaced her. She began to dream of hidden lands, of distant peoples, of wide prospects, of unseen cities.

(KB 67)

This dynamic specularity operating within the narrative functions as a form of surveillance that consolidates the power of the imperial administrative gaze. Unlike Nick Tarvin, who fixes the indeterminate gaze of the concealed other in the figure of Sitabai, Johnston's narrator captures the multiplicity of the "endless myriads of eyes" present in the gaze of Kela Bai. This transforms the anxiety of being the object of the other's gaze and being haunted by that gaze into a spiritually regenerative experience. Simultaneous with the lifting of the veil and the revelation of the "eternal mystery" for the narrator is the refiguring of Kela Bai's own perceptions: in dreaming of "hidden lands, of distant peoples, of wide prospects, of unseen cities" she mimics and duplicates the many dreams that haunted the imagination of colonial men.

It is through this specularity that the temporal and everydayness of the magistrate's colonial labor, including his civil and judicial function, is transformed as the pursuit of timelessness and eternity. Personal accounts of civilians posted in *mofussil* areas during this time often document the loneliness and isolation of white men who found themselves as sole judicial authorities in charge of vast and alien areas (see Graham 1878: 196, 209). In his account of a civil career in Bengal at the turn of the century, R. Carstairs writes that what helped him survive the world of "strife on every side" (Carstairs 1895: 7) was the "dream of race pride, strong and ineradicable," which he regarded as "natural . . . and must continue if we are to hold up the standard of British prestige" (ibid.: 27). For Carstairs, the objective was to work for an "improved instrument of local Government" that could ensure a "partnership between the Crown and the people," but for him it was the *means*– the institutional practices–more than the *ends* that made the difference between simple governing and running the machinery effectively: "Though the instrument itself was the main object, the more duties we could find for it the better; for there is nothing like constant *use to keep an instrument bright and make it efficient*" (Carstairs 1912: 345; emphasis added). The rituals involved in the judicial inquiry against Kela Bai signify how Johnston's civil servant narrator locates himself institutionally as being in charge of the colonial machinery, but, unlike Carstairs, the personal affinity and kinship he establishes with Kela Bai in that process endow him with a new masculinity coded as the power to effect change without the aggressive posturing that characterizes Carstairs's colonial enterprise. If the institutional apparatus is masked by the mission of rescuing a helpless native woman in distress, that mission is also coded in terms of the narrator's own desire to help this woman also to imagine new worlds, realms that lay beyond the here and now. This is achieved strategically by describing Kela Bai's reciprocated gaze: as her friend he "pours" into her, cleansing her consciousness and awakening in her the desire for "hidden lands," "distant peoples," "wide prospects," and "unseen cities." Kela Bai's own desire is here reconstructed in terms of the very gaze that is directed at her by Johnston's narrator. Suffused with the sense of missionary conversion, which was retold in numerous late nineteenth-century biographical and "auto"-biographical accounts of women converts, this gaze concurrently distances Johnston's narrator from the object of his desire.[21]

Furthermore, Johnson's narrator rehearses the classic anthropological stance adopted by the colonizers to define the task of consolidating the knowledge of the colonial subject in the midst of historical change that threatens to alter the status quo:

> The East has met the West; and like a country and a city maiden, they stand face to face, regarding each other with open eyes, half shyly, half curiously. The Western lass is centuries in advance of her sister in experience and knowledge of the world, and will probably go her own gait. But she of the East will be shocked at the license which the other allows herself, and at the contempt in which she holds the tradition of the elders, is already dimly conscious that her clothes are old-fashioned, and her hair not dressed becomingly. Stays and bustle would not suit her figure, and I do not think that she will adopt them. But change she will; and that with a terrible rapidity.
>
> (KB 143)

In fact, like Madge and Kate, the Indian woman had awakened to the call for change, and it was a process that could not be impeded. However, her transformation needed the constant surveillance and intervention on the part of men, so that the threat that this posed could be placed under their restraint.

"The advantage of our mixed condition, civilized at top with the old barbarian under our clothes, is just this, that we can enjoy all sorts of things," wrote Andrew Lang in 1886, adding that, "If we will only be tolerant, we shall permit the great public also to delight in our few modern romances of adventure" (Ledger and Luckhurst 2000: 102). In an age that witnessed dramatic changes in the self-image of the metropolitan subjects of empire—in terms of both what that image signified for middle-class men's and women's attitudes towards their own civility, and how these changes forced a rethinking of gender relations within the colonial context—the Anglo-Indian romances continued to fuel the fantasy of the empire as being another "adventure." In this chapter I have attempted to chart the many-layered formations of that fantasy, formations that are visible in the narratives found in the Anglo-Indian romance, demonstrating how civility played out against this fantasy. In an age that was beginning to depend so heavily on its own image-making machinery, the Anglo-Indian romance offers yet another example of the ways in which the image of the empire was being constantly broken down and reconstituted.

4 Savage pursuits

Missionary civility and colonization in E. M. Forster's "The Life to Come"

For conquering Clive, or Wellesley's mightier name,
The wide world echoes to the trump of fame,
Yet have there been, who loftier praise have won,
Undaunted Schwarz, and saintly Middleton
England hath many such; she little knows
What to their secret championship she owes;
Their prayers, with night and day to Heaven aspire,
Bulwark her empire with a wall of fire,
And arm the happy earth that gave them birth
With power to build the throne of Christ on earth.
Harriet Warner Ellis, *Toils and Triumphs* (1862)

In a letter to E. M. Forster, dated 30 April 1924, T. E. Lawrence conveyed his reactions to a story that Forster had sent him:

> It's abrupt, beyond grace and art: but at my second reading what came out of it strongest was a feeling of pity for the African man. You cogged the whole of life against him . . . and he was no good to wait all that while. None the less his illness was overdone, or his sudden spasm of strength at the end of it. It was too unexpected. Couldn't you have led up to it by some careful hints of force & sinew in the last pages?

> (Forster 1985: 56)

The story was "The Life to Come," and the "African man" in question was no African but a tribal aboriginal belonging to one of the many indigenous forest-dwelling communities of central India. Between the years 1921 and 1922 Forster had served as a private assistant to the local Hindu ruler of the state of Dewas, a province located on the northern boundaries of this tribal area. Generally known by names such as Gonds, Bhils and Khonds, these "primitive" tribes were scattered over a vast area in central India, which in the nineteenth century lay on the geographical edges of the semi-autonomous princely states and the territories officially called "British India." To this day the Gonds represent numerically the most dominant indigenous tribe of India, with a history of political power that extends from the twelfth all the way up to the nineteenth century (Singh 1994: 293). The Bhils, described in Walter Hamilton's *The East India Gazetteer* (1815) as a "jungle people, and in a state of great barbarity" (Hamilton 1815: 146), were often perceived as marauding plunderers.[1] Periodically sweeping down the hills of central India in order to raid communities under the protection of the British, they posed a constant threat to the latter, who, in order to curtail their threat, initially entered into different agreements with Bhil tribal chieftains, guaranteeing them customary payments in return for the security of the territories. However, when the policy of appeasement failed to curb the attacks, British authorities conducted military operations to subdue the Bhils and to annex their lands. By the 1820s and 1830s the region called Khandesh, populated by the Bhils, was eventually incorporated into British India. Almost simultaneously, the tribals were actively recruited into the newly formed Khandesh Bhil Corps, which was established to contain the power of the Bhil chieftains and to fill the ranks in the colonial army with fighting men. Members of the Bhil Corps proved to be exemplary soldiers in the numerous battles Britain fought on the frontiers of its Indian empire in the nineteenth century.[2] The Khonds, who dwelt in the eastern frontiers of this territory, were similarly "pacified" through colonial campaigns for the suppression of the practice of human sacrifice, which eventually led to the establishment of native councils for securing the cooperation of local chiefs in extending civil rule to the region.

Although T. E. Lawrence's misnaming of the tribal people is quite consistent with an imperialist propensity for disregarding the specificity of cultural identities of colonized subjects, Forster's story insists on being read as location-specific. Written in 1922, "The Life to Come" is set in the tribal regions of central India. The story also dealt with a forbidden subject matter—same-sex interracial relations between an Englishman and a tribal, which compelled Forster to withhold its publication during his lifetime, although he sent it for comments to some of his close associates, such as Lawrence, Siegfred Sassoon, and Florence Barger. The narrative revolves around a young English missionary, Paul Pinmay, who comes to the forested region inhabited by the tribes with the intention of converting their most powerful chieftain, Vithobai. However, before he is able to achieve his purpose he sleeps with the chief, who interprets the invitation to "come to Christ" as an expression of the missionary's passion for him. Pinmay wakes up to the horror of the deed, but, too prudent to give up his brilliant conversion of a "wild and hostile potentate," accepts Vithobai into the fold and renames him "Barnabus." Stirred by Pinmay's promise of love, Vithobai remains loyal to his master, while the latter, anxious to keep the affair a secret, asks Vithobai to wait for his love. With the passage of time Vithobai finds himself reduced to a petty convert coerced to live in a stockaded enclosure, while Pinmay, after assuming charge of the entire district, turns into a tyrannical colonial official who forces his ways on the local people. Meanwhile the forests and the surrounding regions are cleared and become valuable sources of timber and mineral ore, inviting land speculators, miners, loggers, and outside labor to work in the mines. Broken-hearted at the postponement of Pinmay's promise of love, and finding himself deprived not only of his religion but of his lands and royal authority, Vithobai falls ill. Apprised of Vithobai's condition, Pinmay—now middle-aged and ready to depart from the district after ten years of service—visits the once powerful chieftain, who now lies alone and naked on his house-top. As a final gesture of comfort to the dying man, Pinmay reiterates his promise of love—"in the real and true sense . . . in the life to come"—and embraces the convert with the hope that a mutual atonement of sin committed ten years ago would free him from guilt. Vithobai seizes the moment to stab the missionary through his heart, and then hurls himself victoriously from the parapet.

The unusual combination of raw sensationalism heightened by a highly charged symbolic language and an unrelenting realism makes the story's underlying colonial narrative unique in Forster's *oeuvre*. Several questions present themselves to the modern reader of the story. Can its setting in the forests of tribal India be read as akin to that of the sexual fantasies found in Victorian colonial pornography, which, as Anjali Arondekar has argued, "becomes the double 'elsewhere' of Foucault's imaginings, a place that is both discursively and literally outside the realm of English bourgeois home-place" (Arondekar, n.d.: 11)? Does the story offer more than a transgressive drama of racial fantasy, heightened by the twin cycles of pleasure and prohibition that seem to propel Forster's other colonial homosexual tale "The Other Boat?" Should the story be read historically as reflecting the nineteenth-century "colonial crisis over miscegenation and interracial desire," as Chris Lane has suggested (Lane 1995: 157–63)? Although all such approaches are themselves amenable to historicization, in this chapter I am more interested in excavating another "story" from the interstices of "The Life to Come," a fugitive story, as it were, containing a radically disruptive kernel that erupts from those interstices. This other story points to a forgotten phase in British colonial history that reaches back to Britain's encounter with colonial India's tribal populations, whose racial, religious, and cultural identities remained a constant puzzle to missionaries and colonizers of the nineteenth century.[3] This story also shows that, if the civility of the colonized subject could only be named in "default of its recognizable name," for the metropolitan subject in the early twentieth century that civility is constituted in relation to the modern state and its disciplinary power. In short, missionary civility manifests yet another face of the state that has morally equipped itself with pastoral power.

Forster's own comments on "The Life to Come" and the way in which it came to be written offer a good starting point for such an exploration. My essay returns to these comments in an attempt to reassemble the fragments of that "other" story and to track the ways in which its emergence radically historicizes the very itinerary of desire that is seen to fuel the story's fantasy narrative. According to Forster's own admission, recorded in his diary of 8 April 1922, his "indecent" writings "were written not to express myself but to excite myself" (quoted in Stallybrass 1972: xiii). However, in a letter to Siegfred Sassoon explaining its genesis, Forster mentions that, in writing the story, which had "[begun] with a purely obscene fancy of a Missionary in difficulties," the "obscenity *went* and a great deal of sorrow and passion that I have myself experienced, *took its place*" (Forster 1985: 45; emphasis added). In his dairy, he also recorded that the story had been written "in indignation" (Furbank 1978: 115). Ann Stoler has suggested that "[a] basic tension in the sexual politics of colonial states was the promise of new possibilities for desiring male subjects," arguing that these states "implemented policies that simultaneously closed those possibilities down for these subjects" (Stoler 1995: 178–9). While the story's underlying sado-masochistic narrative seems to support what Slavoj Zizek has theorized elsewhere as the play of the "libidinal economy of surplus enjoyment" (Zizek 1998: 155–6), the emotions that its writing engendered for Forster–and which he reiterated in so many ways in his comments–invite a new reappraisal of the sexual dynamics underlying its narrative.

Referring to "Kanaya," the erotic piece about Forster's sexual desire for the Indian barber hired by the maharajah to serve him (which was deleted from his Indian memoirs *The Hill of Devi*), Martin and Piggford have suggested that his account of his relationship with the Indian "testifies to Forster's inevitable complicity in the erotics of power" (Martin and Piggford 1997: 14). In a similar vein, Nicola Beauman has described "Kanaya" as being one of the rare occasions in his life when "he [Forster], to whom power and despotism were anathema, confessed to enjoying his own power" (Beauman 1994: 316). Despite the similarities between the two pieces, I argue that "The Life to Come" involved a different relationship to the form of "carnality" identified in the deleted segment of *The Hill of Devi* (Forster [1953] 1983: 323), and this difference is most clearly demonstrated by the story's dramatization of the way in which sexuality is detoured in response to the imperatives of colonial law, causing it to explode elsewhere–in a space that involves the governance by civil law of the tribal man's body. It is important to bear in mind that the issue of power relating to the deployment of sexuality in this story is complicated by Forster's own self-awareness as writer and subject located within the long, and sometimes subterranean, history of colonial violence. It is this history that materializes in the missionary, Paul Pinmay, the figure closest to Forster's own space in the colonial differential. In Pinmay Forster objectifies the erotics of power by situating its operations and effects within the specific sites and apparatus of colonial domination, bringing together the religious and secular under the law of colonial civility. He scripts the narrative of desire and its deferral in accordance with a historical understanding of this itinerary of colonial power, a power that he perceived as having its source in a fundamentally metropolitan fantasy involving the encounter between the colonizer and its absolute counter-image–the savage primitive. This is the same pastoral power that identifies the missionary as an agent of European civility, one who is entrusted not only with the task of civilizing the brute but also with testing the limits of his own civility through an encounter with the potently sexual, colonial subject. The rites of religious conversion, symbolically evoked in the story, therefore, only intensify the sense of how that civil power operates under the law of colonial desire.[4]

The "midnight cry"

In the opening section of "The Life to Come," Forster's narrator appears to imitate the trajectories of the erotic by conveying the power of desire encountered as fantasy:

> Love had been born *somewhere* in the forest, of what quality only the future could decide. Trivial or immortal, it had been born to two human bodies as a midnight cry. *Impossible to tell whence the cry had come*, so dark was the forest. Or into what worlds it would echo, so vast was the forest. Love had been born for good or evil, for a long life or a short.
>
> (Forster 1972: 65; emphasis added)

The temporal and spatial dimensions are deliberately fused and obscured in these opening lines of the story: poised between "somewhere" and "whence," the "midnight cry" becomes an echo whose source is indeterminable. Furthermore, the echo of that cry is also a reminder of the feelings Forster had himself recorded about his own writing of the story: "anger," "sorrow," and "passion." The transformation of the erotic, which Forster claimed took place while he wrote the story, occurs through a hesitancy that is clearly registered in the opening words. It is important to bear in mind that this hesitancy is vocalized at the very juncture at which the story speaks the erotic through the elusive phrase a "midnight cry." The incantatory resonance created through this withholding of a specific time or concrete location appears to highlight the limits of the narrator's own desiring gaze, so that even the concrete details of setting offered in this scene–the "small native hut," the "aged tree," the "stream," the "lamp," and the partly visible bodies of the two figures–appear only to coalesce into the rhythmic reiterations of "Darkness and beauty, darkness and beauty" (ibid.: 65–6). The parallel equivocation–between "trivial" and "immortal" and between "good" and "evil," reminiscent of Professor Godbole's words about the evil in the Marabar caves in *A Passage to India*–similarly evokes an undecidable tenor. The very "origin" of the telling, then, appears to be infected by the shadow of desire, like the bare limbs and golden hair that are barely distinguishable from the light that flickers in the shadows.

However much Forster's reference to Vithobai's "pagan limbs" may concur with colonial orientalism, and however much the story's Arcadian setting–as signified by the description of the singing stream and the tree with its naturally formed throne–may suggest an escape from a concrete material space, "The Life to Come" soon enters a markedly historical domain where the bodies and setting are relentlessly inscribed within the harsh logic of colonial economic extraction and the authority of British civil rule. Juxtaposed with the words "Into what worlds it would echo, so vast was the forest," the harsh realities of an environment soon to be transformed by the forces of civilization are thrown into ironic relief. As Vithobai's pagan limbs get clothed in half-European attire, and as he proves to be "an exemplary convert" (Forster 1972: 69), the darkness of the forest gives way to a visibility that reveals the effects of the real forces at work in the forests–the work of timber merchants, missionaries, land grabbers, and mining agents.[5]

This deliberate shift on the part of Forster–from the mythic realm to the concrete–can be explained in part by his own struggle with defining the place of "prophecy" in art. For example, in *Aspects of the Novel* (1927), he characterized seven different elements–story, people, plot, fantasy, prophecy, pattern, and rhythm–as constituting the basic principles of fiction. Rejecting a purely mimetic function for art, he called for an aesthetic attentiveness to a "secret life . . . for which there is no external evidence, not, as is vulgarly supposed, that which is revealed by a chance word or a sigh" (Forster 1927: 80). By reiterating the fundamental disjunction between the world and language, Forster underscores the fact that what art seeks to represent is achieved through a language that is "always out of place" (Stone 1966: 116). Consistent with this view, Forster contends that prophecy is "an accent in the novelist's voice, an accent for which the flutes and saxophones of fantasy may have prepared us" (Forster 1927: 116). This means—as Forster himself elaborates—that the prophetic author "is not necessarily going to 'say' anything about the universe; he proposes to sing, and the *strangeness of song* arising in the halls of fiction is bound to give us a shock" (ibid.: 117; emphasis added). It is this performativity of strangeness—what Wilfred Stone calls the "bardic strain" (Stone 1966: 116)—that Forster adopts in constructing his fictive world in "The Life to Come." This is a performativity that is infused by a shock of recognition when the world it lyrically describes is suddenly transformed by language into a material space, a space that is marked by the palimpsests of a violent history. This, then, is the "secret" life of Forster's narrative.

Although the colonial narrative in "The Life to Come" invites a comparison with that of Forster's celebrated "Indian novel" *A Passage to India*, no two stories could be more dissimilar, both in form and in content. If the town of Chandrapore, in *A Passage to India*, served as the site for representing the civil side of colonialism—with its officials, schools, clubs, bazaars, and courts—the forests in "The Life to Come" embody the unacknowledged dark underside of the civil station, visible in the brutally extractive economic practices of the British colonial enterprise, with its allocation of mining land-leases to contractors, its development of the timber industry, and the inhumane exploitation of labor achieved by depriving the tribal communities of their land and rights. It is on the body of the tribal who inhabits such a world that the story of colonization is woven. If Forster, as T. E. Lawrence alleged, had "cogged the whole of life against" the tribal chieftain, it was to enact a historical trauma of a region disfigured by the intrusion of colonial industry and missionary activity. As the only story of Forster's where the tribal's abjectness is the focus of its narrative, "The Life to Come" stands out as a genuine and searching examination of the materiality of the colonial encounter and its links to the formation of civil power that Forster would later evoke in *A Passage to India*. That this underbelly of colonial history remained largely unacknowledged in the metropolis is nowhere more evident than in T. E. Lawrence's seemingly innocuous misrecognition of Vithobai as the "African." One may easily surmise that Forster's evocation of a mythic space in the opening sections of the story prompted this easy identification of the setting with the primitive type that had been so relentlessly insisted upon by Victorian anthropological discourses about Africa. Forster's contemporary readers may have been made familiar with this kind of primitive landscape through works such as Joseph Conrad's 1898 novella about the Congo, *Heart of Darkness*. A cursory survey of contemporary scholarship on this story, however, reveals that the tendency to erase the historical specificity of its colonial location and history persists to this day. Satisfied with tracking down the homoerotic tensions in the story or discussing its "astonishing turbulence at the level of sexual demand" (Lane 1997: 169), scholars such as Christopher Lane, Robert Martin, and George Piggford have quietly disregarded its links to colonial history, which are insistently signaled by the story's palimpsests. Although Norman Page's observation about the "socially dense detailing" (Page 1977: 43) of the story has received varying degrees of attention by Frederick McDowell, John Sayre Martin, and Mary Lago, there is little attempt on their part to read that detailing in terms of its discursive historical setting. Even Mary Lago's suggestion that the story reflects "Forster's damning verdict . . . on the colonizers who followed upon the heels of the merchants to consolidate British control of the Eastern Empire: the missionary and the soldier" (Lago 1995: 133) appears to be too reductive, missing its complex negotiation with the historical discourses about the aboriginal tribes of central India. My reading therefore begins at the edge of this critical lacuna. By opening the story with an "echo," Forster gestures towards a narrative of repetition that gradually manifests itself in the palimpsests left by the long colonial history of conquering and pacifying these people. I argue that, in order fully to comprehend the significance of these palimpsests, one has to place the multiple textures and layers of the narrative against the discursive genealogies offered by this colonial history. Using the critical strategies of intersectionality and "thick description" advocated by the new historicists, I foreground a reading of the story's representation of civility in terms of the economic, social, and political issues centering around the formation of "civil rule" from which colonialism derived its authority and legitimacy.

It is true that, except for the name "Vithobai," there is nothing in "The Life to Come" that explicitly locates it in the tribal Bhil and Gond territories of central India; in fact, the description of the forests and the wilderness, of the steady encroachment of the missionaries, and of the gradual transformation of the forest might appear at first to be little more than a routine description of the typical encounter of the civilized white man with the world's darkest regions—be it Africa, Argentina, the Malay islands, or the heart of tribal territories in India. That Forster's story is anchored in a specific history—with its own discursive genealogy—is made evident through its parallels with the accounts left of these regions by British agents, military officials, and missionaries in the nineteenth and early twentieth centuries. Recalling the heroic deeds of James Outram in establishing the Khandesh Bhil Corps in the 1820s, A. H. A. Simcox, the author of the 1912 account of the history of Khandesh, reminds his readers that

> those who dwell nowadays in the Bombay Presidency live in peace so profound that it may seem difficult to imagine any different conditions. That the Marathas were once the most feared race in India, that hordes of ill-paid mercenary Arabs wandered armed and oppressed the country in the name of this or that master, that the Bhils descended from their eyries and swept the plains of many a fair district, that the Pindaris were a constant menace on the eastern frontier; all these things influence modern life as much, and are as often in the public mind, as the Wars of the Roses in England.
>
> (Simcox 1912: 3)

The necessity of evoking the glory of "Pax Britannica" at a time when the history of colonial exploits in the lesser known territories was rapidly lapsing from public memory prompts Simcox not only to chronicle the British military efforts in the region, but also to delineate, in great detail, the local customs, occupations, and language of the tribal Bhils, as well as the physical characteristics of the vast land they inhabited. Extending from a detailed day-by-day account of the founding of the corps to the description of many local insurrections against colonial authorities led by renegade chieftains, this heroic narrative of colonial endeavor and resourcefulness was aimed at reviving a lost history by evoking the lost world of the tribal in the modern era. To this extent, Simcox's work exemplifies the nexus between exoticism, militarism, Victorian anthropology, and the writing of history in the metropolis.

Similarly, in his *Station and Camp Life in the Bheel Country* (1906), the missionary G. W. Blair commences his account of his service in the region by reminding the readers of the history of British efforts conducted "less than sixty years ago" to extend the "benign influence of British rule" and bring the tribes into "subjection." Blair asserts that, under its influence, the Bhils "have become peaceable subjects, peaceful and peaceably disposed, and are no longer looked upon as a tribe of outcast robbers" (Blair 1906: 26). Earlier in the nineteenth century, the suppression of the Pindaris and the Thugees, two of the most notable groups of "outcast robbers," had provided the British authorities with the justification for extending civil rule over regions where, unlike the former Moghul or Maratha states, political power did not derive from any central sovereignty. By negotiating with a select number of tribal chieftains in these regions, the British in the nineteenth century developed a policy of support for power based on lineage and primogeniture, rather than on the existing system of "overlapping authority" which had been the hallmark of precolonial Bhil social order (Skaria 1996: 33). The conferring of legitimacy on a select number of individuals through an immutable system of lineage and succession allowed the British authorities to monitor their power in the regions and to impose a system of civil rule on tribal India that was based on self-serving Western notions. The Bhils' multiple sovereignties had to be fixed as "other"; therefore, the consequent shift in social organization of the Bhils under the guise of legal change was crucial to the imposition of civil society. This is mirrored in the attitudes of missionaries such as Blair for whom the diffusion of Christianity into the land had helped transform savage tribes into members of a civil society, exemplifying the providential role of the evangelical enterprise in introducing civilization through colonization.

Notwithstanding the sanitized nature of these testimonial histories, it is important to bear in mind that their production played a significant discursive role in creating an alternative genealogy for British India. Returning to this genealogy now makes visible those strands of colonial history that had been relegated to the margins of memory in the "modern" twentieth century. Another work of military history that combined a narrative of colonial exploits with a discussion of tribal anthropology and geology had appeared as early as 1864. Entitled *A Personal Narrative of Thirteen Years' Service Amongst the Wild Tribes of Khondistan for the Suppression of Human Sacrifice*, this work by John Campbell, a political agent in British India, provides an early and rare view of colonial expeditions into the territories of the Khond tribe located in Orissa, a region on the eastern front of the central provinces. What makes this narrative compelling for my purposes is the way in which it couples the story of the numerous campaigns conducted for the suppression of human sacrifice in the region with the delineation of the larger political, scientific, and economic interests that these exploits opened up for colonial authorities, interests that were crucial to defining and legitimizing the colonial notions of sovereignty, nationality, capitalism, and modernity in the nineteenth century. Campbell, whose primary aim was to recount the rigors of these campaigns for the suppression of human sacrifice, devotes an entire chapter at the end of the narrative to detailing the geological features of the region, itemizing different kinds of mineral ore, coal deposits, and other natural resources that he claimed could be opened up for commercial use.

Like Simcox and Blair, Campbell begins his narrative by reiterating:

> It is probable that in England few persons possess any great knowledge of that portion of our Indian empire which is formed out of the kingdom of Orissa, and still fewer take any interest in its ancient or modern history.
>
> (Campbell 1864: 3)

Campbell deploys the term "ancient" to allude to the region's forgotten history of fabulous temples and bygone glorious kingdoms lost among the present wilderness and savagery; in fact, for Campbell, the contemporary tribal regions, like Rider Haggard's Africa in *King Solomon's Mines*, are lands that had reverted back to an original and untamed wilderness, waiting to be rediscovered and deciphered by the white man. Consistent with this logic, the term "modern" evokes that historical moment of rediscovery—the more recent story of colonial initiatives undertaken to bring these regions under British civil rule. Simultaneously orientalist and utilitarian in its approach to writing a regional history, Campbell's work is significant to the modern historian in its articulation of the spaces of "national" and "local" as well as the temporalities of "ancient" and "modern," which were key to the formation of nineteenth-century liberal historicism.[6]

The production of such "monumentalizing" histories by nineteenth-century historians of India also exemplifies the efforts of a modern, liberal state to legitimize colonial rule by differentiating itself from the forms of "oriental despotism" into which the pre-colonial world was perceived to have been trapped since the decay of its once magnificent past. It was unilaterally assumed that modern institutions set in place by colonialism not only guaranteed the permanence of private property and rule of law—the hallmarks of any modern state—but also legitimized what Thomas Metcalf calls the "'progressive' world order defined by a newly 'modern' Europe" (Metcalf 1995: 5). Note, for example, how, during the first stages of his campaign Campbell introduces the subject of human sacrifice to the members of the Khond tribals he encounters during the campaigns:

> I was not there to upbraid them with the past, but to inaugurate for them a *better future* . . .

I thought it better to confess that we, like them, had once sacrificed human beings; like them, had indulged in similar cruel offerings; like them, had believed that the judgment of the gods could only be averted by a bloody expiation and the slaughter of our fellow-creatures; but this was in the days of gross ignorance, when we were both fools and savages, knowing nothing, and living a debased and brutal life; *but we emerged from this darkness*, gradually obtained light, and at last gave up for ever our barbarous and unholy practice. And what has been the consequence? I inquired. All kinds of prosperity have come upon us since we abolished those sinful rites.

(Campbell 1864: 70–1; emphasis added)

In an appendix to his work, John Campbell quotes these words from a dispatch he had received from the Court of Directors of the East India Company honoring the initiatives undertaken by the home government in the Khond region:

It is obvious that the germ of an ultimate civilization has been planted in the country, and we may entertain a confident hope that the advance of the population towards a higher social condition will be in an accelerated ration of progress.

(ibid.: 307)

Predicated on a calculative algorithm, the language of progress and prosperity is the mainstay of what Campbell earlier calls the "liberal conduct of government" (ibid.: 269), which had been the defining feature of nineteenth-century imperial ideologies. Here, within this algorithm, we see the circumscribing of the "proper" colonial sense of space in time as well as its material significance. The "savage" must be accepted as a category for conversion to be possible: this is precisely what is required to colonize Vithobai by coercing him into accepting the terms of civility through conversion. Furthermore, it is this configuration that renders Vithobai abject because, in waiting for Pinmay to fulfill his promise of a life to come, he is shown to hold to another "prophetic" sense of space and time that is incommensurable with the norms of civility imposed by Pinmay. In fact, his seeming lack of understanding (or even misrecognition) of the consequences of his betrayal can be read not as primitive naiveté but as a refusal to accept Pinmay's terms of turning the promise into a simple "promissory note" sanctioned by law, which is what the missionary later tries to make it become. As a promissory note, the promise made by Pinmay could easily be rendered null and void through cash payment or compensation for lost lands, all based on the logic of contractual law.

It is no coincidence that, in his "Memorandum of Improvements in Indian Administration" (1858) presented to the British government, the chief examiner of the Office of Indian Correspondence, John Stuart Mill, included an account of the "Protection and Improvement of the Oppressed Races" by claiming that the objectives of the agents of the home government in the tribal regions had been "effected by the admirable power of individual character." Mill proceeds to state:

The mode in which these objects were accomplished was in all cases fundamentally the same. Into fastness, through which bodies even of disciplined troops had vainly endeavoured to force their way, these officers penetrated, [which] is in some cases almost unattended. They trusted themselves to the people. By their courage and frankness they gained their confidence. They made them understand that they were not considered as wild animals to be hunted down; that nothing but their good was intended; and the object which had for years been vainly sought by force, was accomplished by explanation and persuasion.

(Mill 1990: 154)

Like Mill, Campbell casts colonial rule along the lines of paternalism that had been advanced among liberal circles in the metropolis by appealing to metropolitan nineteenth-century ideologies of progress. Mill's appeal to an "ultimate civilization," like the missionary's promise of a "life to come," was central to the colonial task performed by these ideologies. In Forster's story, then, Mill's words become a chilling reminder of the prophecy of servitude that haunts the promise of progress.

"A secret life"

So, how does one locate Forster's story about the tribal in this discursive continuum? The answer to this question lies in section 2 of "The Life to Come." While the story seemingly moves towards its conclusion, which is located in a future as yet to be delineated, Forster interrupts the narrative in this section by indicating that this future has already become a "past." This past is a recorded past, available to Forster's narrator in the form of an "official" pamphlet:

Mr. Pinmay's trials, doubts and final triumphs are recorded in a special pamphlet, published by his Society and illustrated by woodcuts. There is a picture called "What it seemed to be", which shows a hostile and savage potentate threatening him; in another picture, called "What it really was!", a dusky youth in western clothes sits among a group of clergymen and ladies, looking like a waiter, and supported by underwaiters, who line the steps of a building labelled "School".

(Forster 1972: 69)

By incorporating the trace of an official missionary tract into the body of his own narrative, Forster strategically gestures towards the inherent discursivity of his own literary enterprise. His strategy closely resembles Walter Benjamin's re-imagining of the subversive reading of a materialist history—that of the emergence of the historically repressed as the source of re-energizing of the historical consciousness. The image of the woodcut is strongly reminiscent of what Harry Harootunian has described as being central to Benjamin's project—the act of "seeing the historical in the form of a construction resembling a photomontage"

(Harootunian 1996: 63). This act of construction involves a double reading that introduces the "fragment in relation to its 'text of origin' and yet grasps it incorporated in a whole and different totality" (Harvey 1989: 54), the mode of insertion creating a repetition whose performance produces an effect of difference as well as embodying a reunion with remembrance, an impulse prompted by the present. But what this "present" reveals to the consciousness is what Forster calls, in *Aspects of the Novel*, the "secret life" that fuels prophecy. At the heart of this prophetic reconstruction is the issue of pastoral docility understood as the main objective of the evangelical mission in leading the flock safely to the next world—the "life to come." Framed in the language of religious conversion, the image conveys the promise of progressive modernity founded on the transforming power of colonialism's political economy. In short, the image of the civilized convert, whether captured in woodcuts or in photographs, testified to the power of the Church to produce bodies of natives that met the norms of civility dictated by the modern liberal state. Simultaneously, the story's refigurative narrative is produced through a historical understanding of the ways in which uneven development in the colony enabled flexible modes of accumulation through the victimization of the most vulnerable of its subjects—the wild tribes.

As Chris Bongie has argued, by the turn of the century, "those who had been formerly subjected to an 'enlightened and paternal despotism' had now to be represented anew, according to the discursive criteria of 'enlightened paternalism': savagery, and its difference, was to be brought more into line with the now-global pretensions of European democracy" (Bongie 1991: 39). Vithobai's "converted" body is marked by such paternalism, as his partly covered body and the "silver armlets" and the "silver necklet" (Forster 1972: 71) adorning his arms and neck are replaced by "western clothes" (ibid.: 69). Forster's narrator ironically comments on this transformation by describing how Vithobai "moved from his old stockaded enclosure with its memories of independence, and occupied a lofty but small *modern* house ... suitable to his *straitened* circumstances" (ibid.: 77; emphasis added). In introducing this image, Forster may have had in mind a work such as *Battling and Building Among the Bhils*, published by London's Church Missionary Society in 1914, which offered, in addition to anthropological accounts of the manners, racial origins, and social structures of the primitive Bhils, the numerous stories of missionary work as well as photographic representations of tribal converts as exemplary missionary subjects. Therefore, far from being an innocuous detail simply inserted to evoke aesthetic irony, the reference to the missionary pamphlet in the story opens up an entire discursive terrain that had systematically produced the body of the colonized tribal in accordance with the rationale for colonial intervention. By insinuating itself into the fabric of such a terrain, Forster's story not only recuperates a forgotten historical continuum, but reinstalls the very domain of desire that underlined the European attempt to "convert" the tribal into a missionary/civil subject, thereby exposing and undercutting its power. The story's articulation of the play of that desire and its deferral, therefore, takes on a significant political meaning in the context of the politics undergirding the civilizing mission and its promise of a "life to come."

That promise—made by Pinmay during the moment of passion in the first section of "The Life to Come"—is at the heart of the story's political rendering of civility. The missionary zeal behind that promise follows the path dictated by Christian rules of civility: Pinmay's personal challenge of converting Vithobai is presented as an extension of the belief that "conversion," like Macaulay's "education," ensures the path to certain enlightenment and emancipation. In a sense, then, Pinmay's hard civility matches the power of the "primitive" Vithobai, who initially reciprocates Pinmay's attention with a poignant tenderness that makes the task of conversion easier for the missionary. Throughout the story, however, Forster complicates the overt theological overtones conveyed in Pinmay's message of Christian love by placing it at the scene of desire where the line between master and slave seems at first to be indeterminable. This flexibility soon hardens as the emergent power relations between the two steadily serve to promote as well as interdict that desire. Forster fully works out the political repercussions of such action by mapping out its effects on the body of the colonized. In fact, the body itself provides the site of the enforcement of power in this story. The scene of seduction/conversion is set by initially making the experience a test of Pinmay's limitations, a challenge for an "impatient and headstrong" man described as being "surprised" and "delighted" by the sudden appearance of "Vithobai the unapproachable" (Forster 1972: 66–7). Vithobai reciprocates Pinmay's offer of Christ's love by offering his body to the missionary, and it is at this point that the sexual, physical act is transformed through a ritualistic movement into the enactment of power:

> "Come to Christ!" he had cried, and Vithobai had said, "Is that your name?" He explained No, his name was not Christ, although he had the fortune to be called Paul after a great apostle, and of course he was no god but a sinful man, chosen to call other sinners to the Mercy Seat. "What is Mercy? I wish to hear more," said Vithobai, and they sat down together upon the couch that was almost a throne. And he had opened the Bible at I. Cor. 13, and had read and expounded the marvellous chapter, and spoke of the love of Christ and of our love for each other in Christ, very simply but more eloquently than ever before, while Vithobai said, "This is the first time I have heard such words, I like them," and drew closer, his body aglow and smelling sweetly of flowers. And he saw how intelligent the boy was and how handsome, and determining to win him there and then imprinted a kiss on his forehead and drew him to Abraham's bosom. And Vithobai had lain on it gladly—too gladly and too long—and had extinguished the lamp. And God alone saw them after that.
>
> (ibid.: 67–8)

It is worth pointing out that in this scene only Vithobai is named, while the pronominal "he" serves as a signifier that stands in for Pinmay, the missionary. Hence the scene begins with an initial misrecognition, on Vithobai's part, of the names of the Master, "Christ" and "Paul." However, the distinction made by Pinmay between the "godly" and the "sinful" bears no meaning for Vithobai, who can only interpret Pinmay's disquisition on "Mercy" in terms of his own personal passion that he sees reciprocated in Pinmay's words. But this very interpretative move proves crucial for Pinmay because it is what propels the savage potentate to desire the colonizer. Christopher Lane appears to ignore the interpersonal dimension involved in this act of enunciation and interpretation when he claims that, in Forster's colonial homosexual stories, "the narrator seems to merge sexual and racial projection into a wider colonial schema, aligning himself with the white lover by proposing that the black man is responsible for his and his lover's social and psychic collapse" (Lane 1995: 173). Rather, in this enigmatic scene, Forster masterfully discloses the political ramifications behind Pinmay's determination to "win" Vithobai by staging a kind of splitting of the subject Pinmay into "Paul" and "Abraham." The syntactical contortion implicit in the sentence "he imprinted a kiss on his [Vithobai's] forehead and drew him *to* Abraham's bosom" suggests that the act of drawing in to what appears to be a sexual embrace is more than what it appears to be. Not only is this act made richer by the suggestive symbolic over-tones of a biblical sacrifice, but, more significantly, the dual projection of wildness and docility is here disclosed as being inextricably linked to a regulative mechanism through which the "Old Law" asserts itself. The "old" and "new" testaments radically split apart and converge: in this Christian vision, Pauline love is classically meant to supersede a previous inferior covenant. While the "new" claims its difference from the "old" by virtue of its appeal to a common humanity and equality as opposed to the perceived rigidity of the "old," the direction of desire and power in this "embrace" closes the gap between the two. The civilizing principle, the "new" law of love becomes the obverse of desire through which that law is channeled into the service of power, although it initially presents itself as power exercised through mutual consent.

However, as this scene reveals so powerfully, this power rests on wresting a knowledge of the "other" from this scene of desire: it is a knowledge that soon materializes in the social world in the rigidly enforced line between the master and the slave. As possessor of such knowledge, Pinmay,

> ... who had been wont to lay such stress on the Gospel teaching, on love, kindness, and personal influence, he who had preached that the Kingdom of Heaven is intimacy and emotion, now reacted with violence and treated the new converts and even Barnabus himself with the gloomy severity of the Old Law.
>
> (Forster 1972: 70)

The violent "Old Law" that surfaces in Pinmay's perception of the colonial order seems to be intrinsic to, and indeed constitutive of, his knowledge, from which he derives his own sense of power:

> He who had ignored the subject of native psychology now became an expert therein, and often spoke more like a disillusioned official than a missionary. He would say: "These people are so unlike ourselves that I much doubt

whether they have really accepted Christ . . ." He paid no respect to local customs, suspecting them all to be evil.

(ibid.: 70)

Pinmay's insistence on the tribal's difference is indicative of the fact that the law of love that he embodies has to preserve the essential alterity of the colonized and seek new names to mark its difference in order to justify its continued dominance. As Michael Taussig suggests, in his *Shamanism, Colonialism, and the Wild Man*, "wildness is incessantly recruited by the needs of order . . . so that it can serve order as a counterimage" (Taussig 1987: 220). Therefore, while commanding Vithobai not to speak about the incident in the forest, Pinmay continues to incite him with the words: "I said Never speak, not that I would never come" (Forster 1972: 72), which ensures the master's power in offering, and then withholding, the promise. Not surprising, then, the obsessive rage for order that Pinmay's know-ledge produces is also accompanied by an equally powerful sense that this order inevitably threatens to destroy the very object that it acts upon. Therefore, Vithobai's gradual domestication makes him appear to Pinmay as the "somewhat scraggy and unattractive native" (ibid.: 76), resulting in the latter's mounting sense of anxiety which no longer stems solely from his sense of guilt: "Only Pinmay watched him [Vithobai] furtively and wondered where his old energies had gone. He would have preferred an outburst to this corrupt acquiescence" (ibid.: 77). The debasement of the former object into "corrupt acquiescence" is simultaneously the problem and the source for the continued surveillance that is needed to secure the domain of power. This surveillance takes on a political meaning as the narrative continues to chart Pinmay's reactions.

Like nineteenth-century colonial and missionary authorities intent on "pacifying" the tribes, Pinmay's main objective seemed to be to "break" the "spirit" of this "ancient and proud people" (Forster 1972: 70), in which he is aided by the very person, Vithobai, who stands to lose most by the lure of the promise. Possessing all of the institutional authority that Christianity and colonialism had bestowed on him—and which had been utilized to win Vithobai—Pinmay embarks on his ruthless exploitation of tribal power and influence. As he becomes more "like a disillusioned official than a missionary" (ibid.), his actions take up the institutional authoritarianism of a colonial machinery; in fact, the inherent aggressiveness of the "new church" into which he had inducted Vithobai with his promise of love is revealed through the gradual abasement of Vithobai's power, the very power that had initially made the savage man into such a seductive choice for, and a challenge to, a "headstrong" missionary like Pinmay.

Although T. E. Lawrence had sensed the effects of Vithobai's abasement when he stated that Forster had "cogged the whole of life against him," he was unable to comprehend its historical or political basis. Rather, objecting to the unexplained violence, he implied that somehow Forster had failed to achieve a sense of coher-ence in the story. To him, the story seemed flawed as a piece of artistic compo-sition: not only had Forster weighed the odds unnecessarily against the savage, but his illness and the final violent upsurge ("sudden spasm") in the concluding section seemed "unexpected" and undesirably "abrupt." These disjunctive aspects of the story, Lawrence implied, could have been justified only if Forster had prepared the reader more by providing "careful hints of force and sinew." Lawrence may have been suggesting indirectly that the political had emerged too strongly, and that the ideology of "dominating" material had not been realized smoothly enough. Responding to Lawrence's observations, Forster acknowledged the flaws but maintained that he "had prepared for it [the final violent spasm] *all along* and given a rehearsal of it in the cart" (Forster 1985: 55; emphasis added). The incident in question here occurs in section 3, entitled "Day": while driving with Pinmay in a dog cart through the forest, Vithobai offers himself to the missionary, who reacts with a firm "Never" to Vithobai's entreaties. Vithobai's reaction to Pinmay's "Never" is described in the following manner:

> Without replying, Barnabus handed him the reins, and then jerked himself out of the cart. It was a most uncanny movement, which seemed to proceed direct from the will. He scarcely used his hands or rose to his feet before jumping. But his soul uncoiled like a spring, and thrust the cart violently away from it against the ground. Mr Pinmay had heard of such contortions, but never witnessed them; they were startling, they were disgusting.
>
> (Forster 1972: 75–6)

What Forster calls a "rehearsal" to the final violent ending of the story seems at one level to be little more than an encounter with the "uncanny." Accustomed to the convert's submissiveness and his own power to subdue all opposition, Pinmay is startled by the force of Vithobai's retaliatory ire, and interprets the latter's action as something "sinister" and "disgusting." In fact, like Lawrence who read the story, Pinmay misses the full significance of Vithobai's rejoinder to Pinmay's puzzled questioning "Then what ails you?" Vithobai responds: "First the grapes of my body are pressed. Then I am silenced. Now I am punished" (ibid.: 76). It is through the language of desire located in the body that Vithobai communicates the anguish of his own degradation. This is also cast as a language of economic exploitation; Pinmay's inability to comprehend its significance is a mark of his refusal to read the body that he has colonized. Having brought that body into the civilizing fold, he can only interpret Vithobai's violent reaction to his "Never" as a sign of the convert's "illness," and therefore an aberration of his own intended purpose. What that illness might have revealed to Pinmay about himself and the effects of his own violence are here circumvented by the question "what ails you?" Forster's narrator pierces through this question—and the violence masked by it—by progressively tracking the physical, psychic, and economic transformations that wrack the body of the tribal and his land. Not only is Vithobai's continued sub-mission to Pinmay's ways shown to be the result of the missionary's unrelenting determination that "the chief must remain in a state of damnation . . . for a new church depended on it" (ibid.: 71), but that determination is itself ideologically disguised by Pinmay's assertions about the noble objectives of colonialism: "We do not want your kingdom. We have only come to teach you to rule it rightly" (ibid.: 72).

In his 1864 *Personal Narrative*, John Campbell had offered what he called "the existing sentiment of the people" to confirm that after years of colonial intervention the tribals had finally recognized that their interests were being served by the dictates of the civilizing authorities:

> Each chief was invited freely to express his sentiment on this important subject [human sacrifice], which many did without hesitation, saying, that when we first came among them they were like beasts in the jungle, doing as their fathers had before them; they now clearly comprehended that our only object in coming was to stop human sacrifice; not a fowl, or anything else, was taken, not even a fence was injured by the people of the camp; their fields produced crops as good as formerly, and sickness was not more prevalent; it was no use resisting the orders of the Sircar; their Metiahs had been removed, moreover, they cost money, and they were now of one mind, determined never more to have anything to do with human sacrifice.
>
> (Campbell 1864: 113–14)

The act of extracting consensus manifests the authority of the modern enlightened state, in which "the locus of power has shifted from the despotic body of a sovereign figure to an abstract body representing the people" (Bongie 1991: 38). According to Campbell, the tribal man's capacity for "free" expression corroborated what the colonial authorities always claimed—that they had successfully implemented the power of civil rule in a region that had been, until a few decades ago, the site of the most abominable practice of human sacrifice. However, it is clear that, behind the secure assertions about the moral superiority of the civilizers who had successfully implanted such a principle in a savage community, there lay a clear recognition of the force of colonial economic and military might. These people had realized that this force required unquestioned compliance on their part, leaving them with no choice but to concur with its dictates. In "The Life to Come," Forster uncovers the physical, psychic, and economic implications of such compliance, which had been methodically occluded in these nineteenth- and early twentieth-century colonial histories.

Discussing the range and function of colonial territorial operations as practiced in the plantations, Robert Young contends:

> Colonization begins and perpetuates itself through the acts of violence, and calls forth an answering violence from the colonized. Here capitalism is the destroyer of signification, the reducer of everything to a Jakobsonian system of equivalences, to commodification through the power of money. This allows a certain degree of historical specificity: for colonialism operated through a forced symbiosis between territorialization as, quite literally, plantation, and the demands for labour which involved the commodification of bodies and their exchange through international trade.
>
> (Young 1995: 173)

In fact, colonization in South Asia was sustained through this form of abstraction and territorialization, as a result of which the "environment [becomes] a contested site at an ideological as well as a material level" (Arnold and Guha 1998: 16). Pinmay's control over Vithobai and the forest signifies a reterritorialization of the colonial imaginary, whereby the site of savagery and wilderness is inscribed within the larger realm of economic exchange and profit made possible by religious conversion. Through the system of "equivalences," Vithobai's wild power is subjugated by the civilizing influence and employed to secure power over the land as a whole. In the nineteenth century, the control of the timber trade by the British in the Bhil territories called the "dangs" had led to the practice of leasing forests from the Bhil chiefs who had been installed by British authorities. Such a practice of devolving authority on the principle of linear succession had permitted the colonial authorities to exploit the vast forest resources more efficiently. The effects of such a policy become visible in the landscape that Forster's narrator evokes when describing Pinmay and Vithobai's journey in the dog cart:

> They moved briskly through the village, Barnabus driving to show the paces of the horse, and presently turned to the woods or what remained of them; there was a tolerable road, made by the timber fellers, which wound uphill towards a grove.
>
> (Forster 1972: 74)

While modernity leaves its imprint in the form of "roads," the specter of denuded forests, later recalled in the images of "stacked timber" and "polluted stream" (ibid.: 82), looms large in the changing topography. Large timber was a valuable commodity for the British, whose demands grew with the introduction and expansion of the rail system and the mining industry. Even Vithobai does not fail to notice this, as he expresses his concern for the effects of "the galleries extend[ing] deeper into the mountain" (ibid.: 74). David Hardiman has also argued that the reclassification of forests in the dangs into "reserved, protected, and open" was crucial to the consolidation of British economic power in the region, enabling colonial authorities to introduce labor from outside, hire various intermediaries to negotiate timber felling and trade, draw up a code of administrative standing orders, and organize a police force, in addition to developing communication in the form of cart tracks and roads (Hardiman 1994: 133–4).

As "The Life to Come" reveals, the practice of allocating mining concessions by the authorities was based on a systematic exploitation of the tribals, who often signed away their lands without fully comprehending the consequences. A few details interspersed in the narrative clearly indicate that Pinmay's missionary work, far from protecting the tribals, only furthered the interests of the colonial authorities. In fact, Pinmay's alliance with the powerful colonial order—we are told that his brother-in-law served in some capacity as a magistrate—testifies to the collusion between the two. Yet, consistent with his deceptive ways, Pinmay presents himself to Vithobai as a defender of the tribal's civil rights: not only does he admonish Vithobai for signing his rights away without consulting him, but he also offers the assistance of his own magistrate brother-in-law to get him "some compensation" for the lands he had lost. By the end of the nineteenth century, "foresters were in a powerful position within the government. They had *de jure* control over the very lands under the Revenue Department" (Rangarajan 1996: 74). It is significant to remember that not even for a moment does the meaning of the original promise change for Vithobai, who, even at this juncture, persists in asking Pinmay to fulfill it, while Pinmay reads Vithobai's entreaty unequivocally as a demand for economic reparation. As the ravaged forest, earlier rendered in quasi-mythical terms, begins to show its material and historical face, the political implications of Pinmay's "promise" to Vithobai reveals itself in the narrative. A historical reconsideration of that promise, signaled here by Pinmay's reactions, can be undertaken by resituating it within the discourse of "colonial contract," which, as the subaltern historian Ajay Skaria has argued, played a significant role in consolidating colonial interests in nineteenth-century tribal India.

As written documents, these contracts involved a complex system of legal transaction between the tribals and the colonial authorities. Like other practices introduced by the colonial authorities, they ensured that the resources available in the forests could be utilized with maximum efficiency through the exercise of civil rule. Compensation for tribal lands taken over by the authorities was seen to be part of a system of fair exchange introduced by civil rule, although it invariably meant progressive curtailment of tribal power. For example, such compensatory acts often took the form of fixed customary payments offered for leasing out the forests for timber, or of staging elaborate symbolic "darbars" or royal meetings in honor of the tribal chiefs selected by the authorities in order to garner their support. Time and again, the processes of interpreting these contracts involved a subtle manipulation of their legal authority on the part of the colonial authorities, who, Skaria claims, "subverted the binding nature and unilinear implications of the written word in formal ideology, and made possible the derivation from it of diverse courses of action" (Skaria 1996: 37). Three instances stand out: when a written document could be overruled by "appeal to practice"; when a "new written consensus could override the previous one"; or when "'new' meanings could be discovered in the inviolable text itself" (ibid.: 38). All of these, Skaria implies, made colonial domination "supple," allowing the authorities to maneuver the flexibility of contractual language to further their own interests.

Pinmay's verbal promise to Vithobai, although not a contract in the strict sense of the word, is nevertheless homologous to it. It is hard to miss the rhetorical resonance of a legal contract permeating the narrative, as Forster repeatedly situates the drama of Pinmay's promise and deferment within its discursive rims. It is the politics of enunciation and interpretation, crucial to the workings of a colonial contract, that is persistently evoked by Forster to track the strategic operations of a colonial order. This order is shown tenaciously to fashion its exploitative mechanisms by appealing to the progressive principles of modernity, standards that could conveniently be utilized to justify a reinterpretation of an original contract. For example, when Vithobai reminds Pinmay that his promise of a life to come had only resulted in more disease and suffering for the people of the region, the latter responds by saying, "It does, but then so do our hospitals," emphasizing that "under God's permission certain evils attend civilization, but . . . if men do God's will the remedies for the evils keep pace" (Forster 1972: 74). "God's will"—as it becomes increasingly clear in Pinmay's reasoning—is the law of progressive modernity, a law that both embodies and transcends the human. The theological corollary of this line of reasoning was rooted in the notion that as finite beings men could only incompletely comprehend the infinity of divine will; hence, the infinite possibility for discovering new meanings in God's plan. Pinmay's refusal to acknowledge the extent to which the system that he upholds depended on the manipulation of contractual language stems not from an intellectual incapacity to understand, but from his belief that the policy of monetary compensation for lands lost is commensurate with the liberal principle of redressing the "evils" that attend civilization.

Of course all of these justifications occluded the exploitation that lay deep at the heart of the colonial enterprise. Significantly, in 1920, writing in *The Athenaeum*, Forster made the following comment about the work of missionaries:

> On the surface are beneficent schools and hospitals, work in the zenanas, etc, a various and varying interference with their [natives'] sexual habits, an occasional alliance with economic Imperialism.[7]
>
> (Forster 1920: 546)

By making the Christian proselytizing impulse mirror the project of colonial modernity, Forster appears to be putting into question the official liberal position on the empire articulated, for instance, in the influential Earl of Cromer's contention, in "The Government of Subject Races," that Christianity was

> a powerful ally . . . without whose assistance continued success is unattainable. Although dictates of worldly prudence and opportunism are alone sufficient to ensure the rejection of a policy of official proselytism, it is none the less true that the code of Christian morality is the only sure foundation on which the whole of our vast Imperial fabric can be built if it is to be durable.
>
> (Baring 1913: 9)

Given the underlying critique of the colonial/missionary enterprise, it may be worthwhile asking why Forster chose not to show Vithobai openly rebelling against Pinmay's domination. Historical records clearly testify that resentment among the Bhils was a common phenomenon in the late nineteenth century and the early years of the twentieth which led to major outbreaks of tribal insurrection in the region. In fact, the names and deeds of renegade Bhils such as Gumanya Naik, Govinda Naik, Bhima Naik, Bhagoji Naik, Vasudeo Phadke, Anandrao, and Jagtya are numerously recorded in colonial military histories. Does Forster's rendition of Vithobai's willing passivity reflect what Chris Lane calls a "visual and fantasmatic complicity with colonial enjoyment" (Lane 1998: 291), compelling

Forster to preserve the object of his homoerotic desire through its abjectness, even when the attendant historical injustices behind such an action were clearly evident to him? In fact, the description of the "wild" Vithobai throughout the story is suffused with a homoeroticism that continually appears to reinforce the power of the colonial desiring gaze. However, this line of reasoning does not do justice to Forster's richly suggestive narrative, nor does it take into full account his incorporation of significant structural and historical elements that constantly situate the story within the larger story of colonial violence perpetrated under the guise of civil rule. In particular, this line of reasoning also fails to explain the enigmatic ending of the story, when Vithobai is shown ritualistically to sacrifice the agent of his own victimization before taking his own life.

I here return to Forster's own understanding of "prophecy" as delineated in *Aspects of the Novel*. By emphasizing the primacy of "prophecy," I do not intend to avert the question of the conflictual basis of colonial desire as articulated by Forster's narrator, but to indicate that in this story Forster moved towards a new aesthetic that called for a different response to the question of *representing* violence in a colonial text. Rejecting the mimetic mode of "evidence," Forster adopted what he characterized as "accent," so that he could disclose the sedimented effects of colonial violence that had been normalized by the norms of modern civil behavior. When Forster reminded T. E. Lawrence that he had "prepared" for the culminating violence "all along" in the story, he was alluding not to simple narratorial cues to its denouement, but to the fictional possibility of represening this violence. Furthermore, in commenting that the story had been written in "anger," he was perhaps referring to his own inability to disengage himself completely from the violence that lay at the heart of his own liberal colonial society. I suggest that the mode of prophecy, rather than being a simple aesthetic device, provided Forster with a means to engage in a form of fictional defamiliarization through a renewed encounter with the historical uncanny, thereby reanimating the biblical view of "prophecy" as a critique of unjust authority.

This is most dramatically represented in the ritual sacrifice of Pinmay in the final moments of the story. John Campbell and imperial administrators such as John Stuart Mill had seen in the suppression of human sacrifice among India's indigenous tribes the victory of progressive humanism upheld by colonialism. In fact, "human sacrifice" had provided the most extreme counter-image to European civilization, representing the very limits of inhumanity that colonialism had encountered and mastered. By releasing the violence that colonialism had ostensibly suppressed, and by having that violence destroy its victim as well as its prime agent, Forster intensifies the sense of historical trauma in the concluding moments of "The Life to Come." To the extent to which the deaths of Vithobai and Pinmay can be seen to constitute the final apocalyptic vision of the story, or even to embody an ironically logical culmination of Pinmay's promise of a "life to come," it is possible to say that Forster here appears to be gesturing towards the mutually destructive psychic trauma created by the history of civil rule, a trauma that he felt was likely to be repeated as long as the colonizing impulse survived.

This interpretation is underscored by Forster's own comments, made to Sassoon, about writing an additional chapter to the story. Forster writes:

> I tried another chapter, it is true, in the forests of the Underground "where all the trees that have been cut down on earth take root again and grow for ever" and the hut has been rebuilt on an enormous scale. The dead come crashing down through the foliage, in an infernal embrace. Pinmay prays to his God who appears on high through a rift in the leaves, and pities him but can do nothing. "It is very unfortunate," says God: "if he had died first you would have taken him to your heaven, but he has taken you to his instead. I am very sorry, oh good and faithful servant, but I cannot do anything." The leaves close, and Pinmay enters Eternity as a slave, while Vithobhai reigns with his peers. I hear rejoicing, inside the hut, to which occasionally the slaves are summoned. I see them come out again broken in spirit and crouch outside the entrance or lie like logs under the ice-cold flow of the stream. A gloomy prospect you see—except for Vithobhai, who has won the odd trick.
>
> (Forster 1985: 43)

As a graphic reenactment of the dark underside of the testimonial histories left by military and missionary agents, the significance of this scene can best be gauged by placing it alongside the conclusion of "The Life to Come." In the final moment of sacrificial death in the story, Forster portrays Vithobai mounting the body of the dead Pinmay, and as he leaps to his death from the roof top he is phantasmically transformed into a predatory falcon who pursues the "terrified shade" of Pinmay. The falcon represents the image of the fetishized object that had previously adorned Vithobai's silver necklet and which he had been forced to discard in order to be turned into an exemplary convert. By taking on the fury of this fetish object, Pinmay returns the violence that had constituted that change. In the scene that Forster described to Sassoon, there is a similar return to a lost world, but it is a hallucinatory and infernal underworld where the trees felled for their timber are restored only to tighten their grip on Pinmay. Vithobai regains his power while Pinmay, abandoned by his God, is held captive to Vithobai's desires—the potential violence evoked here is a reversal of the violence of the colonizer. In this scene Forster also reverses and reflects back the trauma originally enacted in the forest by representing the world of the colonizer and colonized literally in a "life to come," a life that is the shadowy after-image of the story that Forster writes in "The Life to Come." Enacted in this vision of "life" and "death" is the story's final dramatization of colonialism's uncanny relation to its own law, demonstrating once again the power of Forster's narrative in breaking the very seams of the imperial logic of civility. The "elusiveness" of civility rendered in Forster through the troubled articulations of language and desire, and of power and knowledge, is resolutely historical in nature. As the story demonstrates so powerfully, Forster's delineation of the politics of missionary civility reflects an attempt to think through the materiality of power invested in the modern state under colonization.

5 Civility and the colonial state of body in Leonard Woolf

> Only one person in the world could be as he was, in love. And there he was, this fortunate man, himself, reflected in the plate-glass window of a motor-car manufacturer in Victoria Street. All India lay behind him; plains, mountains; epidemics of cholera; a district twice as big as Ireland; decisions he had come to alone—he, Peter Walsh; who was now really for the first time in his life, in love.
>
> Virginia Woolf, *Mrs Dalloway*

In this scene in *Mrs Dalloway*, Virginia Woolf provides a singularly powerful description of a middle-aged Peter Walsh, a man poised on the threshold of a new life in the post-war metropolis of London after serving for seven years in the colonies. The London to which he returns is a city brimming with the spectral haze of modern consumer goods—shiny motor cars on the streets and shops filled with dazzling new merchandise. How compelling that vision is for Peter becomes clear as he strides out into the city streets and sees his own image reflected on the plate glass window of a motor-car manufacturer in Victoria Street. Captured in Peter Walsh's reflection on this silvery surface of the plate glass is the self-image of a colonial man asserting his sovereign place in the new plenitude of the metropolis. Just moments earlier, he seemed to have stepped clean out of his colonial past into the plush interiors of Clarissa Dalloway's lavish drawing room, hoping to leave behind his memories of death and isolation. Although during his brief meeting with Clarissa he senses that things had changed inalterably for him and for her, he nevertheless convinces himself that he was "really for the first time . . ., in love." The quiet fortitude and self-composure with which he conducts himself in Clarissa's presence is, in a sense, mirrored by the narcissistic emotion that is generated in Peter by the sight of his reflected self-image. The mirroring effect here powerfully suggests the extent to which Peter and other people like him rediscover their identities in a reified spectral relationship to the metropolitan world, a world that presents itself seamlessly through the all-pervasive spectacle of consumer objects. The all-encompassing power of that spectacle is signaled by the spatiality of this world, a spatiality produced in relation to what Marx has called "markets for labor, capital and consumer goods" (Pietz 1993: 148). Londoners are shown to be held by the spectacle of this world—from its goods assembled behind shop windows to its airplanes inscribing product names in the form of clouds of smoke in the sky. Metropolitan individuals decipher the constantly dissolving code underlying the floating signifiers in the sky only by basing it on their own experiences as class-identified consumers of the capitalist world.

What makes this scene significant for my purpose is the way in which *Mrs Dalloway* suggests a possible link between Peter's spectrality and the colonial experience, and between civil identity and colonial history. What becomes obvious, however, is that in this moment of clarity this colonial history is hollowed out of the image of Peter captured on the plate glass. That hollowing out also leads to a flattening of that history into simple fragments of "plains, mountains; epidemics of cholera," as a consequence of which it literally recedes into the background. In other words, set against the fullness of the metropolitan vision, this fragmented colonial order of things is forced out of visibility or simply absorbed into the blinding aura of London's commercial spectacle. I argue in this chapter that this history remains outside the space offered by Virginia Woolf in *Mrs Dalloway*, and the only way it can be excavated is by directing our attention to another source— the colonial stories written by Leonard Woolf after his return from Ceylon. This history, as this chapter demonstrates, is punctuated by the question of civility and its links to colonial desire, to the spectrality that is produced by the fetishization of the colonized subject, and to civility's elusive status as a normative category within the liberal framework of twentieth-century colonialism.

The question of colonial male civility that I examine in this chapter relates directly to my analysis of the relations of power consolidated by the civil magistrate in Charles Johnston's *Kela Bai* (chapter 3) and by the English missionary Paul Pinmay (chapter 4). Both of these male figures represented the dominance of civil authority exercised upon colonial subjects, of a power that also defined their own relation to the colonial state. That this view of colonial civility surfaces quite explicitly in various forms in the writings of the Bloomsbury Group cannot be denied. In Virginia Woolf's *The Waves*, for example, Percival's death in India evokes a sense of crisis in the order of metropolitan civility; its ironically elegiac form is cast as a response to that crisis and evokes an irreparable feeling of loss in the metropolis. But, as Jane Marcus has suggested, that loss indicates the waning of a nationalist ideal sustained by the memory of colonial exploits, challenging the very ground of British culture and its institutions of education, marriage, and vocation. The story of the ideal hero, Percival, who goes to India to serve the empire and subsequently to meet his end in an unfortunate fall from a horse, therefore, embodies the "violent last of the British imperialists" (Marcus 1992: 144), and his death resonates so powerfully in the metropolis precisely because it marks the time of "England's fall from imperial glory" (ibid.), a time when upper-class intellectuals were reminded of the limits to their own authority as bearers of culture.[1] One can add to Marcus's astute observations by noting that this time frame also coincided with the formation of a post-war industrial capitalism in the era of twentieth-century British imperialism, as evident in the description of London provided by Virginia Woolf in *Mrs Dalloway*. In fact, the construction of Percival as a "fallen" colonial hero by his friends in the metropolis can be linked directly to the traumatic effects felt within it of the decay of a global imperial order, now seen as an order that could sustain itself only by demanding the sacrifice of its own civil citizens.

In "Bonga Bonga in Whitehall," Lytton Strachey, another key member of the Bloomsbury circle, openly challenges the liberal credentials of a domestic imperial government by having a visiting African chief question the paternalistic policies of Whitehall on education, justice, and welfare. However, even while directing his satire at the metropolitan government, Strachey falls back on a stereotypical representation of the bumbling African chief in order to convey his critique.[2] It appears that there is no real space of resistance by colonial subjects within the metropolitan imperial order. In *Mrs Dalloway*, on the other hand, Virginia Woolf appears to be testing the very boundaries of the metropolitan imperial imaginary—including the latter's ability to provide the necessary fantasy to maintain its own legitimacy—by relocating the colonial figure, Peter Walsh back in the metropolis. However, her narrative cannot accommodate the colonial site in any substantial manner, as Peter's colonial history remains frozen within the fragments described in his reflected image, imitating in their disconnectedness the very floating letters left by the airplane that the Londoners in *Mrs Dalloway* attempt to connect and decipher.

Upon returning from Ceylon in 1911, where he had served for nearly eight years as a colonial bureaucrat, Leonard Woolf resigned his post in the colonial service. After marrying Virginia, he settled down with her in their new home, Monk's House in Sussex, in 1916. Along with Virginia and Vanessa and their Cambridge friends, Woolf established the "new" Bloomsbury Group as the center of a liberal aesthetic and intellectual culture fashioned after the tradition inherited from the late Victorians. During this period he wrote his novel *The Wise Virgins* (1914) and a novel and three short stories based on his experiences in Ceylon, *The Village in the Jungle* (1913) and *Stories of the East* (1915), respectively. After 1914, Woolf concentrated mainly on his political career as a liberal statesman and undertook projects that involved the writing of political pamphlets in support of the League of Nations, including his famous critiques of imperialism, such as *Mandates and Empire* (1920), *Economic Imperialism* (1921), and *Imperialism and Civilization* (1928). His five-part autobiography was to appear much later, in the 1960s. In many ways, Woolf was the ideal civil bureaucrat and, while his standing as a creative writer remained largely unacknowledged during his lifetime, his political writings played an important role in defining the liberal politics of the times. Despite this reputation of Leonard Woolf as a political instead of a literary figure, Quentin Bell praised *The Village in the Jungle* as a novel of superbly dispassionate observation. Lytton Strachey, Woolf's close friend and confidante, on the other hand, dismissed it, saying that the novel had "too many blacks in it" (Woolf 1989: 197). Curiously enough, Woolf's colonial writings, particularly *Stories of the East*, failed to generate any interest, even from his Bloomsbury friends and peers, who had always been eager to express their personal views on the writings of the group. What is perhaps more striking is that Woolf himself never drew the attention of his peers to these stories. Hand printed and published by the Hogarth Press in 1921, the collection appears to have quietly slipped out of the memory of Bloomsbury.[3]

How, then, does one begin to comprehend this silence? Does it have to do with Woolf's reputation as a creative writer, which rapidly faded after 1916, when he entered the arena of liberal politics in Britain? Did these changes affect the perceptions of his peers regarding his "literary" abilities? Or did the silence stem from an inability on the part of the Bloomsbury circle to comprehend the stories' undercurrents—their persistent and often troubled questioning of the legitimacy of narrative authority derived from, and evoked in, the name of the liberal state? Did these stories challenge the deeply entrenched orientalist impulse within the Bloomsbury circle (as, for example, seen in Lytton Strachey's view of the African chief)? Or did they direct the gaze back at the metropolis by bringing up questions about the fetishization of the colonized world by metropolitan subjects, and by opening up a particularly brutal history of power relations between them and the colony? Was there in these stories an implicit indictment of metropolitan subjects for being complicit in maintaining their own civility by refusing to acknowledge their own power in maintaining and legitimizing these colonial power relations?

What is implicit in all of the questions that I pose here is the disciplinary func-tioning of the modern civil state in relation to colonialism, particularly its role in regulating notions of modern citizenship by disavowing its links to colonial history. I argue that Woolf's attempt to excavate this erasure of history and to highlight the metropolitan subject's complicitous relationship with privilege endowed upon it by its links to the state was met by this silence from the Bloomsbury circle. This silence, which Woolf had himself anticipated, is, however, made visible through the way in which it appears within the stories' metanarrative form, signifying a refusal or perhaps an inability on the part of their interlocutors to read their political meaning. This point will be clarified later when I examine the stories in detail. What is more significant for the purposes of my argument here is to note the ways in which the stories invert the self-conscious orientalist pictorial effect that is found in the cover that adorns the first edition of the collection. Featuring a tiger flanked on either side by two palm trees and images of pineapples and other oriental motifs, the woodcut design by the artist Dora Carrington provides an example of an unabashed orientalism that presents itself in all its exoticism under the guise of Bloomsbury artistic innovation. The form and content of the stories, however, present quite a different picture of the "East" to the one that it is captured on the cover.

Intensely autobiographical and preoccupied with troubling questions about the "real" which Woolf had been posing all along in his letters written from Ceylon to Lytton Strachey, these stories are framed through shifting metanarratives that constantly force the language of the "real" or "reality" out of the realm of objective narrativization. Also implicit in this questioning of the "real" is a particular drama-tization of a trauma through which Woolf links the personal and the political, links that Virginia Woolf could not adequately represent in his portrayal of Peter Walsh. In other words, by remaking his own experience as an imperial bureaucrat into a narrative that poses the question of the "real," he subjects his own history to the violence of representation implicit in the will to know—that is, the will to pin down that "real." The persistence with which Woolf pursues this question in the first story, "A Tale Told by Moonlight," recurs in the story about the pearl divers, entitled "Pearls and Swine." In both, Woolf shows that the very language that claims to establish the domain of the "real" is the very language that represses its own fetishistic drive: this is represented time and again in narrative modes of visibility embodied in the stories. Whether it concerns the body of the native prostitute in "A Tale Told by Moonlight" or those of the pearl divers described in "Pearls and Swine," Woolf's stories clarify how the "visible" in the colonial world is not an empirical but a historical effect. Framed by questions about the authority of the metropolitan civil subject in representing the East, this visibility also marks the place of the metropolitan subject, indicated both by the status of the "unnamed" narrators in the two stories and by the figure of the white man who serves as a bureaucratic official in "Pearls and Swine." Both of these instances of visibility—those that mark the metropolitan subject and those that emerge in the form of the commodified colonized body—bring out what William Pietz has called the "moment of capital's political truth, the moment when 'private enterprise' is revealed as social government . . . and the political-economic reality of capitalist society suddenly appears in public culture as *fetishistic*" (Pietz 1993: 149). Therefore, what can be represented "externally" and "visibly" as an empirically recognizable mark of civility is always haunted by the recurrent question—"what is the real?"

In bringing up this question of the "real" by rerouting it through language, representation, and visibility, Woolf, like Forster, appears to be gesturing towards what Fredric Jameson has described as the "concealment" that lies "beneath the reifying logic of the commodity form" (Jameson 1990: 50), a concealment that is authorized by the logic of "equivalences" instituted by capitalism and imperialism. In "A Tale Told by Moonlight," for example, Woolf identifies that reifying logic through the crisis of naming and understanding the "reality" that one calls "love." What stands out is the way in which Woolf locates the story within a specific performative site. As in Conrad's *Heart of Darkness*, the original setting of the story is metropolitan England, the teller an old colonial who has recently returned from the colonies, the audience four metropolitan male subjects modeled after the Bloomsbury circle, and the story about the "East" narrated by an unnamed male colonial figure. This strategy is repeated again in "Pearls and Swine." Right from the outset, what stands out in "A Tale Told by Moonlight" is the narrator's struggle to identify a language that is adequate to the telling of the story, a language whose conceptual and narrative categories about the "real" can on the one side match the expectations of his metropolitan interlocutors, and on the other capture the "real" experienced in the colony. The war with language that is enacted in the opening sections of the story is in a sense a political war over "meaning"—his metropolitan interlocutors as consumers expect the story to be an interesting oriental tale, while the narrator struggles to communicate another "meaning"—one that can convey how the conditions of narrativity and language in the metropolitan world are themselves constituted by a will to truth that blinds them towards their own history. In fact, as "Pearls and Swine" reveals, metropolitan subjects can confidently discuss the "Eastern question" only in the safety of the metropolitan world.

Following Žižek's analysis of commodity fetishism in *The Sublime Object of Ideology*, one can argue that this history concerns the effect of metropolitan language in reifying metropolitan colonial identity, where the exchange value implicit in language leads to an inherent "misrecognition" produced by the abstraction intrinsic to reification. Žižek explains this phenomenon in the following manner: "Commodity fetishism" consists of a

> certain misrecognition which concerns the relations between a structured network [in this case, language] and one of its elements: what is really a structural effect, an effect of the network of relations between elements, appears as an immediate property of one of its elements, *as if this property also belongs to it outside its relations with other elements.*
>
> (Žižek 1989: 24; emphasis added)

In other words, the structural network of power itself produces a reified "real"–an "immediate property"–which is made recognizable by the language used in the metropolitan world, a language that also expresses the desire of metropolitan citizens. Since this structural effect often occludes its material base, metropolitan subjects are made blind to their own history. Instead what replaces that blindness is a "spectral fictionality" that Michael Taussig attributes to the state, a kind of fictionality through which Peter Walsh can recognize himself in his reflected image, an image that is offered to him in the ideological form of metropolitan civility and its attendant values of freedom, choice, and individuality.

In both of the stories Woolf therefore constantly pushes the continuity of narration out of focus in order to point to those sites where the reality of the fetish lies. Through this form of narrative maneuvering, Woolf provides a political critique of colonialism by returning to, and questioning, its normative order of civility by revealing through the narrative impossibility the limits of that normativity. The quest for the "real" is therefore doomed at two levels–in the narrator's inability to represent the "real" in a form that is consistent with the unnamed narrator's "will to narrate," and in his incapacity to present it in a manner that can be apprehended by his metropolitan audience. No wonder then that both of the stories conclude with the interlocutors dismissing and rejecting the narrator's efforts as being too "sentimental," the very thing of which the narrator had accused his interlocutors, at the beginning of "A Tale." In short, the channels of communication are locked within the precise boundaries of that reifying language.

A cursory reading of these stories makes it clear that this crisis was linked in some indirect way to Woolf's own colonial experiences in Ceylon, experiences that had left him with an inescapable feeling about the incommunicable nature of the colonial trauma he had encountered there. In the novel *The Village in the Jungle*, on the other hand, that feeling is almost absent; in it Woolf had been able to adopt the tone of a detached observer and recorder. The novel's orientalism is discernible in its unmediated evocation of the sense of the "real," the "real" that was based on a faithful rendition of the life and struggles of the rural poor in Ceylon, which Woolf had observed from close quarters. As a political critique of colonialism *Village in the Jungle* has recourse to the power of representing the poverty and destitution of the colony; in fact, the "real" presented itself in all of its objectivity in the obscure regions of rural Ceylon—in the lives of villagers and poor outcasts who lived on the edge of the jungle and whose "primitive" lives crossed paths in unexpected ways with the colonial machinery that had been set in place.[4] Oddly enough, that self-assured felicity of direct observation and objectivity seemed unavailable to Woolf's narrators in "A Tale" and "Pearls and Swine." Instead these stories appear to move unevenly through opaque spaces that open up between the observer/teller and the colonial world evoked by that telling, hovering precariously on the impossibility of ever capturing the "real" world, time and again struggling under the weight of the unnamable and inexpressible. As a result, even the sense of the real—evoked through the visual description of colonial bodies—is often racked by a pervasive narrative unease, by a sense of trauma experienced by the narrators at the level of the physical that could not be communicated through the language of realism. In fact, the struggle in crafting a language that could adequately capture that trauma is reflected by the narrator's own incapacity to locate it in any finite form or to give it an appropriate name.

It is a little curious that, although such questions—about the limits of realism, narrative authority, aesthetic representation, and historical truth—were central to the practices of Bloomsbury writers such as Lytton Strachey and Virginia Woolf, Leonard Woolf's stories awakened no interest, or even curiosity, among them. What is clear, however, is that from the very beginning these stories were relegated to the margins of the literary and political discussions about imperialism that took place within the Bloomsbury circle. I argue that the silence was the result of the fact that they did not lend themselves to a simple liberal reading, based either on the principles of "realism" that Woolf had adopted in *The Village* and that had already been rejected by the other proponents of the Bloomsbury circle, or on the criterion of modernist experimental fiction devised by Bloomsbury. In fact, I argue that the stories complicate our present understanding of the relationship between the discourse of Bloomsbury aesthetics, modernist orientalism, and the institutions of the modern liberal state in relation to capitalism and colonialism. By re-establishing the links between Woolf's professional status as a career colonial bureaucrat and his metropolitan Bloomsbury civility often nurtured by its attendant liberal aestheticism, I offer a reading of the story that explains how the crisis of representation gestures towards Woolf's troubled relationship with his own metropolitanism and with the enterprise of modernity and civility that formed the very ideological core of that metropolitanism. I suggest that, through its ruptures and elisions, the story points towards the structural relation between colonialist/orientalist discourses of fantasy and power and their metropolitan base, which could not be accounted for, within Bloomsbury, in either realist or anti-realist terms. Furthermore, these ruptures also bring to the fore the inherent impossibility of retaining or sustaining the power and credibility of a liberal authorial consciousness to mediate between the fiction of the capitalist state and the political reality of the colony. This impossibility can be understood by taking into account the fetishistic relations instituted by the state that not only constituted metropolitan aesthetic identity for members of the Bloomsbury circle but also mediated their power relationship with the colonial world and its people.

The "real": revisiting the question of civility

> . . . reality is nothing, it is only in writing and imagination that things are wonderful or horrible or supreme; in reality they are sometimes just beautiful, nearly always ugly & always vague & dire.
>
> Leonard Woolf, *Letters*

In October 1904, after completing his Cambridge education but failing to qualify for the coveted Indian Civil Services, Leonard Woolf accepted a cadetship in the Senior Crown Colony of Ceylon. From 1904 to 1911 he was to serve in various capacities as a colonial administrator—in Jaffna in northwest Ceylon, where he was temporary replacement for a magistrate and police officer, undertaking emergency measures for famine relief; in Kandy, where, as an office-assistant, he was involved in the sale and settlement of crown land as well as managing the labor problems of English tea planters; and in Hambantota, a remote district in southeast Ceylon, where, at the age of twenty-seven, he was promoted to the virtually independent post of assistant government agent. In addition to keeping an official diary, as mandated in 1808 by the then governor, Sir Thomas Maitland, in which he noted in meticulous detail his public duties, Woolf corresponded regularly with his friend Lytton Strachey, who had also been a member of the Young Apostles at Cambridge to which Woolf had belonged.[5]

Woolf first started corresponding with Strachey in January 1905 and continued writing to him until 1909, after which his letters grew progressively infrequent. To the modern reader, these letters bear evidence to a whole range of personal emotions that continued to be generated by the various kinds of duties Woolf undertook as a public administrator, which he articulated with a rare sense of intimacy, provocation, and reticence. What emerges intermittently in the letters is Woolf's persistent questioning of the "real," a word he repeats later in "A Tale Told by Moonlight." The word resonates with a particular urgency as Woolf attempts to place his own experiences in the colony against those philosophical debates in which he and his friends had engaged at Cambridge in the early years of the century. Those debates, which had preoccupied the members of the exclusive circle led by the philosopher G. E. Moore, centered around the question of "the good," an issue that had also been at the core of Moore's own philosophical work *Principia Ethica*, whose first edition appeared in 1903 when Woolf was still at Cambridge. I will return to Moore's ideas later in this essay, but here I wish to emphasize the *colonial* route through which Woolf channels the question of the "real" back to the metropolis, testing the epistemological limits of the concept against his own experiences in the colony.

Beginning with his letter of July 7, 1907, and continuing up to November 25, 1908, Woolf's reflective stance on the "real" takes on a form of haunting in these letters: unsure of how to begin articulating ideas about this "real," which increasingly seemed to him to be no longer comprehensible in terms laid out in the metropolis, he searches for an alternative—an alternative that would allow him to move beyond the conceptual categories of metropolitan philosophical reasoning into the colonial world of "affect" in which he dwelt daily as an outsider. However, this world of "affect," as Woolf shows, could not be signified in the form of an unmediated existential experience; rather, it is shown to be produced by the kind of bureaucratic function that Woolf played as a colonial administrator. The agony of confronting the daily tasks of the administrator, witnessing the endlessly fruitless attempts to govern according to the metropolitan principles, and constantly experiencing his own sense of isolation, collided with Woolf's own sense of the goals of imperial rule. The "good," as enunciated by the philosophy of Moore, appeared to be part of that elusive objective category—the "real"—in the colonies, a category that haunts the confessional language of his letters.

The first occasion when he brings up the question of the "real" is in his letter to Strachey in which he is describing his reactions to E. M. Forster's *The Longest Journey*, which he had been reading while performing his official duties:

> The fact is I don't think he knows what reality is, & as for experience, the poor man does not realize that practically it does not exist. Still his mind interests me, its curious way of touching on things in the rather precise & charming way in which his hands (I remember) used to touch things vaguely.
>
> (Woolf 1989: 130)

In these general impressions, Woolf characterizes Forster's work as "fading into humour and the dimmer ghosts of unrealities," suggesting indirectly that the failure of "form" was due to Forster's inability to know "reality." Nevertheless, he qualifies his dismissal by saying that, despite the shortcomings of his novel, Forster's mind still interested him—something about the movement of "touching on things" that he intuited in Forster's narrative indicated that, while the reality might have eluded him, his work, like his habit of "vaguely" touching on things, displayed a kind of subtle tactility that was both precise and indeterminate. To push the sensory body into the domain of narrativity through a paradoxical tactility involving both precision and inexactitude becomes a way for Woolf to establish a possible link between the "real" and the domain of "affect" registered both physically and emotionally. In fact, the act of touching, understood as an apprehension of surfaces, conveyed to Woolf a certain motion of tactile feeling that pointed to the "real," without necessarily moving beyond that surface to penetrate the core.

Woolf's preoccupation with this aspect of Forster's work is repeated once again in another letter he writes to Strachey in November 1908, more than a year after the first one. The book in question is another of Forster's novels that he had been reading—*A Room with a View*. There is a similar indirection and elusiveness in his remarks about Forster's new work. In his inimitably exaggerated style, Woolf communicates his response to Forster's new novel about "sightseeing" by asserting that, although Forster "seems to think that death is real & sightseeing unreal," no final distinction could be made between the two based on "experience" or the evidence of sensory perceptions. Referring to this new novel, Woolf asks Strachey: "Isn't it dominated by a spectral Moore?" (Woolf 1989: 142). Was this characterization of Forster an indirect rejection of Moore's ideas as providing an inadequate basis for artistic representation and a questioning of the objectivist basis of Moore's own thinking, which now seemed to Woolf to be politically empty and meaningless?

To answer the question, it is necessary to examine Moore's ideas about the "good" in some detail. In his *Principia Ethica*, Moore had proposed that the "good" was not definable in a conventional sense because it was "not composed of any parts, which we can substitute for it in our minds when we are thinking about it" ([1903] 1951: 8). Moore had claimed that the good "is one of those innumerable objects of thought which are themselves incapable of definition, because they are the ultimate terms by reference to which whatever *is* capable of definition must be defined" (ibid.: 9–10). The reality of that "ultimate term"–good–rested on "that which is good"–which "therefore [must] be the substantive to which the adjective 'good' will apply" (ibid.: 8). Positing this good to be a singular entity, Moore also rejected the notion that the existence of the means to that singular good had any intrinsic "value," although they were necessary for the latter's existence. This line of reasoning translated into a particular epistemology, which Moore explained in the following manner: "universally the object of cognition must be distinguished from the cognition of which it is the object; and hence that in no case can the question whether the object is *true* be identical with the question how it is cognised or whether it is cognised at all" (ibid.: 141). This idealist and objectivist strain in Moore's philosophy of the real had a significant role in establishing the aesthetic positions on art within the Bloomsbury circle, and, as J. K. Johnstone has noted, its influence on shaping the criterion for defining the "beautiful" as that "of which the admiring contemplation is good in itself" (Johnstone 1954: 21) set the epistemological parameters for Bloomsbury aesthetic theory.[6]

However, separated by nearly 7,000 miles and a world in which those debates seemed distant and alien, Woolf grappled with Moore's ideas, as evidenced by his tortuous and evasive fragments about Forster. Because a simple opposition to Moore's theory of the separation between the acts and objects of consciousness would only lead to a form of elementary monism and totally objectifiable subjectivism, Woolf strove to identify an alternative. However, that alternative appeared to elude him, and the struggle for it appears to have been incarnated in a form of apprehension that I call a "traumatic" encounter with the "real." The telling of the stories is throughout laced with this form of apprehension where the narration of the "real" no longer serves as a "record of the past." Experienced as traumatic, the telling simply "registers the force of an experience that was not yet fully known" (Caruth 1995: 151). As a colonial bureaucrat, Woolf recorded the "real" from the position of an ethnographer; this unknowability, on the other hand, registers in the consciousness as trauma in which the "real" can no longer be "directly available to experience," no matter how intimately unmediated it might have seemed to the subject at some point in time. Given this inaccessibility, the narratorial act performs the trauma by realizing itself in the question of "survival," which, as Caruth has noted, becomes embodied in the question "what does it mean for consciousness to survive?" (Caruth 1996: 31–2). While the urgency of that question of survival is throughout palpable in the story, it is also clear that the narrative act in itself cannot serve as a means to integrate the past to the present. Instead, the historical crisis engendered by the rupture lingers, only to be perceived in what Caruth calls "unassimilable forms" (Caruth 1995: 156).[7]

At this stage, it might be worthwhile asking: what is the implicit link between the disciplinary modern state and its normalizing discourse on civility, and the crisis of representation evoked in Leonard Woolf's stories? The failure of integrating the past and the present represents a historical crisis within the colonial context, a crisis whose rupture begins to signify the vulnerability of the modern metropolitan subject. Woolf's own position as a bureaucrat in service of the empire depended a great deal on his personal sense of social mobility, a point he emphasizes in his *Autobiography*. However, his bureaucratic authority itself depended on those institutional practices of colonialism—the job of supervising the pearl fisheries or serving as a judge in colonial courts, for example—that had behind it a long history of exploitation and violence. In the stories, the inability to retain the centrality and singularity of voice on the part of the narrators signifies the vulnerable status of Woolf's own liberal humanist politics. Forced into forms of reiteration, this narrative voice, with its implicit subject position, is therefore broken into multiply refracted voices. In fact, it is through these disjunctions that the story can speak the history of "brutal things." This psychoanalytic domain—if you will—works within the Foucauldian paradigm precisely because the hesitancy in capturing the "real" is an effect of the crisis in power, a power that is responsible for endowing individual subjectivity with its authority to narrate, govern, or control the world outside itself. As indicating a constant testing of the consciousness of survival in the domain of power, this reiterative process—generated through the disjunctions— is what paradoxically shapes and undermines the narrative in Woolf's stories. The question still remains: what is the status of the "lack" behind these disjunctions, and how are we to conceive its links to the constitution of metropolitan subjectivity?

One possible answer to the question lies in the form of "fantasy" put in place by the narrative, a fantasy experienced both in the ability to tell what the narrator of "A Tale Told by Moonlight" calls "brutal things," and in the "gap" that "speaks" through that narration. In the two stories, "A Tale Told by Moonlight" and "Pearls and Swine," that Woolf forged out of the experiences he recorded in the letters, this fantasy takes on a form of repetition and haunting through which, as Kaja Silverman explains, the subject both strives towards establishing its own coherence and "through which it is jeopardized" (Silverman 1992: 61).[8] This form of repetition and haunting gestures towards, but is unable fully to represent, the "original" trauma. Kaja Silverman characterizes this process as

> an attempt to conceptualize how history sometimes manages to interrupt or even deconstitute what a society assumes to be its master narratives and

immanent Necessity—to undo our imaginary relation to the symbolic order, as well as to the other elements within the social formation with which that order is imbricated.

(ibid.: 55)

I am here suggesting a link between the personal and the public that Woolf was able to discern: like Forster's "vague touching," between being haunted and the desire for an adequate narrative to represent that haunting, Woolf's disjunctive narratives yield an historical conceptualization of specific psychic disruptions. Instead of providing the basis for chronicling a given history, this form of haunting brought up for Woolf questions about colonial power regarding relations about the legal and civil authority of the metropolitan subject constituted within a disciplinary state—and about the very violence of an epistemology structuring the author's urge to represent the "real" for his metropolitan readers.

In his letter of November 25, 1908, written to Strachey from Ceylon, Woolf refers back to a "hanging" incident that he had described in a letter written on September 29, 1907, saying that the spectacle of the dead woman he had seen had triggered a "similar piece of reality" in the "fringe of my brain." That "original" piece of "reality" had earlier been described as a "most appalling spectacle":

> I had to go to see four men hanged one morning. They were hanged two by two. I have a strong stomach but at best it is a horrible performance. I go to the cells & read over the warrant of execution & ask them whether they have anything to say. They nearly always say no. Then they are led out clothed in white, with curious white hats on their heads which at the last moment are drawn down to *hide their faces*. They are led up on to the scaffold & the ropes are placed around their necks. I have [in Kandy] to stand on a sort of verandah *where I can actually see the man hanged*. The signal has to be given by me. The first two were hanged all right but they gave one of the second too big a drop or something went wrong. The man's head was practically torn from his body & there was a great jet of blood which went up about 3 or 4 feet high, covering the gallows and priest who stands praying on the steps. The curious thing was that this man as he went to the gallows seemed to feel the rope round his neck: he kept twitching his head over into the exact position they hang in after death. Usually they are quite unmoved. One man kept repeating two words of a Sinhalese prayer (I think) over & over again all the way to the gallows & even as he stood with the rope round his neck waiting for the drop.
>
> (Woolf 1989: 133; emphasis added)

The modes of a Foucauldian penal discipline and punishment adopted by the colonial authorities lurk at the edges of Woolf's rendition of this spectacle. However, in this scene the other piece of "reality," apprehended earlier when the author had seen the dead woman, returns through the unconscious through a reiterative assembling of fragments of memory. Personal memory can be seen to represent another disciplinary site of "subjectification" that allows Woolf to speculate whether this was the "real" that his consciousness had apprehended. But that personal memory cannot be isolated from Woolf's own consciousness of his public role expressed in his letter to Strachey—the role of a "policeman, magistrate, judge & publican" (ibid.: 141). The sight of the dead woman stirs up the memory of the hanged man, but that memory is no longer a purely private one since it returns Woolf to the scene of the symbolic as the site of colonial law and its institutional authority. What is revealed fragmentarily in that moment is the way in which an individual such as Woolf had been "accommodated" to the institution of law via "an ideological facilitation" (Silverman 1992: 2). In order to function as law, the symbolic simultaneously required that the "criminal" be turned into an anonymous object—with his face covered by the hat being drawn down over it—and that the agent of law—Woolf himself—be present as a witness to its action and to give the final "signal." Reminiscent of Foucault's description of the technology of penal semiotics which he elaborates in *Discipline and Punish*, the scene also gestures towards the modern technology of colonial power which "combines the idea of the social contract with the theory of representation and a principle of utility" (Owen 1994: 173). It is assumed that the criminal is being punished for having broken the law, and that his punishment attests both to the terrible power of the state and to his quiet willingness to present his own body for a spectacle that necessitates the witnessing presence of the supervisor.

Although physically placed at a safe distance from where he escapes being drenched by the prisoner's blood, Woolf is haunted by the memory of that scene. The kind of trauma registered in that memory appears to have its origin in the "efficient" functioning of the colonial machine that Woolf served. Kafkaesque in its presentation of the workings of this machine, this scene links the machine to the operation of law and justice. This is highlighted by Woolf through a deft narrative turn: linked to the staging of the entire scene—from the criminals being "led out clothed in white," to ropes being placed around their necks, to the giving of the signal, to the bodies dropping, and to the unexpected streaming of the blood—is the "gap" revealed within the very order of efficiency. For Woolf, what had seemed to be a "clean act" turns out otherwise: as the blood streams out, spills over, and drenches the priest standing nearby, it rips open the veneer of methodological precision with which the law operated. Simultaneously, the scene itself produces the "excess" that the law had attempted to contain through its own precise and clean operations. The tearing of the man's head from his body and the subsequent drenching of the gallows and the priest by his blood forces a form of visibility from which the agent of law himself cannot escape (although he remains untainted by the actual blood). In other words, the poised civility of the witness is disrupted, and, as I will demonstrate later, the kind of stark visibility that marks the event begins to resonate in the stories with a force that can only be represented by the visibility of the fetish.

How do the scenes that evoke this excess insinuate themselves within the domain of "affect" to which Woolf returns constantly in his letters to Strachey? One can speculate that after Woolf returned to England he began to shape these images into a formal narrative, but recognized that the "excess"—the spilling over, as it were—could only be represented by evoking once again the question of the "real." It is therefore not surprising that the first story opens with this question, and persists in raising it for its entire length. But that questioning, I argue, is intimately linked to the crisis of representation as well as to Woolf's own growing awareness that any re-creation of an illusory whole to serve as a mirror of the objective "real"—described and narrated in the form of a "real' story—would simply occlude the complicitous relationship between narrative visibility and colonialism's fetishistic practices, and reproduce the very violence that he wished to identify in them. It is precisely because of this impasse that these stories provide a compelling site for examining the discourse of civility as the elusive node that brings together the historical violence of colonialism and the violence of representation, a relationship in which the "real" is not an entity to be located as a thing per se, but is the very texture of fictionality through which the colonial state and its citizens mask the violence inherent in its own civil and cultural identity. Woolf seems to have suspected that the Bloomsbury circle, despite its unorthodox views on representation, could not see beyond that fictionality.

"A Tale Told by Moonlight": civility, desire and the colonial traffic

"A Tale Told by Moonlight"—the first story in the collection—appears in the form of several embedded narratives. The outermost narrative shell shows the un-named narrator and his metropolitan friends gathered under a moonlit sky on a fine summer evening in England to talk about their first "love." The group comprises a poet, a critic, a novelist, and a statesman. Inspired by the sight of two young lovers kissing in the moonlight, they all start speculating on the true definition of "love." When asked about his definition of love, the narrator initially struggles to define it and, failing to come up with an appropriate answer, opts to tell them a story from his own life. The story he relates is the second narrative shell and concerns the narrator's friend in the colony, Jessop, who once invites another friend, Reynolds, to pay him a visit in Ceylon. Reynolds is a struggling novelist, worn out by life in England and looking for an opportunity to revive his failing artistic inspiration. He arrives in Ceylon and is introduced by Jessop to a local prostitute, Celestinahami. Attracted by her, Reynolds eventually marries the prostitute and settles down with her in a little cottage by the ocean. He starts to write again, and this time it is a novel about the "East." However, as time passes Reynolds loses interest in the woman, and eventually leaves her to return to England after making a monetary settlement with her. Soon after Reynolds's departure, Celestinahami's Western attired body is found floating on the waters outside the cottage. This is the point where the narrator ends his second narrative, and we return to the first, where are left with his interlocutors wondering if the story they had heard was not just another "sentimental" tale about love.[9]

One of the outstanding features of Woolf's "A Tale Told by Moonlight" is its persistent concern with defining and capturing the "real," a word that is repeated so obsessively that it begins to dominate the language of the narrative. What makes the story stand apart from Woolf's letters to Strachey is the fact that this obsessively repeated word occurs within a narrative where the original relationship between the narrator (Woolf) and the interlocutor (Strachey) has shifted. Instead of the man, Leonard Woolf, communicating in his letters the events that he experiences (and the affect triggered by those experiences) to a friend on the other side of the globe, we have their fictional rendering in the form of a story within a story, with multiple narrators and characters, and dual fictional settings. The framing of the fictional narrative occurs through the use of double narrators and double locales. This narrative distancing is also intensified by the constant interruptions and reiterations in the early sections of the story, which introduce a kind of modernist doubleness. As a result of these interruptions, the representational impulse is constantly destabilized by being caught between visibility and invisibility, the factual and the interpretive, knowledge and desire, determinism and randomness, and self-presence and the imagined "other." The constant reiteration of that elusive "it" (referring to love)—that stands in for but cannot itself be the "real"—haunts the very telling, which makes it impossible for the story to occupy its own imagined center.

What, then, is the connection between Jessop's narration of the story and his desire to tell "brutal things" (Woolf [1921] 1963: 255)? In this story, those "brutal things" ironically concern love and the question what is the "real" when we think of love? Set in the metropolis, the inciting moment of the narrative in "A Tale" comes when the sight of two lovers kissing in the moonlight prompts four individuals to tell stories of their first love. Jessop's four interlocutors are clearly modeled after the Bloomsbury circle—the narrator, an ex-colonial; Alderton, the novelist; Pemberton, the poet; and Hanson Smith, the critic. Within this group, Jessop is presented as a singular, brooding individual, as a man whose knowledge comes from elsewhere—from outside of the familiar setting of the metropolitan world. Commenting on the nostalgic romanticism of his interlocutors who are intent on knowing the reality of love, Woolf's narrator comments with characteristic cynicism: "You talk as if you believed all that: it's queer, damned queer. A boy kissing a girl in the moonlight and you call it love and poetry and romance. But you know as well as I do it isn't. It's just a flicker of the body, it will be cold, dead, this time next year" (ibid.).

When the primary (unnamed) narrator of "A Tale" claims that the "things" his friend Jessop "fishes" up out of life "fascinated as well" (Woolf [1921] 1963: 255), a link is made between the narrative act and "fantasy." The word "fascinate," as defined by the *Oxford English Dictionary*, points to the state of being deprived of power by a look representing "a state between attraction and repulsion." As Jacqueline Rose has argued, "fantasy, even on its own psychic terms, is never only inward-turning; it always contains a historical reference in so far as it involves, alongside the attempt *to arrest the present, a journey through the past*" (Rose 1998: 5; emphasis added). The "present" that is arrested in the narrative when the narrator opts to tell his story is, therefore, a point from which a specific history gets linked to an itinerary of narrative desire and will. That this itinerary of narrative desire and will is aligned with the story of "brutal things" makes Woolf's story work with the burden of a history, a history of colonial desire.

As I have already mentioned, in the context of the first narrative presented in "A Tale," those "brutal things" concern "love" and the question what is the "real" when we think of love? This question was foreshadowed in the letters Woolf had written to Strachey from Ceylon in which he alluded to his confused sense of the link between sexuality, love, power, and eroticism (see Woolf 1989: 73). In these letters, Woolf had referred to his own desperate attempt to confront his individual sexuality in a land where most colonials found themselves caught between protecting their own status and their fantasies of power as white men, and his personal feelings for the woman waiting back home (Virginia Woolf). However, right from the outset, Woolf's fictive narrator Jessop struggles without much success to name what he calls "love": when he reiterates that "the real thing, it's too queer to be anything but the rarest; it's the queerest thing in the world" (Woolf [1921] 1963: 257), he conveys both a sense of its immensity and the impossibility of categorizing or reducing it to its essence. The slippages register at the level of language; for example, as soon as he posits that love is "immense, steady, enduring," he undermines it by asserting that it is experienced for not more "than a second, and then it's only a feeble ripple on the smooth surface of [people's] unconsciousness" (ibid.). Similarly, he explains that love's queerness lies in the fact that it isn't "animal," but neither is it "vegetable or mineral" (ibid.). It appears that all definitions/categorizations of love inevitably fall into this predicative paradox: each definition is provisional since its relational (or predicative) reality cancels out the kernel of definitional meaning—its nominal reality. Clearly, it is Moore's specter that looms behind this portrayal of Jessop's struggle to "name." That struggle is further heightened as Jessop undertakes to narrate his own tale—of what he had "seen" (ibid.)—as a way to account for the "mysterious" thing called love. The turn to narrative then marks a significant moment in the story's attempt to force the idea into some form of representational and narratorial clarity.

Although that clarity remains elusive, the exotic is ready at hand: in acknowledging that love comes "in strange ways and places, like most real things, perversely and unreasonably" (Woolf [1921] 1963: 258), Jessop locates the reality of love in his own experiences in the remotest outpost of the empire, the den of the local prostitute. It is at this crucial point that the colonial terrain makes itself explicitly visible: what the reader encounters is Jessop's own desire—the desire to fulfill what he claims to be the wish of his friend Reynolds to "see life" in the colonies, "to understand it, to feel it" (ibid.: 259). Such a sense of the palpable, of the original and unhampered, by the illusionary haze of the metropolis is what Jessop offers to his exhausted friend. However, this invitation to "see life" is also an invitation to an initiatory rite that Jessop extends to his friend almost immediately after he reaches Ceylon, and it is not surprising that Jessop fulfills that promise by taking him to the den of the local Colombo prostitutes.

That rite of initiation brings up specific questions about metropolitan civility—its imbrication in the form of visibility available to the white man in the colonies, and its relationship to the objectification of the colonial body. What the uninitiated Reynolds had "never seen before" (Woolf [1921] 1963: 259) yields up a form of visibility to both of these white men, one that is typically fashioned in accordance with the logic of yet another form of orientalist fantasy: "all the smells of the East rose up and hung heavy upon the damp hot air in the narrow streets" (ibid.). By appropriating this orientalist trope, Jessop's voyeuristic narrative penetrates through the overwhelming mass of sensations right to the interior of the den:

> There was one of those queer native wooden doors made in two halves; the top half was open and through it one saw an empty white-washed room lighted by a lamp fixed in the wall. At the other end were two steps leading up to another room. Suddenly there came the sound of bare feet running and giggles of laughter, and ten or twelve girls, some naked and some half clothed in bright red and bright orange clothes, rushed down the steps upon us. We were surrounded, embraced, caught up in their arms and carried into the next room. We lay upon sofas with them.
>
> (ibid.: 259–60)

As a European man of the environment, Jessop is able to conduct himself as the master of the scene. The staging of this scene is also organized around the progression of the gaze of the narrator, with its ability to move through the material frames of the doorway into the heart of the den. The suddenness, registered in the words "embraced, caught up in their arms," implies a sense of entrapment, which is immediately followed by Jessop's assertion of his own ability to contain and master that entrapment through the knowledge of the "other," the entity located in the interior of the frames. This act of knowing, enunciated at this point in the narrative, is constructed as the narrator's ability to grasp and fix the objects—here the bodies of the naked prostitutes—both sexually and epistemologically:

> They knew me well in the place, you can imagine what it was—I often went there. Apart from anything else, it interested me. The girls were all Tamils and Sinhalese. It always reminded me somehow of the Arabian Nights; that room when you came into it so bare and empty, and then the sudden rush of laughter, the pale, yellow naked women, the brilliant colours of the clothes, the white teeth, all appearing so suddenly in the doorway up there at the end of the room. And the girls themselves interested me: I used to sit and talk to them for hours in their own language: they didn't as a rule understand English. They used to tell me all about themselves, queer pathetic stories often. They came from villages almost always, little native villages hidden far away among rice fields and coconut trees, and they had drifted somehow into this hovel in the warren of filth and smells which we and our civilization had attracted about us.
>
> (ibid.: 260)

Knowledge is transacted in a mode of seeming reciprocity: "they knew me well" and "the girls themselves interested me." Jessop's words, however, point to two stories that seem inextricably intertwined in this moment of discovery—one that unfolds in a measured progression of surprise towards the vision of the women revealed at the center, and the other that remains frozen in the "pathetic stories" of destitution narrated by the girls themselves. Furthermore, Jessop's ability to speak their language, and the inability of the girls to speak his, encourages the narrator temporarily to subsume their individual histories under his own orientalist pastoralism. Since the women have no recourse to the master language, their stories can be easily disavowed by Jessop. But this disavowal itself opens up questions about the power of a metropolitan language in fetishizing the "other," and suggests that Jessop's desire to initiate Reynolds into the "life of the East" will necessarily occlude the story that the "East" may have to tell. Furthermore, this moment suggests that if historical circumstances, propelled by colonial rule, had coerced these young women into a life of prostitution, perhaps they could simply be described as "drifting" from the villages to the urban center. Did the "filth"–with its double implication of sexual contamination and destitution–exist prior to colonial rule, or was it produced by it? In what ways did the colonialist "attract" that filth, and how does that "filth" in turn continue to attract these women as well as men like Jessop? At this point in the narrative, these questions can be articulated only in such ambiguous terms precisely because the master language deployed by Jessop to describe Reynolds's initiation is complicit in pushing them beyond the story's margins.

However, it is the power of Jessop's language that provides him with the will and the ability to continue to narrate the tale of the "perverse." Celestinahami, the prostitute (who we are told later had another "name"), becomes simultaneously the object of Reynolds's desire and the object of Jessop's quest. By being deployed to play this role, she is constantly subjected to a form of visibility that is engendered by the narrator's scopic relationship with her figure: "Her skin was the palest of pale gold with a glow in it, very rare in the fair native women" (Woolf [1921] 1963: 260). That physicality, which constructs her innocence in her nakedness, is also made possible by forcing her eyes–and her vision–to yield what the narrator himself desires, reminiscent in every way of the way Kela Bai is visualized by Johnston's narrator. However, that yielding up is registered in uncertain terms in Woolf's story: "Her eyes [were] immense, deep, dark and melancholy which looked *as if* they knew and understood and felt everything in the world" (ibid.; emphasis added). As the possessor of the body upon which the narrator's desiring gaze is directed, Celestinahami presents both the immediate possibility for knowing the "real" in all of its immensity and the necessary illusion that sustains that quest. Therefore, her presence is necessary, but she has also to be emptied of all subjectivity and agency: "He looked into her eyes that *understood nothing* but *seemed to understand everything*, and then it came out at last; the power to feel, the power that so few have, the flame, the passion, love, the *real* thing" (ibid.: 261; emphasis added). Thus Reynolds's initial misrecognition–articulated by Jessop–of Celestinahami's "realness" generates in Reynolds the "power to feel . . . the flame, the passion, love, the 'real' thing," and, in Jessop, the power to enunciate it. This misrecognition occurs as soon as the narrative merges the parallel perspectives of Jessop and Reynolds.

It is clear that this misrecognition is fired by their mutual construction of the woman as both sexually singular, mysteriously silent, without history, and available for the mutual traffic of desire: "She never wore anything colored, just a white cloth wrapped round her waist with one end thrown over the left shoulder. She carried about her an air of slowness and depth and mystery of silence and of innocence" (Woolf [1921] 1963: 260). The "real" thing that appears in this encounter is both the object that is made to signify and the affect produced in the desiring subject, but it also generates another "lack" that produces another deferred desire—the desire to "want *something else*: the same passion, the same fine strong thing that he had felt moving *in himself*" (ibid.: 261). It is clear that male civility is itself inadequate to capture the object of desire: what impels both of the metro-politan subjects is the perceived movement of commodity in exchange—always available to satisfy and re-create desire in its multiplying forms. "Sameness" and "something else" are conjoined in Reynolds's imaginary: his "read[ing] in the depths of her eyes" is simultaneous with Celestinahami's being cast as an object that is looked at—"she *was* what she looked" (ibid.), rendering everything that "was beautiful and great and pure" as part of this lack. What moves him is precisely what is rendered still in the other by his own desiring gaze, a stillness that recalls the objectifying function of the fetish.

It is in this context of the native woman's objectification via the projection of male desire that the story moves into the realm of the logic of the fetish, here seen as an economic force that Marx had identified as a characteristic feature of commodity fetishism. This logic is founded upon the fetishizing spectrality necessary to uphold the colonial white man's power and the power of the colonial state that interpellates him. By asking Reynolds to buy Celestinahami out for twenty rupees and settle down with her in a "little house down the coast on the seashore" (Woolf [1921] 1963: 262), Jessop employs a new economic language to represent the authority of the white man to insert the woman into a system of colonial exchange, and thereby to hold on to his own fantasy of power. As Rosemary Hennessy has commented: "When the commodity is dealt with merely as a matter of signification, meaning, or identities [as Woolf's narrator attempts to do], only one of the elements of production—the process of image-making it relies on—is made visible" (Hennessy 1994–5: 54). In the story, however, that process of pure signification is punctuated by a discourse about money, exchange, and market speculation, which, although part of the verbal exchange between the two friends, relentlessly gestures towards a colonial political economy in which Reynolds is invited to take a "risk." When Reynolds hesitates to act on his desire, Jessop tells him: "But it's no good shooting yourself with that thing. You've got to get on board the next P & O, that's what you've got to do. And if you don't do that, *why practise what you preach and live your life out, and take the risks*" (Woolf [1921] 1963: 262; emphasis added). "Risk" is about desire and the fantasy of future investment: one does not necessarily invest in success—risk is playing the possibility of success. As an item of exchange the native woman is little more than the embodiment of that challenge for colonial men. As soon as he possesses the woman, Reynolds's fortunes take a new turn. Not only does he teach her English, but his own literary energies are refired as he begins to write the long-awaited novel about the East. And even when his disillusionment with the woman sets in, he risks giving her up simply because he can easily reclaim his own freedom through economic reparation by offering her a "generous settlement" of property. Commenting on Reynolds's decision, Jessop says: "How wise, how just, isn't it? The past cannot be immoral; it's done with, wiped out—but the future? Yes, it's only the future that counts" (ibid.: 264). This future, of course, is guaranteed to the white man by the civil authority of the colonial state and its legal mechanisms.

However, in this future what remains for Celestinahami is not abjection (Jessop does not tell us how she responded to Reynolds's decision to leave her), but death, death by her own hands. Celestinahami's action can therefore be seen as a symbolic act of defiance against the entire colonial civil and legal apparatus fashioned in order to secure the privilege of the white man, but it is a defiance obtained through self-annihilation. Her still body, found floating in the sea at the end of the story, "bobbing up and down in her stays and pink skirt and white stocking and shoes" (Woolf [1921] 1963: 264), is a far cry from the orientalist image of native women with "bare feet running and giggles of laughter" (ibid.: 260) evoked at the beginning. At this point in the narrative, she appears in her commodified form, emptied of all pretensions to subjectivity—translated, fixed, fetishized, and irrevocably transformed by Western accoutrements which still cling to her body like a wet doll's dress. Turned into a fetish, she evokes a form of visibility, whose effects resonate with a quiet clarity when one considers Peter Walsh, in *Mrs Dalloway*, looking at his own reflection in the plate glass of a window in metropolitan London. The political power of the fiction of the colonial state embodied in its legal apparatus and agents—the deed, the settlement, law—are thrown into relief by what Michael Taussig calls its fetish spectrality, its "powerful insubstantiality" (Taussig 1993: 219), much like the way in which post-war metropolitan Londoners are shown to be interpellated as phantom citizens and consumers in an industrial, capitalist society.

Both at the metropolitan and the colonial site this insubstantiality conceals the real power of the state—its ability to constitute and regulate the desires of its citizens. In Woolf's colonial story, this power is reflected in the state's ability to incite, direct, and sustain the white man's fantasy of simultaneously being able to take risks and to have his future and liberty secured by the authority conferred on him. The death of the colonial woman is necessarily part of this dynamic: while the heroic image of the dead Percival in *The Waves* is constantly revivified in order to be made more glorious, the dead woman in Woolf's story (whose other name, as I have indicated before, is never revealed) can exist only as a lifeless fetish. However, like the hanged man Woolf had described in his letter to Strachey, Celestinahami's dead body does reveal both the power and the limits of the order of efficiency adopted by the colonial state. The "excess" that had spilled out in the form of the hanged man's blood appears here in Celestinahami's Western accoutrements, which clash with the bucolic scene of lapping waves and coconut trees.

Furthermore, the difference between her image as a "soft little golden-skinned animal" (Woolf [1921] 1963: 261) and that of the bizarre dead body found floating on the waters only heightens the interrelationship between the sexual and the political levels of such fetishization within the context of the disciplinary state. In

Mrs Dalloway, Peter Walsh's pocket knife serves as his fetish object, helping him to maintain his connection with his own masculinity. His civility dictates that he should never openly flash that knife in the face of Clarissa. However, Peter cannot be recuperated into Clarissa's metropolitan world precisely because that fetish object—with its potential power to cut and therefore produce a kind of temporary seeing—is a threatening object for the inhabitants of London (it is enough to have shell-shocked figures such as Septimus Smith throwing themselves out of windows). In the remote colonial world, located thousands of miles away from the metropolitan center, the power of the fiction of that fetish is palpable, but only to the extent to which the dead woman's image can represent that threat in the form of the culminating crisis in Jessop's own narrative of the "real." That this moment could also be an encounter with the powerful fictionality of the state is accentuated by the fact that Jessop's interlocutors dismiss his story as yet another tale of "battle, murder, and sentimentality," concluding, "You're as bad as the rest of them, Jessop" (ibid.: 264).

Is this the kind of response that Woolf expected from his Bloomsbury circle of friends to his own story? Does Jessop trade one set of abstractions about the "real" for the more elusive "story" about the fate of Celestinahami he chooses to tell, only to be dismissed for being "sentimental?" Is Woolf/Jessop's narratorial authority— legitimized as a "teller" of "brutal things"—subject to the same illusionary haze that his metropolitan interlocutors reject while still missing the "real"—the powerful fictionality of the state that is evoked by the story? By attempting to embody that fictionality, Woolf's "A Tale Told by Moonlight" thickens the silvery self-image that Peter Walsh encounters in the metropolitan world of *Mrs Dalloway*. In this story Woolf not only utilizes the subtle tactility that he had admired in Forster, but forces the question of the failure of representation into the domain of colonial ideology, particularly its spectral power to invest metropolitan subjects with their freedom and individuality while blinding them to their own fictionality. Finally, one may extend this idea of the "real" to re-establish the link between metropolitan civility and the orientalist impulse that moves the metropolitan self, revealing how that fantasy is sustained in the metropolis through a denial of its own history.

"Pearls and Swine": civility, labor, and the modern state

In his *India: Impressions and Suggestions*, J. Kier Hardie, the maverick Labour MP who toured the subcontinent in 1907, advanced his own critique of the economic effects of imperialism on colonial India. Referring to the conventional eighteenth-century image of India that associated it with the "unlimited wealth" of "merchant princes," Hardie asserts that, although we "hear less now-a-days about India's great wealth . . . at no period has there ever been such a regular soaking drain upon its people as now" (Hardie 1909: 1). Diagnosing the present ills besetting the country, he attributes their cause to the changes ushered in by colonial administration of property and revenue, observing that before the imposition of British rule "the revenue was not due from individuals but from the community represented by the headman." Structural changes made by Britain within India's political body, he argues, had led to the universalizing of money as a system of exchange, as a result of which the "individual cultivator has to pay his revenue direct, not as collective part of the harvest, but as individual rent . . . paid in coin and not in grain as formerly" (ibid.: xiii). Extending his argument, he alleges that the colonial government was directly responsible for the widespread occurrence of famine by instituting the policy of exporting food grains, and for the religious disaffection that had been created by "new division behind caste and religious communities" (ibid.: xv). Hardie's diagnosis of colonial rule and its impact on the country is throughout patterned on a left critique of imperial economic policies.

Focusing on the system of taxation, for example, Hardie shows how Britain's extractive policies are revealed in the unequal statistics: "The burden upon India— "5% interest on £500000000 to bondholders in Britain. 80% taxes raised by revenue assessment." He then explains the impact of such policies on the taxation of the peasantry that lead to "continuous extortion" (Hardie 1909: 3):

> The amount of taxes raised direct from the peasants from 50% to 65% of the value of the yield of the land; in addition to which they have to pay local cesses . . . so that probably not less than 75% of the harvest goes in taxes. To most people this will seem incomprehensible. A 5% tax on income at home leads to heavy and continuous grumbling; and yet the 5% is assessed not on the total produce of the land, but on the profits; but 75% on the harvest reaped? . . . It is this fact which keeps the people of India in a condition of perpetual, hopeless, grinding poverty.
>
> (ibid.: 2)

Writing in 1920, in *Mandates and Empire*, Leonard Woolf drew upon the spirit of Hardie's polemic in order to highlight the exploitative impact of colonialism in Africa and Asia:

> It is widely recognized that imperialism, with its economic penetration and exploitation and its autocratic government of Africa and Asia, has been accompanied by very serious evils. . . . The Great Powers, when they divided up Africa among them and began the same process in Asia, incorporated enormous stretches of territory in their dominions and claimed and exercised unfettered sovereignty over those territories and their inhabitants. The motives behind this acquisition of territory were economic or strategic. The "subject races" as they are called, had no control over their own Government, and the Government had subordinated the interests of the inhabitants to the economic interests of its European citizens or to the "imperial" strategic and political interests of the mother-country.
>
> (Woolf 1920: 5–6)

Woolf's historical perspective on the emergence of imperialism as a global phenomenon is aimed at tracing its impact on the balance of powers within metropolitan Europe. He also distinguishes between two systems of administrative and economic control that had evolved on the African continent as a result of colonialism—one that had allowed natives to retain their rights over the land by refusing to "alienate it to Europeans," and the other in which they had been completely deprived of their legal rights over land as a result of its being alienated to "white settlers or to European joint-stock companies" (ibid.: 9). Woolf's critiques of imperialism may also have been shaped by his relations with the two Fabian socialists Beatrice and Sidney Webb, who are said to have "discovered" Woolf through the article he wrote for the *New Statesman* in 1914, and who were responsible for his entry into labor politics (see Woolf 1989: 583). Both Beatrice and Sidney Webb had toured India in the early years of the century. In the years after his return from colonial Ceylon, Woolf ruminated about economic imperialism with the acute awareness of its present "reality." As he states in *Imperialism and Civilization* (1928), "imperialism is a *real thing*," adding that it is a "menacing movement which has developed a political philosophy peculiar to itself and has caused great political, economic, and social upheavals all over the world" (Woolf 1928: 30; emphasis added). The use of the present tense evokes a sense of urgency about colonialism's power that he sees as being consolidated through a "political philosophy" whose world-wide impact was based on a rationality rooted in European civilization. Perhaps the most compelling expression of that rationality is to be found in Woolf's story "Pearls and Swine"—a story that evokes the phantasmatic power of the disciplinary colonial state in regulating labor among the pearl divers and in constituting a racial imaginary that established the very conditions for the production of value through that labor. By situating a white bureaucratic individual at the heart of this experience narrated in the story, Woolf calls into question the legitimacy of a metropolitan civility that both gives assent to that disciplining body and constitutes its chief functional cadre.

The story is set in a fictional landscape among the pearl fisheries of southern India. The action centers on the story of a "little Anglo-Indian" (Woolf [1921] 1963: 268), a returned civil servant who had been in charge of supervising the pearl fisheries. The man relates his experiences as an observer and participant in the work of the pearl divers to his metropolitan interlocutors, who all claim to have their views on the so-called Eastern question. What distinguishes this story's rendition of the "Eastern formula" (ibid.: 265) from the critiques of imperialism that Woolf authored in the 1920s is the former's complex dramatization of the actual fashioning of the phantasmatic power of the colonial state. At the beginning, Woolf presents a chorus of voices belonging to the old India-hands, representing all of the standard political positions on the empire, but soon the story focuses on the single narrator's point of view, one that gestures towards the formation not only of an authorizing consciousness but also the effects of power exercised by the modern colonial state. However, in her discussion of "Pearls and Swine," Elleke Boehmer does not discern any political meaning in the story, claiming that Woolf casts his narrative as an exotic oriental tale that depends on the romanticization of the native. As I have suggested in my analysis of "A Tale Told by Moonlight," the story "Pearls and Swine" presents the unassimilable form of the fragment, as opposed to "official" narrative, as a way to narrate the violence that lurks within the spectral fictionality of the colonial state. It is the very fictionality that Woolf later describes as the powerful "real thing" that emerges from European political philosophies and takes the form of imperialism.

In "A Tale Told by Moonlight," Woolf's narrator gestures towards that spectral fictionality by breaking off the narrative with the image of the colonized body, one that is represented as being transformed and ultimately destroyed by the violence of colonial traffic. Within its narrative, then, Celestinahami's "life" and "death" remain as markers of an itinerary of colonial traffic, one that is enabled by securing the primacy of the colonial man's freedom to make a "choice" and to take a "risk" in securing a future for himself. In "Pearls and Swine" Woolf returns to this theme by delineating the spectacle of colonial labor as a site of the disciplinary regime of the colonial state, and not as a simple tableau of dignified labor, as Boehmer has argued. In this story he presents two dead bodies—one that of the white man (referred to as Mr. White) and the other that of the Arab pearl diver. While Mr. White dies of a contagion caused by the tropical disease infesting the fisheries, the diver meets his death in the depths of the ocean. In juxtaposing these two deaths, "Pearls and Swine" serves as an allegory of the political economy of the colonial state that opens up the very limits that constitute the colonial desire for extraction and accumulation in the name of "freedom." In short, while Mr. White's death represents the demise of the fantasy of unlimited colonial exploits, that of the native diver represents the victimization of the worker that is necessary in order to uphold that fantasy.

In January of 1906 Leonard Woolf was appointed superintendent to the pearl fishery in the coastal village of Marichchukkaddi, where he was put in charge of supervising the divers of the famous Ceylon pearls. On March 21, he wrote to Strachey:

> I sometimes wonder whether I shall commit suicide before the six years are up . . . Depression is becoming, I believe, the mania with me . . . You don't know what it is to be, as I am now, so tired at 10 p.m. that every muscle in your body seems to be felt & to know that you have to keep awake until 2:30 a.m., only to begin another day of the same sort at half past seven. And then there are flies—they are bred in the millions of rotting oysters that lie about the camp. All day long they fly about in clouds, hundreds & hundreds swarming over every-thing: not a scrap of food can be left uncovered for a second without becoming black with them. They infect the food in some foul way, for all day long I feel horribly sick & many people are actually sick four or five times regularly a day. They are crawling over one's face & hands all day long & owing to the putrid filth on which they feed every little scratch or spot becomes sore . . . Can I write to you about Duncan or Society out of this?
>
> (Woolf 1989: 115)

Faced with the raw immediacy of his own experience as a supervisor of the pearl fisheries, and with the real possibility of his own mental breakdown (which seemed inevitable in the face of the infection and illness he saw all around), Woolf communicated his thoughts of torment about the vast chasm he sensed between his own world and that of his friend at home, Lytton Strachey. In the letter, the "real" had once again invaded his mental world, but in a manner that seemed essentially incommunicable since the world he currently inhabited presented such a different image of life and labor to what he imagined Strachey experienced in the metropolis. As a man committed to the state-ordained principles of efficiency, order, and hard work, Woolf had been totally unprepared for the kind of toll the supervisory job would take on his mental and emotional life. In an earlier letter, written on January 28, 1906, he had likened his job to that of the laboring "cooly":

> It is merely cooly work supervising this & the counting & issuing of about one or two million oysters a day, for the Arabs will do anything if you hit them hard enough with a walking stick, an occupation in which I have been engaged for the most part of the last 3 days & nights.
>
> (ibid.: 114)

Here Woolf envisioned his job in paradoxical terms, likening it to that of a manual laborer while simultaneously asserting his own mastery over the work-force he had been supervising. Leonard Woolf's contradictory identification with the workers is based on an imaginary alignment, which, as Kaja Silverman notes in discussing T. E. Lawrence's relationship with the Arabs, was "facilitated not only by the intimacy of his working relationship with them, but also by the fact that they are displayed for him within a literal and metaphorical tableau which conforms to his fantasmatic" (Silverman 1992: 337). This personal "fantasmatic" corresponds, in the story, to a type of scenographic tableau that is structurally ordered in terms of the requirements of a colonial economy based on the extraction of value from laboring bodies. Within the microcosmic world of the pearl fisheries, the conditions of proximity to, and visibility of, colonial labor were necessary not only for envisioning such labor as a source of value but also for producing and maintaining the colonial racial divide. Correspondingly, the singular identity of the white man in charge of the system of extraction is simultaneously produced and threatened by the heterogeneity of racial identification of the native divers, itself necessary for the distribution and deployment of labor. Given this scenario, the story is often charged with an abiding sense of "degradation," a word that Woolf obsessively repeats in his letters to Strachey (1905–9). Keeping "Pearls and Swine" in view, I will argue that the sense of personal degradation intimated in the letters assumes a wider political meaning in the story—it not only signifies the vulnerable boundaries between the civil self of the colonizer and the governed bodies of colonized labor, but also relates civility to the workings of the state and the logic of bureaucratic labor (represented by Woolf himself as he describes his duties as being those of a "policeman, magistrate, judge, & publican"; Woolf 1989: 141).

For nearly half a century, the civil service that Woolf joined in 1904 had remained largely unchanged in the crown colony of Ceylon. British rule was still maintained by a small majority of white men—mostly British assistant government agents in charge of the districts and the government agents in charge of the provinces, whose authority rested on the power to make on the spot decisions without being directly responsible to the headquarters in Colombo. The hierarchy of power was itself patterned on a feudal system inherited from the Sinhalese kings, in which the British civil servants employed Sinhalese to manage local affairs (Wilson [1978] 2003: 31–2). Thus, in significant ways Ceylon's administration, unlike that of the rest of the Indian subcontinent, still remained unchanged. Solely responsible for the management of entire districts—whether it involved serving as overseer of the pearl fishery or acting as magistrate and policeman— Woolf constantly evokes the rigor of his own labor in his letters to Strachey and the effects it has on him. From administering the new laws of salt collection to controlling the rinderpest epidemic in 1910, from working on new irrigation projects and the maintenance of schools and hospitals to regulating the cut and burn practices of "chena" cultivation, Woolf found himself both serving the economic interests of the government and arguing for the need to prevent the gradual extinction of local agricultural practices perceived as harmful by the government. His letters often allowed him the opportunity to exchange with Strachey ideas about what it meant for the colonizer and the colonized to be laboring, living, and desiring subjects; how his own middle-class aspirations for social mobility had been channeled as bureaucratic labor into the service of maintaining the principles of civil society based on a paternalistic colonial order; how the clockwork timing of work and the knowledge of native character and racial difference, central to the ideas of change and efficiency, also designated a desire to exploit an unequal system of exchange, enabling the extraction of surplus; and how that work tested the limits of "experience" and of "reality," as they had been philosophically conceived in the rarified air of the metropolis.

By setting his own labor as a supervisor against the working bodies of the colonized, Woolf described the effects of surveillance on the consciousness of the colonizer. Writing to Strachey, he had once confessed:

> I get your moments sometimes when nothing seems to matter & I suppose that most of the time we, or I at any rate, are passively inert to happiness or unhappiness. I mean that we are so persistently automatic that most of the day is a trance. When I do think or feel, it is usually with rage or despair. Don't you feel often or always that there is so little time to lose, & that we are losing it so fast.
>
> (Woolf 1989: 77)

The suspension of consciousness is symptomatic of the troubled relationship between his own labor and the affect produced by it, one that is recurrently described in ambivalent terms. For example, he says that his work became an obsession that aided him in warding off his own impending madness and that the experience of resting from work was like "gliding into the vegetable state of the East" (ibid.: 120). The instability of the "psychic sphere" is registered at the level of the body of the colonizer that is seen to be threatened by cessation from work, although it is the same work that makes him "half-dead from weariness and want of sleep" (ibid.: 114). This paradoxical encounter with the laboring body lies at the heart of "Pearls and Swine," written after Woolf's return to England in 1911 in the secure environment of the metropolis. This story also represents an effort on Woolf's part to narrativize that encounter in terms of his personal contradictory engagement with his own labor and the labor extracted from the bodies he supervised. By being placed at the remote colonial site of the fisheries, the narrative penetrates the heart of the "real," represented by the scene of extraction— that of precious pearls from the flesh of the oysters fished from the very depths of the ocean that lapped on the edges of colonial *terra firma*.

As in "A Tale Told by Moonlight," this story initially organizes itself through multiply embedded narrative frames and narrators before the actual story can be presented. The primary narrator—the "I"—an ex-colonial, is described as being in the company of three interlocutors—a retired colonel, a stock-jobber, and a clergyman with a missionary background, a group that is later joined by the "Anglo-Indian man." We are told that this man had served as a superintendent overseeing the pearl fisheries in south India. It is the narrative of the latter, the Woolfean alter-ego, that forms the core of the story that is recounted by the primary narrator, the "I." The Anglo-Indian's assistant, Robson, described as "a little boy of twenty four fresh-cheeked from England," who had "passed the Civil Service 'Exam'" (Woolf [1921] 1963: 270), serves as yet another authorial persona, although he does not narrate any part of the story. This form of narrative embeddedness—with multiple personas refracting different facets of Woolf's own experience—can, of course, be interpreted as an attempt on Woolf's part to secure a distance from the raw immediacy of his own experiences as recorded in his letters, so that the "real" could be explored by partially surrendering the experential self to these multiply-narrated (and narrating) selves. This is initially achieved through the separation of the two narrators, both of whom are united by a common colonial history, and through the iteration of the distance between the metropolitan setting, from where the story is narrated, and the colonial site where it is originally located.

However, the link between the fetishization of body, labor, and power begins to emerge as soon as the story moves into the colonial scene. The primary (unnamed) narrator's claims to possess a superior understanding of India is based on an orientalist trope utilized earlier in "A Tale Told by Moonlight": knowledge of the colony is figured as an ability to access the core of the East through the body of the colonized woman: "They hadn't been there . . . they hadn't even seen the brothel and cafe chantant at Port Said suddenly open out into that pink and blue desert that leads you through Africa and Asia into the heart of the East" (Woolf [1921] 1963: 266). This coupling of the sexual with knowledge of the "heart of the East" is reminiscent of Jessop's own narrative impulse for "fishing things out of life" (ibid.: 255). Just as Celestinahami's body provided the site for unraveling the elusive operations of desire in relation to the "real," the brothel here is imagined as a space of entry into "the real" that lies beyond the metropolitan frame. Similarly, the second narrator, the Anglo-Indian man, presents Robson, his young assistant, as a spokesperson for liberal philosophy and the self-assured belief in scientific rationality and progressive social engineering. As a product of metropolitan board school education, Robson sees the empire as a vast crucible for social experimentation (ibid.: 272). Robson's views, as I will argue later, reflect an ethos of scientific management that had provided the economic and political basis for imperialism in the new century, and which was to find support from capitalist industrial interests operating in far corners of the globe, who all claimed to be intimately familiar with local affairs. Furthermore, the use of scientific knowledge as the basis for moving the colony into a new progressive era meant greater access to its resources and its laboring masses, and to more efficient systems of extraction.

Once the main actors have been located, "Pearls and Swine" begins to track the political and psychic effects of extracting the pearl from the core of the oyster—a task that thrusts the norms of colonial civility, modern industrial rationality, and management of work, as well as the security of colonial knowledge, to those very limits that had been called on to consolidate the colonial divide. The pearl fishery industry has had a long history, which is recalled in quasi-mythic language:

> They were doing it centuries and centuries before we came, when—as someone said—our ancestors were herding swine on the plains of Norway. The Arabs of the Persian Gulf came down in dhows and fished up pearls that made their way to Solomon and the Queen of Sheba. They still come, and the Tamils and the Moormen of the district come, and they fish 'em up in the same way, diving out of long wooden boats shaped and rigged as in Solomon's time, as they were centuries before him and the Queen of Sheba.
>
> (Woolf [1921] 1963: 270)

At the turn of the century, when Woolf was put in charge of Marichchukkaddi, the industry came under the renewed scrutiny of the British authorities.[10] Its economic viability was evident, although doubts were raised as to whether the operations were being carried out with maximum efficiency. Invariably this meant looking to experts—marine biologists, owners of companies, and civil bureaucrats—for the reorganization of the industry, achieved by introducing new norms of scientifically authorized forms of surveillance and by recodifying the bodies of divers in order to comprehend the link between racial types and extraction of maximum value from their work. The work of the expert—embodied by Robson—is anchored in an understanding of modern "biopower"—that is by constituting the colonial people as a laboring population. Consistent with Foucault's account of "biopower," statistical and ethnographic records of different ethnicities of the divers, their nationalities, and racial forms provide the categories through which the work of diving for, and collecting, the pearls is instituted. In "Governmentality," Foucault has shown how the individualizing and totalizing modalities of power define what David Owen calls the "parameters of modern political reason" (Owen 1994: 188). In the colonial context of this story, these modalities of power are shown to be related to the economic government of the colony and the moral government of the bureaucratic self, the latter signified by the narrator's constant questioning of the ethical role of the colonial administrator.

The site where the operations of this modern political reason are most visible is of course the pearl fishery located in the colony. One of the earliest accounts in the twentieth century of the growth and consolidation of the pearl fishery as an important economic endeavor is to be found in James Hornell's 1907 *Report on the Operations on the Ceylon Pearl Banks*. Hornell, a manager and marine biologist, refers to the enormously intimidating task of surveillance of the working bodies to prevent theft:

> This task is one of the most wearisome I know, as it is one that requires constant personal oversight if theft, with constant vitiation of results, is to be avoided. From 7 a.m. to 5 p.m., one has to sit over a trough full of decayed oysters in process of being washed by the coolies, or else keep ward over the cloths on which the oyster washings are laid out to dry in the broiling sun.
>
> (Hornell 1907: 7)

The need to replace this form of wearisome surveillance with a more "modern" system is reiterated by the principal owner of the Burma Shell Company, John I. Solomon. Solomon refers to the losses incurred by an inefficient system of surveillance by reminding his readers that the "final nett profits accruing to them as a result of a fishery represent but a tithe of the actual value of pearls which are contained in the oysters which grow on the pearls banks of Ceylon" (Solomon 1914: 2). Like Hornell and Solomon, Sir West Ridgeway acknowledges that the "pearl fisheries in the gulf of Mannar have been for centuries a lucrative source of revenue to the Government of this Island" (Ridgeway 1903: 111), but is emphatic about the defective method of fishing and washing, which he claims "is an excellent type of Eastern organization, but is hardly suited to modern conditions." To him the main defect is that:

> under the old system an undue proportion of the profits of the fishery accrues, directly or indirectly, to the divers and, more especially, to the merchants, as compared with the Government share. These defects would all be cured by the substitution of a new system under which the whole of the operations— both the dredging of the oysters and the extraction of the pearls—would be conducted by the Government with a much smaller number of labourers in its own employ.
>
> (ibid.: 114)

Hornell's suggestions for improving the efficiency is to "raze the old edifice," by limiting the size of the diving fleet, landing the day's catch in sealed bags instead of in bundles, and remodeling the store (Hornell 1907: 12–13). Solomon's recommendations include, in addition to Hornell's, reducing and streamlining labor, ensuring that the bulk of the work is done by local Sinhalese and not "foreigners" who are "not British subjects" (Solomon 1914: 7), and investigating the possibility of radiographing pearl oysters, a new and relatively undeveloped scientific technology at that time.

The attention drawn to ethnic and racial categories among the workers is closely linked to the details about the working bodies found in Hornell's *The Biological Results of the Ceylon Pearl Fishery of 1904 with Notes on Divers and their Occupation* (1905). His description of the process of washing the oysters after they have rotted illustrates not only the system of surveillance set in place to observe the details of the work in order to prevent theft, but also a scrutinizing gaze aimed at specific bodies that could ensure greater efficiency in the extraction of value:

> After the oysters are rotted, it is time to wash them. The covers are removed from the ballam and coolies fill it to the brim with water. . . . The washers range themselves in line along either side, squatting on anything convenient. They are stripped to the loin cloth, and are not allowed to take their hands out of the water save to drop out the empty shells, rinsing the shells, separating the valves, and rubbing the outside of one valve against the other to remove any detritus in which a pearl might lodge.
>
> (Hornell 1905: 30)

The process of identifying and collecting the pearls ends only when the shells of the oysters are removed, and the "men stand up and stretch their cramped limbs" (ibid.), and the "final search," Hornell continues, is carried out by children and women. He remarks: "it is amazing to see what a large quantity of small pearls their keen eyes and fine touch enable them to obtain, chiefly by winnowing" (ibid.). The range of visibility offered by this form of surveillance on workers who are literally tethered to the work compares in some degree to the observation of the tactile abilities of women and children who harvest the pearls that escape the normal eye. Furthermore, this form of visibility depended on a biological reasoning to ensure a productive division of labor: women's and children's bodies were regarded as being most conducive to work that ensured the maximum extraction of value, while the racialized bodies of the divers provided a greater knowledge to the colonialist for ensuring the greatest security and efficiency in the harvesting of oysters. Hornell categorizes the major "racial types"–coastal Tamils, Moormen drafted from villages on the Madura coast, Malayalam men from the Travancore coast, and so-called Arabs from Colombo and Jaffna (ibid.: 31)–in terms of their physical and moral attributes, claiming that, while the behavior of the Arabs and Moormen were "generally excellent"–they "worked energetically without complaining even in the rough weather"–the Tuticorun Parawa divers engaged in "purposeless sailing about" in order to "mask and give opportunity for wholesale and illicit opening of oysters for the purpose of extracting the best pearls" (ibid.: 33). Following Foucault's line of reasoning in "Governmentality," it is clear that, by constituting the working population as both *subject* (with known and unknown motives) and *object* of government, a political rationality is circumscribed that has an essentially disciplinary function.

The power as well as the vulnerability of the disciplinary regime is signaled by the continuous call for renewed surveillance in the face of "deception." In "Pearls and Swine," this shadow of deception enters through the story of Mr. White, the itinerant planter and pearl merchant who the narrator describes as drifting one day out of the blue into the fishing village. A great talker, he is the picture of self-confident posturing of an empire builder, but soon he is racked with delusions and pain after his first attack of "D.T." Tied to the pole on the beach to prevent him from harming himself the hallucinating Mr. White serves as an extreme image of colonial delusion, as his paranoia rips apart the structure of colonial surveillance, including the thin line separating the surveyer and surveyed, the visible and the invisible.

But before that can happen, the narrator evokes the vast land and seascape that surrounds Mr. White and the pearl fishery. Gesturing spatially towards those surfaces and depths that reflect the uncertain structure of visibility and invisibility built around them, the narrator also provides the most dramatic scenographic representation of biopower—with its production of the "truth" about native bodies and the systems of surveillance deployed to regulate them, its management of health, sanitation, and civil design, and its control over the processes of economic extraction and accumulation.[11] After describing the location of the fisheries and the population of the divers in the area, the narrator depicts the surrounding land-scape as a vision that operates between an expansive order of visibility and invisibility, evoking a form of spatiality against which he can identify the tiny pearl that lies embedded in the oyster:

> Well, Providence had so designed it that there was a stretch of coast in that district which was a barren wilderness of sand and scrubby thorn jungle—and nothing else—for three hundred miles; no towns, no villages, no water, just sand and trees for three hundred miles. O, and sun, I forget that, blazing sun. And in the water off the shore at one place there were oysters, millions of them lying and breeding at the bottom, four or five fathoms deep down. And in the oysters, or some of them, were pearls.
>
> (Woolf [1921] 1963: 269)

Although the working bodies of the natives are significantly absent, the scene metonymically links the ownership of the gaze to the extraction of pearls harvested from this expanse: "Well, we rule India and the sea, so the sea belongs to us, and oysters are in the sea and the pearls are in the oysters. Therefore of course the pearls belong to us" (ibid.).

However, this direct and unmediated link between the gaze and the "com-modity" made visible by the gaze is hampered by the awareness that the process of extraction and accumulation involves an "immense gamble" (ibid.: 270). This sets the body of the colonial master against the multiplicity of racialized bodies of colonial subjects produced by the system of knowledge—those of "Tamils, Telegus, fat Chetties, Parsees, Bombay merchants, Sinhalese from Ceylon, the Arabs and their negroes, Somalis." Although the government claims "its share of two-thirds of all the oysters fished up" (ibid.), the risks involved in this gamble range from the government superintendent having to discern among the various claims to the ownership and distribution of the pearls to the prevention of "Known

Depredators"—"small pox and cholera"—to maintaining order and sanitation in a town that had "[sprung] up in a night" to accommodate the swarming masses of people. As part of the fantasy of pure extraction, this risk, like Reynolds's desire in "A Tale," is also about the willingness to participate in the play of possibilities, in the game—as it were—of life and death, often evoked through the phantasmagoric images of disease, rotting oysters, maggots feeding and reproducing in the flesh of the oysters, and of shining pearls extracted from the core of these rotting oysters.

Although both human bodies at work—of divers and cleaners—and the swarming flies and maggots feeding on the rotting oysters are captured through a singular vision of the empire extending beyond the land into the ocean, this vision soon begins to be threatened by the enormity of the task. Behind the frenzied activity is the specter of death: "He [Robson] saw men die—he hadn't seen that in his Board School—die of plague and cholera, like flies, all over the place, under the trees, in the boats, outside the door of his own hut" (Woolf [1921] 1963: 270). The dizzying interplay of life and death is further accentuated by the sense of putrefaction and the unmitigated feeding frenzy of the maggots, which conveys not only the raw power of colonial accumulation, but also the accompanying consumption of bodies that produces the clear visibility of the pearl, the object that is the end-product of the process of extraction. The fantasy of pure extraction, earlier conveyed by the narrator, is here coded across the image of the laboring body, pushing *beyond* the turmoil, death, and putrefaction: "Why is it allowed? The pearls, you see, the pearls: you must get them out of the oysters as you must get the oysters out of the sea" (ibid.: 270–1). In this sense, the fantasy of pure visibility also asserts the intrinsic simplicity behind the process of extraction:

> They rot very well in that sun, and the flies come and lay eggs in them, and the maggots come out of the eggs and more flies come out of the maggots, and between them all, the maggots and the sun, the oysters' bodies disappear, leaving the pearls and a little sand at the bottom of the canoe.
>
> (ibid.: 271)

The gaze is seen to have direct access to the heart of that which constitutes value: as the bodies of the flies reproduce, they feed on the oysters, leaving them with bare shells, from which the deft hands of men, women, and children reap the precious pearl. In short, what yields the pearl is both the gaze of surveillance and the labor of working bodies, with the former subsuming the latter.[12]

In the pearl fishery, bureaucratic work lay mainly in the acts of observing and monitoring the bodies of these working men. Time stretches out in this kind of work, creating a sense of ennui: as the narrator says, "forty eight hours at a stretch doesn't leave one much time or inclination for thinking,—waiting for things to happen" (Woolf [1921] 1963: 275). The other action occurs in the story as the narrator observes

> the dark shadows, which lay like dead men about the boats, would leap into life—there would be a sudden din of hoarse voices, shouting, calling,

quarrelling. The boats swarmed with shadows running about, gesticulating, staggering under sacks of oysters, dropping one after the other over the boats' sides into the sea.

(ibid.: 277)

In March of 1906, when Woolf described in his letter to Strachey his physical and mental condition after a day of supervision spent among hundreds of swarming flies and men toiling in their boats, he was able to perceive the link between the bodies of men exhausted by labor and the oysters consumed by the maggots and flies. What happens in this period of "waiting" in "Pearls and Swine" is the sudden reversal in Mr. White's self-assured stance. The narrative juxtaposes and contrasts two different kinds of spectacle—that of the hallucinating Mr. White and that of the divers in their particularly visible inactivity. The very embodiment of the spirit of colonial enterprise, Mr. White is consumed in slow degrees by the precise object on which he had set his eyes—the valuable pearl. Tied to the pole, where he comes to occupy the center of the divers' gazes, he becomes a spectacle for them:

They gathered about him, stared at him. The light of the flares fell on their dark faces, shining and dripping from the sea. They looked calm, impassive, stern. It shone too on the circle of the eyes: one saw the whites of them all round him: they seemed to be judging him, weighing him: calm patient eyes of men who watched unastonished the procession of things.

(ibid.)

The very man who had "talked a great deal about the hidden wealth of India and exploitation," and who had said that he "would work for the good of the native" (ibid.: 273), is himself immobilized by his own delusional fever.

Figures who had appeared as anonymous bodies in Hornell's statistical accounts of native workers suddenly acquire specific features that threaten to overcome the singularity of Mr. White's racial identity:

The Tamils' squat black figures nearly naked watched him silently, almost carelessly. The Arabs in their long, dirty night-shirts, black-bearded, discussed him earnestly together with their guttural voices. Only an enormous negro, towering up to six feet at least above the crowd, dressed in sacks and an enormous ulster, with ten copper coffee pots slung over his back and a pipe made of a whole coconut with an iron tube stuck in it in his hand, stood smiling mysteriously.

(Woolf [1921] 1963: 277–8)

Is this another version of the spectacle of oriental barbarism embodying all of the hidden fears that coalesced and gave shape to colonial anxiety in numerous other colonial narratives, or is it the flip side of the very disciplinary regime founded on colonial biopower? Do the figures evoke Conrad's shadowy forms or are they animated in their inactivity by the very force that harnesses their labor for profit? What is clear is that, faced with these spectacles, the narrator describes himself as retreating to his position as a mere recorder of events, one who continues to "write his report" in the midst of the unfolding scene of Mr. White's madness. That self-imposed equipoise—signified by the act of reporting—is soon disrupted when he confronts the lifeless body of the Arab diver brought up to the shore. The man, the narrator states, had "lived, worked and died" (ibid.: 278). However, this quiet acknowledgment of the labor of the diver is followed by an image of his lifeless body brought up to the shore, repeating the description of the naked dead woman that Woolf had recorded in his letter to Strachey (Woolf 1989: 141). In both of these descriptions, the toes are described as "pointing up, very stark" (Woolf [1921] 1963: 278). Unlike Mr. White, who dies in the midst of putrefaction, the dead Arab's body is concretely located at the site of life and labor. While the narrator has to move away immediately to "make arrangements for White's funeral," the effect of the diver's death on his fellow workers is signified by the mournful words of the Arab sheikh who presides over the funeral— "Khallas"—"all is over, finished." This solemn ceremonial scene, repeated almost verbatim from his letter to Strachey of March 4, 1906, can be read as an attempt on the part of the narrator to counter the finality of the word "Khallas," but it is through the repeated echoes of that word that the narrative enacts its own reiteration of memory as well as its own impossibility. If the word signifies the end of a life, it also marks the interrupted moment in the narrative—signifying a "nothing beyond what is"—when the archdeacon says, "It's too late, I think. . . . Don't you think you've chosen rather exceptional circumstances, out of the *ordinary* case?" (ibid.: 279; emphasis added).

The narration of this link between the colonial and metropolitan worlds unites "A Tale Told by Moonlight" and "Pearls and Swine" through a common concern with the disciplinary modes of the modern civil state. They both point towards the relationship between the objectifying and reifying discourses of colonialism as it mediates the power relations between these two domains and gives metropolitan civility its functional authority. If Woolf represents this relationship through a narrative of crisis that eludes the "real" story, the interruptions contained in the stories only magnify and highlight the conditions within which civil authority evokes and maintains modern forms of metropolitan subjectivity.

Conclusion
Civil conduct

> Colonialist discourse does not simply announce a triumph for civility, it must continually produce it, and this work involves struggle and risk.
>
> Paul Brown, "This Thing of Darkness" (1985)

Civility operated on identities in changing historical and material contexts by marking them as normative subjects of race, gender, class, and nation. It also allowed the relational links between these categories to be subjected to a form of rationality that has been called the "governing-effects on colonial conduct" (Scott 1995: 204). Repeatedly our attention is brought to bear on the centrality of this notion of conduct, a notion that made civility a contested site of making and unmaking, and a differential node from which imperial culture both registered and worked out its narratives of identity and alterity. In fact, throughout the nineteenth and twentieth centuries the historical exigencies facing the modern state provided the necessary forms of incitement and interdiction through which conduct became the defining structure for the establishment of identity. Whether it is the mercantile agent of empire, the *baboo*, the soldier, the imperial magistrate, the *nautch* girl, the missionary, the native convert, or the colonial supervisor, the emphasis on their "conduct" is inescapably visible in the history I have attempted to chart. In fact, the essential historicity of civility is made visible in the kind of work that is performed to sustain the dynamic set in place by conduct, folding together varying discourses that relate to questions about law, inheritance, nationhood, and class.

In chapter 2, I argued that this historicity operates through a specific negotiation of the relationship between the metropolitan self and colonial governance, and between the private–public dichotomy that is found in John Stuart Mill's liberalism. As Mill's colonial writings demonstrate, this negotiated relationship manifests the normalizing power of civility and its ability to consolidate the patriarchal authority of the modern liberal state in the colonial era, which is exemplified by the liberal philosopher's ongoing preoccupation with conduct and imperial governance. Therefore, Mill's salvific possibilities for new political and radical states of being can be considered only in relation to a form of civility underwritten by the colonial legacies of government and the familial lineages of control. As manifested in the representation of the *baboo*, these authorizing lineages are consolidated on the colonial site through the deployment of liberal ideas about education, family, inheritance, and legacy, which in turn required the normalization of specific ethnic, racial, and national identities. In this concluding chapter, I wish to pursue the questions raised earlier in the study by suggesting that this historicity of civility is also intimately tied to the creation of new sites *within* the metropolis that opened up supplementary boundaries of conduct over which civility could perform its work of normalization. My objective here is to reiterate the manner in which the discourses of civility were aimed at setting up and testing these supplementary limits within the metropolis, boundaries across which citizenship, gender, class, and nationality could be reidentified, linked, and instituted. As I will demonstrate through my examples, this necessitated making available and objectifying colonial bodies and objects within the metropolitan site in ways that enabled certain forms of visibility to perform the narrative rituals tied to the "governing effects of colonial conduct." My examples are taken from two very different texts set in metropolitan Britain–D. H. Lawrence's *Women in Love* (1920) and F. Anstey's *Baboo Jabberjee* (1897).

Lawrence's study of the crisis of the modern industrial state in *Women in Love*, as exemplified in his delineation of the dominant subjectivity of the "industrial magnate," is a symptomatic scrutiny of the pathological power of the modern system of bourgeois patriarchy, ownership, and organizational management. Into this scenario–one that is already imbricated in questions of governance–Lawrence introduces two specific "objects" drawn from the colonial orbit and placed within the familiar site of the bourgeois living room–the "Hindu" manservant and the West African wood-carving of the naked woman. While the manservant is presented in his "borrowed" clothes obediently serving the master, the African statue is constructed as a "strange and disturbing" object whose strange power immediately draws the attention of Gerald, who reads it as "conveying the suggestion of the extreme of physical sensation, beyond the limits of mental consciousness" (Lawrence [1920] 1987: 74). In their respective ways, both of these colonial bodies are represented as things that point beyond what is immediately palpable or graspable to the metropolitan consciousness, indicating a site beyond its safe boundaries.

Anstey's *Baboo Jabberjee*, on the other hand, is a piece of journalistic satire written for the purpose of unmasking the cultural pretensions of a university-educated Bengali *baboo* visiting the imperial metropolis. Although the book's satire is directed primarily at the figure of the *baboo* represented by Kipling in *Kim*, it also forces its metropolitan readers to revisit the familiar sites of imperial culture (the "shrine of Shakespeare"), as well as the metropolitan public sphere ("the Ladies' Debating Club" and the university), the judiciary (the English court), and the government (the "India Office") from the point of view of the marginalized colonized subject. This double movement, barely visible in Kipling's *Kim*, opens up the struggle within the metropolis to establish a singular rationality for civility, indirectly pointing to civility's function as a dually organized normalizing force. Therefore, despite the apparent differences between the two texts, they appear to be united in one common preoccupation—that is, they are both concerned with the shifting ethos of metropolitan civility, especially with the ways in which the metropolitan investment in cultural capital often involved developing strategies for managing its own contradictory demands for coherence. Both suggest that, for the metropolitan subject, the engagement with civility stems from a form of desire constituted through opposition—between the ostensible fixity of the norm and its operational maneuverability—an opposition that is played out and managed in strategic ways throughout these two texts.

As *Women in Love* and *Baboo Jabberjee* indicate, such a stake essentially involves an ideological struggle that simultaneously reinforces and exposes the operations of the metropolitan will to be subject to the imperatives of civility. Irrespective of whether they are articulated in the form of a crisis of "civilization" and of masculinity, or as effects of a class-defined organizational order, these imperatives are shown to be defined by the boundaries that can be rendered visible—both within the private space of the metropolitan living room or the public space of the English court house. Furthermore, and perhaps more significantly, the struggle enacted at these boundaries' simultaneity gestures towards civility's links with cultural capital in a manner that opens up, once again, the forms of surveillance under which colonial conduct operated. Early in the novel *Women in Love*, Lawrence describes a scene in London where four of his male metropolitan protagonists, Halliday, Gerald, Birkin, and Maxim, are met at the door of Halliday's apartment by an exotic-looking manservant who is described first as a "Hindu" and later as an "Arab." As the manservant busies himself serving the men, he is constantly subject to their scrutinizing gazes. His closely guarded "reticence" and physically marked nobility, accentuated by his "tall and slender" figure (which Gerald finds rather attractive), set him up as an inscrutable oriental fantasy figure. That inscrutability is, however, produced through a sustained discursive incitement: although the man performs the normal functions of an attending servant, Gerald's first impression on seeing him is that he could be a "gentleman, one of the Hindus down from Oxford," an impression that is quickly dispelled by his host, who tells him that the man was no more than a mere destitute who had been rescued from the streets and offered shelter and clothing by his benefactor, Halliday. Clarifying that he was "anything but what he seems to be" (Lawrence [1920] 1987: 73), Halliday adds that the man's attractive demeanor had more to do with the borrowed clothes that Halliday had so generously given him than on any intrinsic trait. In this short exchange, it becomes clear that Gerald's uncertain reading of the man and Halliday's clarification of that reading are attempts to locate a fixed site for the colonized subject. Interestingly, his "clothing" serves an important function in these multiple readings, providing the clues to work on the perceived disjunction between his outer self and his real identity.

Serving as an external marker of his identity as a strangely hybrid figure, the man's Western clothing continues to incite Gerald, whose gaze pursues him throughout this short scene. Moving from his visible body to the clothes that, in a sense, conceal that body, Gerald's gaze performs a kind of surveillance through a shifting structure of visibility and invisibility. This act of constant surveillance ultimately constructs the man as an erotically produced "enigma," and, working through this shifting structure of visibility and invisibility, Gerald's gaze produces a mysterious core for the laboring colonial subject. In short, civility works through that elusiveness of desire and power, and this scene exemplifies and marks a special moment in the construction of civility at the very heart of the metropolitan society where the master–servant structure has already been instituted. That elusiveness is in a sense mastered by Birkin as he reflects on another colonial figure—that of the African statue he finds in Halliday's living room. Offering his own critique about modern "culture " (Lawrence [1920] 1987: 72) by directing his gaze at this "primitive" statue of an African woman in labor, Birkin expresses to his metropolitan interlocutors his longing for a "culture in sensation" (ibid.: 79) that he perceives as being unavailable to the alienated modern industrial consciousness. Just as the statue is displaced from its position within the colonial traffic and made to stand in a pure space of Birkin's aesthetic contemplation about culture, the "Hindu" manservant stands naked to the gaze of the metropolitan subject, whose own discomfort and hesitance is constantly produced by the elusiveness attributed to him. Here we see reflected Birkin's "longing" for that missing "sensation," a longing that is structured around a simultaneous ordering of risibility and opaqueness, producing the object for scrutiny that will both mark and erase the difference between the knower and the known. Although the African statue initially creates a sense of dissonance among the others in the room, it eventually provides a stable and silent body for Birkin to engage in his critique; the colonized body of the manservant, on the other hand, becomes a source of persistent discomfort among all of the viewers, presenting an ambivalent form of disclosure where his physical body and his clothes mark him simultaneously as both original and derivative. This disruptive permeability between the "inner" and the "outer" makes the colonized man the object of continual scrutiny, a process that is eventually worked out in the novel by foreclosing that permeability and restoring the stable gaze of the metropolitan subject.

Although this event can be seen only as a passing—and even inconsequential—moment in *Women in Love*, one can argue that its unexpected eruption makes Lawrence's delineation of the crisis of modernity—at the heart of which is the question of civility—resonate in specific ways. The resonances are clearly discernible throughout the novel's dramatization of the crisis of modern industrial society. At a more specific level, this crisis is defined and inflected by questions of class and gender, and embodied in Lawrence's portrayal of the fate of his male characters. In particular, Gerald's maleness most clearly represents the ethos of the imperial managerial proprietorship adopted by Britain's rational industrial order; that maleness is not only set against the bourgeois feminine domain but also made to negotiate a specific place within Birkin's fantasy targeted in part at the colonized body of the male subject. While throughout the novel both Gerald and Birkin attempt ironically to harness the power of the feminine as a way to achieve their respective fantasies, the larger crisis (marked in the novel as the crisis of "culture" or "civilization") is only aggravated by renewed demands placed on their own respective masculinity. As the scene with the manservant demonstrates, the necessary enactment of masculinity requires the colonial site: it is this site on which the struggle to define civility is articulated as a struggle with desire and interpretation. As I have indicated, the colonial "enigma" constitutes the very form and object of that struggle, indicating that in the case of *Women in Love* the performative does serve as an embodied form of normalization: objects are produced and manipulated with the same dexterity with which the norms of civility are inscribed and transgressed. As an aesthetic object, the statue of the African woman in labor is readable because masculine intellectual labor serves as the invisible center from which the form of primitive (maternal) labor can be marked as being outside the limits of metropolitan bourgeois life. As a result, cultural alterity and gender difference are mutually reinforced by such an arrangement of knower and the known. On the other hand, as a physically attractive man who is dressed in borrowed Western clothes, the manservant tests the boundaries between masculine knowledge and homoerotic desire: cast as a enigma, he evokes a discomfort that only serves as a source of incitement for his metropolitan viewers, who are already consumers of the primitive. He appears in a space where private authority, obedience, ownership, and control interface with the regulative ideals of governance, consumption, and conduct. However, he also becomes a mark of the tenuous line demarcating the "savage" from the "civilized," a line that cannot easily be accommodated even by Birkin, who serves, like John Stuart Mill, as a hyphenated father-son figure intent on establishing his father-like authority while appealing to a new ethics of transgression that necessarily relies on the call to return to the primitive.

That said, it is worth pointing out that, unlike the loquacious nineteenth-century *baboo*, the colonized subject in *Women in Love* is never given a voice, although his discontent with his employer is reported indirectly through the words of his master, Halliday. Questions about language and silence are crucially linked to his enigmatic presence. Lawrence's delineation of the relationship between civility, language, and power within this construct of the enigma is first explicitly voiced by Halliday's two comments about the man: "He's anything but what he seems to be" and "his only advantage is that he can't *speak* English and can't understand it, so he's perfectly safe" (Lawrence [1920] 1987: 73; emphasis added). Halliday's authority to read the man who ostensibly cannot "speak" enables him to defer the threat evoked by his deceptive exterior; however, the man's visible docility remains as a question for his metropolitan viewers. When Gerald hears him speak in his halting English for the first time, his perceptions of the man undergo a change: while he is still struck by his looks and his "aristocratic" bearing, he also reminds himself that the man "was a half savage." Again, the conversation he later overhears between the man and Halliday reinforces Gerald's feeling that the man was anything but "safe." As he soon discovers (after Halliday returns to the room), the servant was quite capable of quarrelling with his master about money, demanding that he be paid to buy a new set of underclothes, clearly contradicting earlier assertions about his inability to understand or communicate in English. Two conflicting images of the man emerge in this scene: his initial aristocratic bearing and muteness, both of which are transformed as soon as he is described as being capable of speech. However, before this transformation can take place, there appears to be an awkward vacillation between the white man's desire to produce the man as an enigma and the desire to pierce through that enigma in order to reveal the missing core, his "deceptive" muteness. Is the "grinning" man merely a deceiver who exploits his master, or does he simply cloak his otherness by refusing to be completely readable? Or is he, underneath the savagery, a civilized human being after all, who like all respectable Englishmen cares for—and demands—underclothing? Is he "passing" as a civilized subject by reconstituting himself as respectable or simply demanding, as a worker, what is his due share—to protect himself from the cold and the draught of London?[1]

The questions are never fully articulated in the novel so that the elusive core remains in place at the heart of the unsaid; confronted with this, the narrative predictably situates the man into the space defined by the original boundaries separating the "savage" from the "civilized." Questions about class and ownership, gender, and race are all subsumed under this classic binary, and what persists until the very end of this scene is the tantalizing elusiveness of the manservant. After breakfast, the men appear dressed in their best, while the manservant is described bringing in a "great deal of toast," looking "exactly as he had looked the night before, statically the same." His affect is measured and compared with that of Pussum, the woman of the street earlier picked by the men for their pleasure. The colonized man and the woman of the street present the same face: they both wear "masks" that are described as being "sinister" (Lawrence [1920] 1987: 80). Again, the manservant goes about his chores—disappearing and appearing unexpectedly with "tea, bending in a slow, strange leopard-like fashion" (ibid.). Ironically, it is Birkin—the man most concerned with questioning the norms of bourgeois civility—who completes the circle of comprehending the enigma that had been set in motion when the man first appeared at the doorway. At this point in the narrative, Birkin fixes the man once and for all by describing the "slight greyness" visible in him as the sign of "an ash of corruption," and suggesting that behind the "aristocratic inscrutability of expression" lay "a nauseating, bestial stupidity" (ibid.). The nausea triggered in Birkin represents the most extreme form of "sensation" he longs for—here, manifested as a form of aversion. Even in these last lines about the "Hindu," one senses its lingering effects, but now the binary through which he had earlier placed the African statue as an embodiment of "pure culture in sensation, culture in the physical consciousness" (ibid.: 79), becomes unsafe and tenuous.

Written during World War I, *Women in Love* is punctuated with questions about the value of bourgeois civility—manifested in the ways in which it questions the basis of sexuality and economic and cultural power in modern colonial industrial society. Whether it is the civility of the modern industrial magnate or the civility of the bourgeois woman, the novel seeks to disclose the often-suppressed rage for power and dominance that lies beneath that civility. The aggressive individuality of the modern subject is revealed time and again in the ways in which the characters in the novel act out their anxieties, simultaneously resisting and expressing their ties to the imperatives of metropolitan civility. However, in this attempt to diagnose it, the novel often resorts to producing the counter-image of that civility—

in this case, the enigmatic civility of the colonial servant—making that enigma an object/text that can be read and translated. When considered from this perspective, the piece of African art becomes another item of consumption, a commodity made available through colonial traffic, which also tests those boundaries of civility from which Birkin has claimed to have freed himself. It is Birkin's moral task to make Gerald, the industrial magnate, realize his own incompleteness as a man; that task also necessitates the freezing of the colonized subject in its place as a "found" object. None of the metropolitan subjects are aware of their own fragmented understanding of the manservant: they are never given his history— one that would explain how he made his way to England or about the causes of his destitution. Instead, he is made continually subject to the gaze of the men, a gaze that moves in accordance with their desire to know him. It is the task of Birkin—the supreme reader and translator—to fix him in his objecthood (even as he is unable to overcome his own nausea). The normative value of civility that Lawrence wishes to interrogate in his novel is therefore seen to possess a particular calculus that requires the simultaneous presence of the Western man, the colonial subject, and the colonial artefact—all within the space of the Western living room. And in this play of simultaneity *Women in Love* registers a particular relationship between colonialism and the modern industrial state, between civility, ownership, and aesthetic value.

Like *Women in Love*, F. Anstey's *Baboo Jabberjee* opens the colonial rims of metropolitan culture. Written as a satirical autobiography of a young educated Indian on his visit to imperial Britain, it belongs to a popular subgenre that also includes a popular work such as *A Bayard from Bengal* (1902), a work that mocks the attempts of the Bengali *baboo* Mr. Bhosh to adjust to life in Britain. Kipling's Hurree Babu is also a contemporary of Mr. Jabberjee: like the former, Mr. Jabberjee is a Calcutta-educated Indian man who speaks as a "translated" subject. Like Hurree Babu, Mr. Jabberjee is mocked and parodied in the very language that he has adopted from his master. With his injudicious language and combination of outrageous pomposity and deferential demeanor, he is the quintessential *baboo*. But unlike Hurree Babu, Mr. Jabberjee is an Indian inhabiting the hallowed spaces of the imperial metropolis; in fact, he can be considered as the *baboo* who had finally made his way to the imperial center. In this humorous tale, Anstey describes two incidents that mark his protagonist as the mimic man—his "pilgrimage" to the shrine of Shakespeare (Anstey 1897: 125–34) and his appearance in court accused of luring an English woman to marriage (ibid.: 216–55). In these scenes, he is made to speak the master's language in a manner that can only reveal the grotesqueries of his mimicry. He is also made to wear European clothes so that his darkness can be accentuated. However, that mimicry reveals the very structure and hierarchical system authorized by colonial governance. Above all, he is made to stand as a witness to the normative categories of civility circumscribed by culture, government, and the court, the symbol of imperial judicial institutions, and it is in this role that the work opens up the spaces within the colonial/metropolitan circuit of civility and governance.

One of the first places where this occurs is when Mr. Jabberjee is described as visiting Stratford to honor the greatness of Shakespeare. Culture as the site of civility is embodied in Mr. Jabberjee's own comments about Shakespeare's greatness, and, while he exaggerates in his inimitable "Eastern" manner, his comments also indicate that the normative standards of culture across which mimicry is authorized in the colonial context are themselves contradictory in nature:

> It has been remarked, with some correctness, that he did not exist for an age, but all the time; and though it is the open question whether he did not derive all his ideas from previous writers, and even whether he wrote so much as a single line of the plays which are attributed to his inspired nib, he is one of the institutions of the country, and it is the correct thing for every orthodox British subject to admire and understand him even when most incomprehensible.
>
> (Anstey 1897: 125)

As these words indicate, even the greatest genius of English culture was an imitator. His imitations have been recast as "original" by the authority of metropolitan culture. We are told that Mr. Jabberjee commits to memory "select passages to his works" (ibid.), suggesting that an educated Indian can generate cultural capital by following the fetishistic practices of metropolitan culture. In short, the pristine world of the metropolis is itself "counterfeit," based on "imitation." In this situation, attempts to understand the "true" merit of Shakespeare's genius could at best be an expression of the value of imitation as a cultural practice in which no one can claim the original. Furthermore, imitation is part of what defines culture and the forms of education received by the colonial subject. When the *baboo* arrives at the "hallowed and sacred spot" (ibid.: 126) he is reminded that the "counterfeit" statue of the bard placed in the doorway resembled images of Buddha found in certain places in India; however, when he questions the literary merit of the "spurious cryptogram" inscribed on the slab holding the statue of the poet, American tourists respond by "exclaim[ing], indignantly, that such irreverent levity was a scandal in a spot which was the Mecca of the entire civilized universe" (ibid.: 127). Proceeding to the room where the poet was said to have been born, Mr. Jabberjee is shocked by the dinginess of the room, but approaches the window where he wishes, as a "distinguished Shakespearean student," to scratch his own name in order to mark his visit. However, Anstey's efforts to mock the cultural pretensions of his own society through the mouth of the colonial subject are possible by making him repeat the fetishistic practices of England—that is, by making him imitate the very hollowness that Anstey simultaneously wishes to expose. The colonial subject, therefore, emerges in this contradictory space that suggests, as I have indicated before, the contradictory space of civility itself. This is again highlighted in the chapter where Anstey describes Mr. Jabberjee visiting the India Office in London. Mr Jabberjee follows the very rituals mandated by colonial bureaucracy—influence, obedience, entreaty, patronage, favoritism—in order to reach the inner sanctum, although at the end he is refused an audience by the chief. In all of his attempts to enter civil society in London based on his knowledge of the system, he is continually frustrated, and on one occasion exclaims: "as a patriotic Baboo gentleman, my blood will boil occasionally at instances of stuck-up English self-sufficiency" (ibid.: 186). The contradictions within the space of civility are rendered both visible and invisible in Ansty's satire: whenever Anstey slips into mocking the exaggerated mannerisms of his *baboo*, he also gestures towards the disciplinary function of civility and to the highly fraught ground on which the operations of civility are secured.

Notes

Introduction

1 This kind of reasoning is also reflected in the view, expressed in the *Calcutta Review* 90 (1893), that the newly educated class of Indians have "forgotten their ancestral craft but have not required any shame faced reluctance to assert their fitness for all and every form of occupation under Government that may fall vacant." Correspondingly, nineteenth-century theories about heredity are deployed to explain the consequences of such change: educated Indians, it is argued, had "forsaken the paths of life to which they were born, and for which by heredity they were fated, and for which they have become a sort of non-descript community, describing themselves as enlightened" (p. 153). The *Calcutta Magazine* calls for the need to have a "counter-balancing power" (1883: 70) to combat the effects of education on Indians.

2 The Indian reformer Raja Rammohan Roy and the English educationist William Hare pioneered English education in Bengal with the founding of the first regular English school in Calcutta in 1813. Meant for male students from noted Hindu families, the school—named Hindu College—was built with the aid of private funds and modeled after Western institutions of higher learning. The government's reluctance to allow missionaries to set up their own institutions of higher learning led to the founding of the first missionary college in the Dutch-controlled town of Serampore in Bengal in 1818. The controversy over the government's role in supervising education continued till the mid-century. Although trained as a missionary, Alexander Duff, another eminent educationist, opposed missionary efforts to introduce religious instruction, preferring that these institutions emphasize teaching rather than preaching. In 1833, the British government passed the India Act, urging the government in India to play a direct role in the establishment of public education, which led the latter, in 1835, to adopt the education scheme proposed by Lord Macaulay. The growing bureaucratization of education is reflected in the gradual increase in the number of committees appointed to review education—for example, the Committee in Public Education that was chaired by Lord Macaulay in 1835. Maintaining neutrality in religious matters, the governor-general, William Bentinck, continued to work for the expansion of a publicly supported higher education with English as the new medium of instruction and as the new language of the courts, instead of Persian. For details, see Oak (1925).

3 Viswanathan (1989) is of special relevance. Viswanathan astutely charts the ways in which the consolidation of the study of "English" literature at Indian universities in the mid-nineteenth century paved the way for setting up a hegemony of Western learning among the colonized elite in India, a process that led to the consolidation of British political power. As I highlight in the following pages of the Introduction, the political consequences of such a policy become evident in the establishment of specific class and racial hierarchies that are deployed in the education debates.

4 See Chatterjee (1996), pp. 9–27, for a discussion of the formative role of English-language education in the rise of the new intelligentsia.

5 The *Calcutta Review* refers to the universities established by the British in India as "a mistake, an anachronism" and "a somewhat clumsy counterfeit" (*CR*, 96 [1893]: 296). The idea of the *baboo* as a counterfeit parallels the notion that the educational institutions in which he was trained was likewise fraudulent.

6 F. Anstey, a contributor to *Punch*, was the author of *Baboo Jabberjee* (1897), a parody of a Bengali gentleman on his visit to England. Note that the *Hobson Jobson*, the dictionary of Anglo-Indian terms, which originally appeared in 1881, has an entry on the term "Baboo," with examples from three different sources, the first dating back to 1866 (from Arthur Lyall's *The Old Pindaree*).

7 See Bhabha (1994) on the discomfort and ambivalence associated with the racialized and sexualized colonial stereotype.

8 In the preface to "*Baboo English*," the author describes *baboo* as "a name applied to native clerks in Bengal, and some parts of upper India, although it really is a term of respect equivalent to Esquire, and to enable them to obtain this coveted title, youths are crammed until they can stand no more, and in many cases they become utterly worthless" (p. 2). Most nineteenth-century Anglo-Indian periodicals of this period feature essays on the *baboo*: for example, the *Calcutta Magazine* describes the *baboo* as someone "who pretends to know the language of the *sahib logue* [English folks]" ("The End of Education," *CM* 1883: 126), and the *Calcutta Fortnightly Review* describes him as being "the flatulent grotesque of Anglo-Indian tradition" ("British Rule," *CFR* 1881: 59). Worth noting is the similarity between this and the physical traits of Kipling's Hurree Chunder Mukherji, described as the "obese Babu whose stockinged legs shook with fat" (Kipling [1901] 1998: 207).

9 For discussions about Kipling's representation of Kim's hybrid identity, see Brody (1998), pp. 148–50; Said (2002); and P. Roy (1998).

10 My purpose here is not to take on the task of mapping the complex profile of "modernity" as it has been theorized in contemporary discourse. Appadurai's work is particularly instructive, given his critical intervention into the form of orientalism advanced by Edward Said and his delineation of the process of collecting colonial data, which helps substantiate the ways in which orientalism's "enumerative" function was embodied in the exercise of bureaucratic power and applied in the name of "modernity."

11 Lauren Berlant's discussion of the relation between "Law" and the "National Symbolic" is useful here for thinking about the formation of this national narrative in the colonial context. According to Berlant, "Law" defines the "field of citizenship" by constructing "technical definitions of the citizen's rights, duties, and obligations," while the "National Symbolic" links those definitions to "desire, harnessing affect to political life through the production of 'national fantasy'" (Berlant 1991: 5).

12 Educated Indians in the nineteenth century, while continuing to support the government's initiatives in education, often attacked its economic and political policies. Take the example of Romesh Chunder Dutt, the first Indian to qualify for the civil services in 1869, who on the occasion of Queen Victoria's Diamond Jubilee, commended the "present administration" for being "honest and able" (Dutt 1897: ix), but also offered a scathing attack on the government's political and economic policies. Quoting John Stuart Mill, Dutt shows how these policies had impoverished the people of India, particularly the manner in which British frontier policy was beginning to "drain the resources" of the nation, and its "unlimited borrowing of English capital" had led to "the increasing of public debt in time of peace" (ibid.: x). Similarly, Parbati Churn Roy, an eminent lawyer, argued in the pages of the *Calcutta Review* that, contrary to what many Anglo-Indians felt about the mounting costs of publicly funded education, there was a marked disparity between what a province such as Bengal contributed to the public treasury and what it received back in the "shape of the Education Grant" ("Higher Education," *CR* 1887: 232). Both Dutt and Roy contributed to the *Calcutta Review*.

13 Here I have in mind, among other ideas, Foucault's notion of a historical a priori, which he delineates in *The Archaeology of Knowledge*. According to Foucault, historical a priori

can be seen as a "positivity" that provides "not a condition for the validity of judgment," but the rules that "characterize discursive practice." Emphasizing "practice," Foucault explains that these "rules" are "caught up in the very things that they connect," and "are transformed with them into certain decisive thresholds" (Foucault 1972: 127). In other words, the historical a priori is formed not out of historically stable, self-evident norms or standards but out of a dynamic productive relationship—what he calls multiple "points of contact, places of irruption or emergence, and domains or occasions of operation" (ibid.: 128). My argument is premised on a similar principle that the normativity of modern disciplinary society is not a manifestation of "a great, unmoving empty figure that irrupted one day on the surface of time" (ibid.), but a productive field of discursive practices in which "normative standards" are constituted in relation to competing fields of ideological work. For a succinct discussion of Foucauldian methods of historical ontology, see Owen (1994), pp. 140–62. For the relevance of Foucault to the study of colonial discourse, see Mufti and Shohat (1997), pp. 8–9. For a questioning of the idea that postcolonial critiques rely on a derivative discourse already elaborated by Foucauldian poststructuralism, see Chakrabarty (2000b), pp. 6–11.

14 Under the broad category of "civility," I evoke notions of "civil," "civic," "disciplinarity," and "governmentality." The connections between these terms become clear in the course of the study, particularly by the specific discursive contexts I evoke to discuss the texts.

15 On October 8, 1881, the Governor-General in Council appointed a committee to draft a code for regulating the conduct of European education. Questions about the role of men of "English descent" continued to be posed in the 1880s in periodicals such as the *Calcutta Review* and *Calcutta Magazine*. The views expressed often emphasized the significance of character-building as a way to overcome the present handicaps: "Every inch on their road to success must be gained for themselves and by themselves, amidst healthy rivalry, the play of interests, and the force of character" ("Eurasians and Poor Europeans," *CR* 1881: 55).

16 It is interesting to note that Indian writers contributing to the *Calcutta Review* were often able to see through this ploy, although their challenge often yoked together "power" and "weakness" in order to explain them as being "natural" manifestations of national traits. For example, Ram Chandra Bose, in his essay in the *Bengal Magazine*, argues that "European hauteur" was "the product in unregenerate European nature of conscious power," while "Asiatic treachery" was "the product in Asian human nature of conscious weakness" ("Modern Civilization," *BM* 1882: 332).

17 Note how Arnold cites the "Indian virtue of detachment" while explaining the idea of aesthetic "disinterestedness" in his essay "Function of Criticism" (Arnold 1954: 351).

18 In his essay "A Definition of Culture," Charles Johnston remarks: "We are to supplement muscular effort by education and humanity by culture" ("Definition of Culture," *CR* 1899: 128).

19 Colonel Creighton is the most stable representative of European civility in *Kim*, partly because his actions and thoughts are never subject to the kind of anxious narrativization that we find in the portrayals of Kim or Hurree Babu. See Said (2002), pp. 340–3.

20 Like Ann Stoler's *Race and the Education of Desire*, in which she fills in a key critical lacuna in Foucault's *History of Sexuality* by examining the intersections of race and sexuality in modern colonial culture, my work attempts to map out a colonial genealogy by proposing why we need to consider civility as constituting an important discursive element in the historical formation of metropolitan (and liberal) disciplinary society under colonialism. Moving beyond Stoler's consideration of race and sexuality, my study points to questions of race, class, and nationality that are imbricated in the formation of normativity within colonial disciplinary society.

21 Anthony Smith's *Nationalism and Modernism* offers a succinct overview of the ways in which imperialist initiatives departed from the European Enlightenment views of progressive development and instead adopted a policy of "exploitation of the cheap

labor and resources of peripheral regions of the world by metropolitan capitalists and states" (Smith 1998: 49).

22 If my analysis brings attention to this "psychological' Freudian/Lacanian dimension in Woolf, it is simply to underscore the fact that, as a liberal, Woolf had to negotiate his own metropolitan civility in terms of an affect-laden response to its imperatives. The stories therefore articulate Woolf's own understanding of the historical effects of colonization, a process in whose fashioning he had played a significant role during his eight-year service in Ceylon.

23 I should add that Foucault's ideas about governmentality which I use to frame my analysis of Mill are also relevant to the notion of "biopolitics" that I utilize in chapter 5 in my analysis of Leonard Woolf's "Pearls and Swine."

24 In *Culture and State*, David Lloyd and Paul Thomas contend that, although Foucault's analysis of "governmentality" is useful at a descriptive level, his ideas "veer towards a virtual positivism that lacks any real analytical capacity" (Lloyd and Thomas 1998: 4). It is true that Foucault ignores the colonial context in which the modern state takes its specific form as a "disciplinary" society. My own strategy in invoking Foucault has more to do with pushing his line of inquiry onto the colonial terrain than to quarrel with the viability of using his analysis in any simple manner to talk about colonialism. It is clear that their interest in spelling out the causal relations affecting governmental institutions puts Lloyd and Thomas in quite a different domain of inquiry than the one I am interested in pursuing in this study. I take as my starting point not the historical veracity of any single proposition in Foucault but the possibility of locating the questions of colonial difference within the structure envisaged in Foucault's analysis of disciplinary governmentality. Both François Ewald and Michael Donnelly are especially useful in working out the critical implications of Foucault's genealogical analysis specific to this understanding of "disciplinarity."

25 See Foucault (1991), pp. 98–104.

26 Perhaps the most sustained critique of Edward Said's *Orientalism* appears in Aijaz Ahmad's *In Theory*, in which Ahmad claims that the contradictions in Said's arguments stem from his attempt to combine Marxist elements of realist epistemology with a Foucauldian analytic of power as a discursive category. Other scholars who question Said's methodological approach are James Clifford (in *The Predicament of Culture*); Robert Young (*White Mythologies*); and Dennis Porter ("*Orientalism* and its Problems"). For a succinct overview of these positions, see Moore-Gilbert (1997).

27 Elizabeth Jane Bellamy's discussion of Spivak's deployment of "affect" in her work on the postcolonial subaltern is relevant here since it provides a useful way to think about the production of civility in colonialist discourse. Bellamy clarifies how the story of Jashoda in Mahasweta Devi's "Stanadayani" ("The Breast-Giver") provides Spivak with the opportunity to explicate the ways in which value is produced through the mechanism of labor power acting on the female body. In case of Jashoda, affect's relationship to labor and value emerges with the "domestic" being inscribed as the site for the production of exchange-value and surplus labor (Bellamy 1998: 350–1). The processes of affective coding underlying these material relations between the nation and the subaltern are singularly important for comprehending the normative function of civil discourse in producing the colonial body. My chapters on E. M. Forster and Leonard Woolf indirectly address these concerns.

28 This is a rich terrain to be explored here and in much pioneering work, from Gauri Viswanathan's exploration of the literary curriculum to David Arnold's discussion of policing, to Jyotsna Singh's analysis of the "discovery" as performing the master trope of colonization, and to Catherine Hall's investigations of the formation of the British white working-class subject and its institutions in differentiation from colonial subjects. What distinguishes these studies, and others like them, is the attention both to discursive formations and to the analysis of the institutional practices that are informed by them and through which they circulate. Indeed, the value, one might say, of Foucault's work

lies in this articulated attention to disciplinary mechanisms or practices and to discourses. However, in my work I do not evoke theoretical notions developed by Foucault, such as "biopower" and "governmentality," in order to study the institutional practices of colonialism: it should be borne in mind that this is not a *historical* study of disciplinary practices but one that works out a hermeneutic that takes into consideration the effects of these practices in regulating discourse. For example, in my chapter on Scott, I analyze the ideational and symptomatic structures of the oriental tale, the social and political anxieties, and the constitution of racialized subjects within a wider field of racialized subjects, taking into account the history of the "Jewish question," although in discussing the history of the East India Company I do not offer a historical account of, say, the modes of discipline through which East India Company officials or military cadets were formed and regulated. Similarly, although I refer to specific policies such as the Contagious Diseases Act and the establishment of lock hospitals in chapter 3 to discuss questions about sexual policing, I do not go into details about the construction of specific legal and civil codes that helped institute the practices. Again, the focus on education debates in the Introduction necessitated a reference to the formation of education codes for colonized subjects, but in my analysis I do not offer specific details about their implementation or the costs involved. Such an inquiry, although outside the present scope of my study, certainly deserves scholarly attention.

1 Colonial civility and the regulation of social desire

1 All citations to Scott's *The Surgeon's Daughter* are taken from *Chronicles from the Canongate*.
2 The clearest and most direct expression of the social and economic behavior spurred by these developments at home are to be found in Herman Merivale's *Introduction to a Course on Colonization and Colonies*: "The colonies," he claims, "afforded an outlet for the enterprising and the discontented; they stimulated commerce by the offer of fresh markets, not indeed secured to a particular class of producers, as their founders had imagined, but furnishing rewards eventually to superior energy and industry alone. The object was attained; prosperity and colonization advanced together; but it was he whose development of strength, the zeal and the activity thus aroused, the substantial means and not the imaginary end, which remunerated national enterprise" (Merivale 1839: 39). Merivale's vision, that the colonial enterprise, initiated by a certain class at one point in history, now provided an avenue for economic advancement by all the classes, provided a powerful ideological tool to justify the national basis for colonialism.
3 It is worthwhile reminding the reader that, although Scott's tale is about Scottish characters, it does not set "Scottish" identity in opposition to an "English" identity, but seeks instead to identify a common "Saxon" culture that unifies the two and sets them apart from the "Jew" and the "Indian." The "tricky balance" that Scott maintains between "assimilation and independence" (Sorenson 1997: 31) with regard to the relations between England and Scotland can be explained in part by his own political and ideological stand, and in part by Scotland's historic involvement in the establishment of the British empire. A detailed discussion of this issue, however, remains outside the scope of the present chapter. Also see Garside (1933).
4 Critical assessments of *The Surgeon's Daughter* are few. Andrew Lang wrote an introduction to the novel in the Border edition of the Waverley novels in 1894. With the exception of some scattered references in general studies on Scott, the work has enjoyed no extended treatment in modern scholarship. While noting that the first two stories in the *Canongate Chronicles* had been widely acclaimed as being among Scott's best works, Christopher Harvie fails even to mention the tale. Edward Wagenknecht dismisses it as singularly bad, poorly conceived, and "not worthy of attention" (Wagenknecht 1991: 95). The work receives only marginal comments in Martin Green's otherwise richly suggestive appraisal of Scott's Indian connections in *Dreams of Adventure* (1979).
5 Graham McMaster, in *Scott and Society*, acknowledges that there may be "contradictory

impulses" (McMaster 1981: 6) within Scott's own political opinions, noting that, in spite of his concern for the "poor problem," Scott's "Tory paternalism" never "accepted the need for more than a token attempt at reform" (ibid.: 100).

6 Fiona Robertson claims that Mr. Croftangry is "an extended portrait of the artist . . . [who] draws the reader into his confidence as he describes the preparation of his tales" (Robertson 1994: 137). Robertson, however, fails to comment on the way in which this fictive narrator engages in incorporating and legitimizing post-mercantile/industrial metaphors in order to establish his own narratorial authority in a work such as *The Surgeon's Daughter*.

7 In addition to the works considered in this chapter, see James Scurry's *The Captivity, Sufferings and Escape of James Scurry*, a work that enumerates the hardships encountered by the writer when he was detained as a prisoner by Hyder Ali and Tippoo Sahib. Casting these native princes as diabolical figures, the narrative reminds its readers of the inherent dangers in a colonial military career.

8 John Trelawny, who was a friend of P. B. and Mary Shelley and Byron, created in his hero the image of a romantic rebel whose story of adventure and bravado was to prove very popular in his time. The power of the typical Promethean hero is, in many respects, reminiscent of the violence of Trelawny's enigmatic privateer: both are over-reachers precisely because they are driven by an abiding sense of social injustice.

9 *Twelve Years' Military Adventure* details the military campaigns of the British against the powers of Mysore and the Mahrattas in 1803. Significantly, the author comments that, upon his return to England, "the first thing that struck me on landing in my native country was the smallness of the houses into which Englishmen thrust their magnanimous souls; for I had pictured to myself every thing about a Briton as being great" (vol. 2, p. 125).

10 The exchanges between supporters and opponents of free trade were conducted through numerous pamphlets written by stock-jobbers, merchants, military men, and East India Company officials. See Jackson (1829). The missionary James Peggs comes out in support of free trade: in his *India Cries to British Humanity*, he declares that "the utility of colonization in India [is] apparent in the improvement of its produce—the increase of British trade and commerce with India, and the Eastern world" (Peggs 1832: 418), and that the greatest "advantage of European colonization would be—the permanence of the British power in Hindostan" (ibid.: 433). In his *A Sketch of the History of the East India Company*, Robert Grant expresses his concern over the disorders produced by the "interference of Europeans in the inland trade," stating that as a result of this the "native population suffered an aggravated load of oppression" (Grant 1813: 246).

11 Cecil Roth notes that historical figures such as Samson Gideon and Joseph Salvador, both Sephardic Jews, were key members in London finance in the eighteenth century. The latter was the only Jewish government underwriter, and also served as a governor of the East India Company. Families such as Lopes Suasso and Agular assumed "nobiliar titles, albeit only baronies of the Empire" (Roth 1978: 294). Harold Pollins calls attention to the fact that the colonial diamond trade was virtually in the hands of the Jewish-Portuguese community of London (Pollins 1982: 48).

12 Sussman has noted the close association made between the "unmanly Jew" and "the Harpy, the monstrous female" (Sussman 1995: 21) in Thomas Carlyle, and argues that such figures constituted notions of masculinity in Victorian England.

13 In his *Sirdhana* (1889), William Keegan provides an account of the life of Begum Sumroo [spelled Somre in the work]. The begum, called Zeeibool Nissa, was the wife of William Reinhard, or "Sumroo" as he was popularly known, who had once been a private soldier in the French East India Company. After the defeat of the French, Sumroo left the company and independently undertook the training of the troops of the Nawab, who was fighting the English. After his death, his wife retained control of his troops and gained notoriety as an inveterate English hater. There are other similar examples of eighteenth-century female adventurers whose stories were chronicled at this time. One

such example is a work published in 1750 entitled *The Female Soldier, or, The Surprising Life & Adventures of Hannah Snell*. Snell was woman who took the name of James Gray and was drafted into the regiment that fought in the colonial war against the French in Pondicherry, India (see Dowie, 1893).

14 The ritualistic presentation of Richard's execution conforms to the visual representations of such macabre deeds often found in illustrated books, such as Robert Knox's *An Historical Relation of the Island of Ceylon in the East Indies* (1681). See Lach and van Kley (1993).

2 Writing the liberal self: colonial civility and disciplinary regime

1 Mill saw the middle-class individual as a "rational" economic agent—one who embodies the "national" values of industry and self-sufficiency by being fully conscious of his/her own interests (see Ryan 1973).

2 Maria Koundoura tracks a similar reasoning process in Mill's *Considerations on Representative Government*. She argues that "culture," for Mill, "allows for the production of a normative temporality that places unequally constructed contestations against each other." Mill's example in this work is the Breton's archiacness set against French nationality's "particular time," which "is made universal and concrete, world-historical and forward-moving" (Koundoura 1998: 76).

3 Mill's *Autobiography* is a good example of a Victorian *Bildungsroman*. The working out of the dialectic between "continuity" and "rupture" can be comprehended in psycho-analytic terms in what Daniel Bivona has described as "vaulting an order of discourse which escapes the mirroring of the Imaginary and accedes to the representational power of the Symbolic in Lacan's sense" (Bivona 1998: 91). While the Imaginary can be said to represent the statis of historical determinism, signified by James Mill the despotic father, the Symbolic represents the order spurred by a self-creating organic entity whose allegiance to the Symbolic makes it simultaneously capable of exercising free choice and recognizing that the subject is part of the historical, political world in which the moral choices are dictated by the reigning ideological values of individuality.

4 Bhikhu Parekh's comments on Mill's ideas of man as a self-creating being are worth noting in this context. He writes:

> Man's "comparative worth as a human being" consisted in becoming "the best thing" it was possible for him to become. He was constantly to improve himself, develop new powers, cultivate a "striving and go-ahead character," dominate his natural and social environment, experiment with different ways of life, and to evolve one best suited to his "natural constitution." To Mill, only such an autonomous and self-determining being had character or individuality. "One whose desires and impulses are not his own has no character, no more than a steam engine has character."
>
> (Parekh: 11)

5 Note in particular the argument in Chakrabarty 2000a: 34–5.

6 Here it is worthwhile noting Tejaswini Niranjana's comments: "The universalizing move, which is, after all, part of the West's constitution of itself as subject, contributes to erasing the violence of colonialism. Non-Western people attain maturity and subjecthood only after a period of apprenticeship in which they learn European languages and thereby gain a voice" (Niranjana 1992: 164).

7 In 1833, Mill had published his "Thoughts on Poetry and its Varieties," where he engaged in a lengthy discussion of the essentials of poetry. Distinguishing between the "poetry of a poet and the poetry of a cultivated but not naturally poetic mind" (Mill 1981: 357), he praised Wordsworth over Shelley for having shown a culture "reared from his own *inward nature*" (ibid.: 359; emphasis added). It is clear from this relatively early work that, for Mill, unlike Shelley, Wordsworth's appeal lay in his poetic ability to evoke the apolitical power of this "inward nature," a power that he later invoked to write about his life in the *Autobiography*.

8 It should be noted that, in the early decades of colonial government, policies relating to land reform, ownership and taxation had played a significant role in consolidating the company's political power, allowing it to create new sites of power that could be exploited to serve its own interests. During the 1830s and 1840s, company authorities were forced to consider alternatives as these policies came under new forms of scrutiny. For example, colonial administrators such as Munro, Malcolm, and Elphinstone argued for the need to recognize the power and efficacy of indigenous rural systems of India, such as the *ryotwar* system of revenue prevalent in southern India, instead of imposing centralized programs from the metropolis and thereby averting the possibility of handing power to the wrong people. As Eric Stokes has demonstrated, Mill's own views regarding the rationale and feasibility of Benthamite programs were often inconsistent, leading him to support conservative ideologues like Munro, while still upholding the principles of his father's utilitarian policies. However, this inconsistency proved to be rather productive in dealing with the provisional and fluid nature of existing colonial politics of that era.

9 Throughout Britain in the late eighteenth century, Quakers, evangelicals, and rational Dissenters gave voice to powerful abolitionist sentiments, whose appeal lay in the fact that anti-slavery success promised to usher in a proper moral order that would ensure a greater social and political harmony. Enlightenment values as well as the principles of Christianity appeared to lend support to this appeal. For a full discussion of this history, see Turley (1991) and Porter (1970).

10 It was in 1853 that a system of entry into the civil service by competitive examinations was established. Before that candidates were directly recruited by the company through a system of patronage.

11 For details concerning the construction of India's past predating the introduction of Islamic rule, see Kopf (1969).

12 It is worthwhile noting that, unlike the narratives of colonial cadetship, this comparison is not made between "happy slave" and toiling cadet, but between the rigor of a slave's life and that of a poor peasant who lives at the mercy of the system.

3 Policing the boundaries: civility and gender in the Anglo-Indian romances, 1880–1900

1 The term "Anglo-Indian romance" is taken from reviews appearing in the popular press of the day. For example, praising Alice Perrin's *The Stronger Claim*, the reviewer for *The Scotsman* writes: "The book is steeped in Oriental hues and feeling and atmosphere, and probes further, perhaps, than any Anglo-Indian romance yet written into the mysteries of Hindu faith and worship and love" (advertisement for the novel in Alice Perrin's *The Waters of Destruction*. London: Chatto & Windus, 1905). Benita Parry's analysis of five women novelists, whom she calls "Romancers"–namely, F. E. Penny, Bithia Mary Croker, I. A. R. Wylie, Maud Diver, and Alice Perrin–offers new insights into this colonial genre.

2 Reviewers of such novels did not fail to note that there was a public ready to consume the "romance of India." For example, in *St. James's Gazette*, the reviewer for Flora Anne Steel's *On the Face of the Waters* says: "Her position is now established as the writer of the truth and romance of India. She is a fine writer, and she has written a fine novel about an epoch in our history which Englishmen can never cease to weep over and glory in" (advertisement for the novel in *Romantic India* by Andre Chevrillon, trans. William Marchant. London: Heinemann, 1897).

3 This genealogy, which has underpinned most of the existing scholarship on colonial Anglo-India, covers writers such as Flora Anne Steel, E. M. Forster, and John Masters, also includes more recent writers of the Raj, such as Paul Scott and M. M. Kaye.

4 In *Double Talk*, Wayne Koestenbaum argues that the return to pure romance by men such as Haggard and Lang offered a "refuge not only from women's fiction, but from an England that they imagined Queen Victoria had feminized" (Koestenbaum 1989: 153).

5 The late Victorian period also saw the emergence of a didactic fiction for adolescent girls that served a patriarchal nationalist cause. See Rowbotham (1989).

6 In *Effeminism*, Krishnaswamy explains the "cult of masculinity" as being a "historical product overdetermined by various intersecting ideologies that are metropolitan as well as colonial" (1998: 53). Exploring a wide range of literature, from Kipling to Forster, she argues that this cult also produces a "deeply divided figure" of masculine authority (ibid.: 3).

7 Barry Milligan asserts that "the appeal of the exotic Indian diamond is a peculiarly appropriate choice of metonym for the obsessive English fascination with India, for the historical playing out of that attraction was also mediated largely through Indian gems" (Milligan 1995: 71).

8 What follows are some biographical details about the authors considered in this essay (I have deliberately excluded Kipling from this list).

Born in 1857 in London, and educated at Owens College, Manchester, Morley Roberts worked as a clerk in the War Office and the India Office. Traveling all over the globe–from Texas, to the American West, to Chicago, Iowa, Minnesota, and British Columbia–he visited Australia, South Africa, and the islands of the South Seas. His circle of friends consisted of W. H. Hudson, George Gissing, and R. B. Cunninghame Graham. A popular writer of fiction in his day, he authored thirty-one novels and well over a hundred short stories, most of which were published in the *Strand Magazine*. Later Roberts won his fame as a scientist who wrote about malignancy and cancer, elucidating them by applying explanation drawn from the study of human societies. According to John Sutherland, *A Son of Empire* was his most successful work (Sutherland 1989: 596).

Charles Johnston served in the Bengal Civil Service in the 1880s and 1890s, and was a translator of key Hindu texts, such as the *Mahabharata*, the Yoga Sutras of Patanjali, the works of Shankaracharya, and the *Upanishads*. He was also a member of the Theosophical Society of India and contributed regularly to the *Calcutta Review* from 1890 to 1899. In writing the story of Kela Bai, Johnston might have been influenced by the Therigatha, songs of renunciation and release written in Pali by Buddhist nuns in 6 BC (see Tharu and Lalita 1991: 65–70).

Married to an officer in the Royal Scots in the 1870s, Bithia Mary Croker spent fourteen years in India and Burma with her husband. Her Anglo-Indian works include *Interference, Mr. Jervis, Proper Pride, Pretty Miss Neville*, and *A Bird of Passage*. Like Croker, F. E. Penny spent many years in south India as the wife of a missionary. In a literary career that spanned nearly three decades, Penny wrote more than fifteen Anglo-Indian novels, including *Caste and Creed, A Mixed Marriage, The Forest Officer, The Malabar Magician, The Tea-Planter, The Inevitable Law, Dark Corners, The Rajah, Sacrifice*, and *The Sanyasi*.

9 Early twentieth-century Anglo-Indian romances, such as Mary B. Turner's *Collision* (London: Duckworth, 1913) and Sara Duncan's *The Burnt Offering* (London: Methuen, 1909), depict English suffragists involved in the early nationalist struggle in India. In Duncan's novel, Joan, who falls in love with a native nationalist while visiting India with her socialist father, Vulcan Mills, reflects on her own struggles back home, saying: "As for my life of committees and campaigning at home, I am a little tired of it . . . Such things have their uses, but compared with a nation's awakening they are like the beating of a nursery drum. Looking back, it is all tawdry and feverish, full of expediency and vulgarity. I love the larger peace and the deeper dream of India" (p. 124).

10 Throughout the 1880s and 1890s, the close and interlinked network of friends established by women's groups had been successful in "drawing many of its ideas from the liberal economic and political beliefs that were so important for the middle class" (Caine 1997: 89). This sense of political organization, which had gained its rationale from the existing political ideologies, ushered in a sense of agency for middle-class women activists, giving rise to the idea that the new woman's resourcefulness and resoluteness were part of a "new" identity. Predictably, the Anglo-Indian romances, in portraying strong women, strategically eliminate any possibility for women to bond

together in the "spirit of sisterhood" that Hadria, the woman protagonist of Mona Caird's *Daughters of Danaus*, wished for.

11 This is not to suggest that the "orientalizing" of the East is abandoned, but that new geographical boundaries are drawn for its construction. Note, for example, this statement in *Bibliotheca Pastorum: A Knight's Faith: Passages in the Life of Sir Herbert Edwardes* "Whatever is West of Indus is Abrahamic, and progressive, like a tree; whatever is east of Indus, Brahmic, and somehow or other, evaporating into air, or so crystallized into changeless shape like a jewel" (Ruskin 1885: 23). Sir Herbert Edwardes was the great hero of the Indian Mutiny, and such hagiographies of heroes of the Indian Mutiny were very popular in the 1880s.

12 For details on Britain's Afghan policy, see Moore (1966), pp. 17–21.

13 For a detailed discussion of Kipling's correspondence with Teddy Roosevelt, the American president most closely associated with the rise of American imperialism, see Carrington (1955).

14 The most prominent writers whose work focused on the "new woman" were Sarah Grand and Allen Grant.

15 In many of the novels, women were seen to be particularly responsive to the call for improving the condition of their Indian sisters. In Evelyn Green's *Half-a-Dozen Sisters*, the heroine, Gypsy, hears the call of suffering Indian women in India, and undergoes a three-year medical training to fit her for a life-time of work as a medical missionary in the zenana.

16 Colonial literature on the nautch girl is fairly extensive. The popular form of the "nautch girl" was derived from a wide variety of images—those of the *tavayif*, or courtesan, as well as the *bayadere*, or temple girl. See George Dance, *The Nautch Girl, or, The Rajah of Chutneypore: A New Indian Comic Opera in Two Acts.* London: Chappell & Co., 1891; K. Raghunathaji, *Bombay Dancing Girls.* 4th edn, Bombay: Education Society's Press, 1884; *Nautch Woman: An Appeal to English Ladies on Behalf of their Indian Sisters.* Madras: Christian Literature Society, 1893; *Opinions on the Nautch Question.* Lahore: Punjab Purity Association, 1894; Thomas Duer Broughton, *Letters Written in a Mahratta Camp During the Year 1809*; London: John Murray, 1813 [1892 edn]; *Our Plague Spot: In Connection with our Polity and Usages, As regards our Women, our Soldiery, and the Indian Empire.* London: Thomas Cautley Newby, 1859. In *Writing under the Raj*, Nancy Paxton describes the *devadasi* as a "figure of abjection" (Paxton 1999: 87). She identifies the *devadasi* almost exclusively as a Hindu temple dancer, while the term "nautch girl" is a more composite figure in the Anglo-Indian romances, drawn from various colonial discourses about Hindu and Islamic religious and secular traditions.

17 Nancy Paxton has also noted that the figure of the "nautch girl" expresses not only the author's "personal commitments to Christian evangelicalism . . . but also the effects of the larger forces driving colonial anthropology and imperial medicine which worked in concert with evangelicalism and with the social purity movement to reshape the figure of the *devadasi* in the last two decades of the nineteenth century" (Paxton 1999: 90).

18 As Ella Shohat, Lisa Lowe, and Nancy Paxton have argued, the zenana is a significant site for the enactment of masculine, imperial power. Paxton contends that Kipling's "troubled reflection of the zenana" mirrors the "actual, historical, ideological, and symbolic tensions of life in British India in the 1880s and 1890s" (Paxton 1992: 18).

19 For a detailed discussion of the "uncanny" in relation to Kipling's narrative vision, see Sullivan (1993), pp. 20–1.

20 Christian missionaries, such as the Church of England Zenana Missionary, were engaged throughout the later nineteenth century and the early twentieth century in promoting the cause of conversion of Indian women.

21 Stories of such conversions are available in the Zenana Mission official journal, *India's Women: The Magazine of the Church of England Zenana Mission.* See in particular, Rev. W. H. Jackson Picken, *From an Indian Zenana: The Story of India's Muttulakshmi.* London: Charles H. Kelly, 1892; Miss S. Joseph, *Zenana Work.* Benares: Medical Hall Press, 1887;

Josephine A. Evans, *Kali-Dassie: The Servant of the Goddess Kali*. London: CEZM Society, 1904; *Kardoo, the Hindoo Girl. By a Zenana Missionary*. London: Religious Tract Society, 1870; G. Arnold Fernandez, *The Romance of the Zenana*. Madras: Hoe & Co., 1900; Armstrong Hopkins, *Within the Purdah: Being the Observations of a Medical Missionary in India*. New York: Eaton & Mains, 1899; William D. Hockley, *Tales of the Zenana*. London: n.p., 1874; E.A.L.O., *The Zenana Reader*. Madras: Christian Vernacular Education Society, 1880; Milly Cattell, *Behind the Purdah*. Calcutta: Thacker, Spink & Co., 1916.

4 Savage pursuits: missionary civility and colonization in E. M. Forster's "The Life to Come"

1 Demographic reports on the Bhils continued to be produced throughout the nineteenth century all the way up to 1916, when R. V. Russell published *The Tribes and Castes of the Central Provinces of India*, in which they are described as a "non-Aryan tribe" (Russell 1916: 278). Horatio Rowney's account in *The Wild Tribes of India* (1882) confirms that the savagery of the Bhils had been contained through the intervention of the government: "The Country of the Bheels is still as wild as ever; but a great portion of the population . . . has now been thoroughly tamed, and accustomed to industry and labour" (Rowney 1882: 33).

2 Perhaps the only direct allusion Forster makes to the Bhils is found in his novel *A Passage to India*, where, along with Gurkhas, Rajputs, Jats, Sikhs, Punjabis, and Pathans, Bhil fighters are mentioned as being the ideal fighting men in the British army (Forster 1924: 184).

3 Missionary interest in the Bhils dates back to the nineteenth century, when the first conference on "non-Aryan tribes" organized by the Christian Missionary Society was held at Salisbury Square, London in 1877. Missionary pioneers, such as Charles Stewart Thompson and J. W. Goodrun, helped establish schools and hospitals in the Bhil regions of Western India. Missionary accounts of India's tribal regions and the history of British control over the territories are to be found in works such as Ellis (1883), p. 16.

4 Missionary rhetoric about "civilization" reiterated the belief that "civilization appears to advance in society in the same proportion as Christianity is diffused. . . . Degraded indeed was the condition of the inhabitants of pagan countries before Christian missionaries commenced their arduous labours, which have already been attended to all who feel a just desire for happiness to mankind" (Ellis 1833: 1). The efforts of Reginald Heber, the famous nineteenth-century missionary, are recalled in many of these missionary documents, including his encounter with the "Bheels" (see Peggs 1832: 403). In 1871, Captain James Forsyth of the Bengal Staff Corps drew a detailed picture of the central highlands by furnishing a history of the immigration of its original populations as well as the geology and forest life of the Gonds, the Bhils, and the Kols. The language of Forsyth's account is characteristically anthropological: "Few parts of India present so great a range of interesting natural objects for investigation as this" (Forsyth 1871: 21), adding that the "ethical, zoological, botanical, [and] geological" features of the area provide a rare site for scientific inquiry. Forsyth's work also displays a rare interest in Gond language and traditions, including the songs of the Gond "troubadours" (ibid.: 95).

5 In 1832, James Peggs, a missionary in Cuttack in the southeastern region of Orissa, provide an account of the rich mineral sources—primarily iron ore—ready be exploited from the forests, saying, "the Indian forests hardly afford any commodity fit for foreign exportation, because the Indians know not how to turn them to account" (Peggs 1832: 393). Commenting on the indigenous methods of extracting the ore, he says: "if we look to the mining operations of the Indians, we shall find (as every one capable of taking a rational view of man in such a condition of society must expect) conspicuous examples of carelessness, incapacity, want of capital, and want of enterprise" (ibid.: 394).

6 Colonial historiographical work undertaken by figures such as Alexander Dow, the

author of the eighteenth-century *History of Hindustan*, and in the nineteenth century by James Mill, Charles Trevelyan, Thomas Macaulay, Sir William Hunter, J. R. Seeley, and Alfred Lyall had similarly deployed these spaces and temporalities to chart India's history and to explain the historical necessity of European intervention to bring the subject nations under colonial rule.

7 Relations between the missionaries and the East India Company in the nineteenth century have been briefly explored in Carson (1991). Also see Rachel Tolan's essay for a discussion of the collaboration of the Salvation Army and government agencies on projects relating to the reform of criminal tribes in India (Tolan 1995: 91).

5 Civility and the colonial state of body in Leonard Woolf

1 In *Virginia Woolf Against Empire*, Kathy Phillips argues that Virginia Woolf's whole *oeuvre* expresses an exultation in the dissolution of the empire. In her analysis of Woolf's short story "Thunder at Wembley," Phillips shows how Woolf conveys a sense of the "passing of the Empire" by revealing the "arrogance of the puffed-out members of the band" at the British Empire Exhibition, wondering how the public could be held in thrall by their "spell" (Phillips 1994: xxix–xxx).

2 "Bonga-Bonga in Whitehall" appeared in the *New Statesman* on January 17, 1914.

3 The most recent, and in my view the only, study of Woolf's colonial stories is to be found in Elleke Boehmer's "'Immeasurable Strangeness' in Imperial Times: Leonard Woolf and W. B. Yeats." Among other things, Boehmer notes Woolf's Conradian technique and his use of a "bricolage of voices" (2000: 105) to communicate the "intense uncertainty" over the "question of received meanings from points of view external to England" (ibid.: 107–8). That this epistemological impossibility has to do with Woolf's own understanding of the limits of metropolitan civility is the focus of this chapter.

4 In his autobiography, Woolf writes that the "jungle and the people who lived in the Sinhalese jungle villages fascinated, almost obsessed me in London, in Putney or Bloomsbury, and in Cambridge. *The Village in the Jungle* was a novel in which I tried somehow or other vicariously to live their lives" (Woolf 1960: 78).

5 For a detailed account of Woolf's career in Sri-Lanka, refer to Duncan Wilson's biography ([1978] 2003).

6 Rosenbaum makes a distinction between the two stages in Moore's development as a thinker—the first stage he describes as being a "monistic mentalism," and the second as resting more on a "dualist" conception of the mind–matter relationship. For details, see Rosenbaum (1987), 222–30.

7 Cathy Caruth's reading of trauma is derived from Freud's discussion of the returning traumatic dream in *Beyond the Pleasure Principle*. Freud provides the example of accident victims whose dreams reproduced the catastrophe they had suffered so that they could retrospectively gain some control over the unsettling occurrence. Freud explained that traumatic neurosis was not simply a reaction to any horrible event, but a response to the "perplexing experience of survival" (Caruth 1996: 31). This suggests a sense of indirectness, which results from the fact that trauma is not directly available to experience, and that there is an unmediated link between the consciousness that suffers and the life-threatening events. In fact, trauma is the "strange connection between the elision of memory and the precision of recall" (Caruth 1995: 153). Since I am more concerned with questions of narrativity in this essay, I have deliberately avoided seeing the "real" purely in terms of the Lacanian "Real."

8 Kaja Silverman's discussion of male subjectivity is relevant here because of its attempt to discern the dynamic formation of a "normative male ego" through repetition. Repetition is necessary to protect the "coherence" (1992: 61) of male subjectivity, being ideologically invested in protecting its own boundaries, but repetition also opens it up to the contingencies of history and power relations.

9 The page numbers given in parentheses refer to Leonard Woolf's "Three Stories on

Ceylon by Leonard Woolf." The story "Pearls and Swine" also appears in *Stories from the Raj: From Kipling to Independence*, ed. Saros Cowasjee (London: Bodley Head, 1982), and the critical appraisal of the same story is in Elleke Boehmer's edition of *Empire Writing: An Anthology of Colonial Literature* (Oxford: OUP, 1998).

10 Here it might be worth noting what Daniel Bivona has argued about Kiplings's vision of "work." According to him, it represented a "complex form of social endeavor" based on a "complex division of labor" that fitted into an image of organic and "natural" order, instead of being part of a specific historical arrangement in industrial societies. Bivona suggests that this bureaucratic vision rested on the sense that hierarchies within the order were "founded on inequalities of power and ability" (Bivona 1998: 71) which, unlike the traditional patterns of Indian caste relations, served "utilitarian rather than cosmically authoritarian ends" (ibid.: 72). Although the native population of divers were never imagined as being part of a "natural" order, the distinctions of nationality and race being so evident to the colonial observer, the systems of surveillance operating in these pearl fisheries were founded on observable and calculable utilitarian distinctions. The level of specificity in describing the different kinds of labor involved in the process highlights a modality of order that is based on what I have described as "modern biopower." Such biopower also rested on determining the level of health and sanitation in the pearling station and in preventing diseases such as cholera and smallpox.

11 In *The History of Sexuality I: An Introduction*, Foucault describes "two poles of development" in the exercise of power over life, "linked together by a whole intermediate cluster of relations." He describes one of these poles as centering "on the body as a machine: its disciplining, the optimization of its capabilities, the extortion of its forces, the parallel increase of its usefulness and its docility, its integration into systems of efficient and economic controls, all this was ensured by the procedures of power that characterized the disciplines: an anatomo-politics of the human body." The second pole, he says, serves "as the basis of the biological processes: propagation, births and mortality, the level of health, life expectancy and longevity, with all the conditions that can cause these to vary. Their supervision was effected through an entire series of interventions and regulatory controls: a biopolitics of the population" (Foucault 1978: 139).

12 This form of territorialized landscape as reflecting capitalism's symbolic role in recoding the socius is discussed by Robert Young in *Colonial Desire* (see pp. 168–9).

Conclusion: civil conduct

1 Lawrence's representation of the manservant relies on nineteenth-century descriptions of working-class people and vagrants from Ireland and India found, for example, in Henry Mayhew's *London Labour and London Poor* (1851–62).

References and bibliography

Nineteenth-century Anglo-Indian periodicals

CR = *Calcutta Review*
"Modern Civilization," by Ram Chandra Bose. *Bengal Magazine* 10 (1882), 325–48.
"British Rule in India." *Calcutta Fortnightly Review* 1.9 (1881), 57–60.
"The End of Education." *Calcutta Magazine* 53 (1883), 123–30.
"Anglo-Indian Romance." *CR* 50 (1870), 180–208.
"A Contribution to the Education Question." *CR* 94 (1892), 346–58.
"Bengal European Code School," by G. S. Gasper. *CR* 84 (1887), 112–29.
"Cram and Crammers." *CR* 59 (1874), 285–320.
"A Definition of Culture," by Charles Johnston. *CR* 108 (1899), 115–28.
"The Education Code for European Schools in Bengal," by L. W. D'Cruz. *CR* 84 (1887), 381–91.
"Education in Bengal." *CR* 90 (1893), 152–63.
"Eurasians and Poor Europeans in India," by Edward Thomas. *CR* 72 (1881), 39–55.
"Higher Education in Bengal," by Parbati Churn Roy. *CR* 84 (1887), 232–42.
"Indian Universities–Ideal and Actual I," by H. R. J. *CR* 100 (1895), 383–401.
"Indian Universities–Ideal and Actual III," by H. R. J. *CR* 105 (1897), 139–62.
"The Native Press of Bengal." *CR* 43 (1866), 358–79.
"Race and Language," by Charles Johnston. *CR* 96 (1893), 294–307.
"Review of *Considerations on Representative Government* by J. S. Mill." *CR* 37 (1861), 188–223.
"The Teaching of English," by H. R. J. *CR* 96 (1893), 294–307.

Books and articles

Ahmad, Aijaz (1992) *In Theory: Classes, Nations, Literatures*. New York: Verso.
Anderson, Benedict (1983) *Imagined Communities*. New York: Verso.
Anstey, F. (1897) *Baboo Jabberjee B.A.* London: J. M. Dent & Co.
Appadurai, Arjun (1996) *Modernity at Large*. Minneapolis: University of Minnesota Press.
Appeal to the Scientific World: Being a Scientific Exposition of the Study of Vice or Humanity in Vicious Aspect (1894). Bombay: Ripon Printing Press.
Aravamudan, Srinivas (1999) *Tropicopolitans: Colonialism and Agency, 1688–1804*. Durham, NC: Duke University Press.
Ardis, Ann (1990) *New Women, New Novels: Feminism and Early Modernism*. New Brunswick, NJ: Rutgers University Press.
Arnold, David (1993) *Colonizing the Body*. Berkeley: University of California Press.
Arnold, David, and Ramachandra Guha (1998) *Nature, Culture, Imperialism: Essays on the Environmental History of South Asia*. Delhi: Oxford University Press.

Arnold, Matthew (1954) *Matthew Arnold: Poetry and Prose*, ed. John Bryson. London: Rupert Hart-Davis.

Arondekar, Anjali (n.d.) "The Story of an India Rubber Dildo: Un-doing Victorian Pornography." Unpublished paper.

Asad, Talal (1992) "Conscripts of Western Civilization." *In Dialectical Anthropology: Essays in Honor of Stanley Diamond*, vol. 1, ed. Christine Gailey. Gainesville: University of Florida Press, 337.

Austen, Jane (1970) *Sense and Sensibility*. New York: Oxford University Press.

"Baboo English": On our Mother-Tongue as our Aryan Brethren Understand It. Amusing Specimens of Composition and Style, or, English as Written by Some of Her Majesty's Indian Subjects (1890). Collected and edited by T. W. J. Calcutta: H. P. Kent & Co.

Balibar, Etienne, and Immanuel Wallerstein (1991) *Race, Nation, Class: Ambiguous Identities*. New York: Verso.

Ballhatchet, Kenneth (1953–4) "The Home Government and Bentinck's Educational Policy." *Cambridge Historical Journal* 11, 224–9.

Ballhatchet, Kenneth (1980) *Race, Sex, and Class under the Raj: Imperial Attitudes and Policies and their Critics*. London: Weidenfeld & Nicolson.

Barber, William (1975) *British Economic Thought and India 1600–1858*. Oxford: Clarendon Press.

Baring, Evelyn, Earl of Cromer (1913) *Political and Literary Essays 1908–1913*. London: Macmillan & Co.

Barrell, John (1991) *The Infection of Thomas De Quincey: Psychopathology of Imperialism*. New Haven, CT: Yale University Press.

Battling and Building Among the Bhils (1914) London: Church Missionary Society.

Baumgart, Winfried (1982) *Imperialism: The Idea and Reality of British and French Colonial Expansion 1880–1914*. Oxford: Oxford University Press.

Beauman, Nicola (1994) *E. M. Forster: A Biography*. New York: Alfred A. Knopf.

Bellamy, Elizabeth Jane (1998) "'Intimate Enemies': Psychoanalysis, Marxism, and Post-colonial Affect." *South Atlantic Quarterly* 97, 341–59.

Berlant, Lauren (1991) *The Anatomy of National Fantasy*. Chicago, IL: University of Chicago Press.

Bhabha, Homi (1985) "Sly Civility." *October* 34, 71–80.

Bhabha, Homi (1990) *Nation and Narration*. London: Routledge.

Bhabha, Homi (1994) "Of Mimicry and Man." In *The Location of Culture*. New York: Routledge, 85–92.

Bignold, Thomas Frank (1888) *Leviora: Being the Rhymes of a Successful Competitor*. London: Thacker, Spink.

Bivona, Daniel (1998) *British Imperial Literature, 1870–1940: Writing and the Administration of Empire*. Cambridge: Cambridge University Press.

Blagdon, Edward (1931) *A Cadetship in the Honourable East India Company's Service, 1805: Being a Short Memoir of Edward Blagdon. Born 1788. Died 1806*, ed. Florence Mostyn Gamlen. London: Oxford University Press.

Blair, G. W. (1906) *Station and Camp Life in the Bheel Country: A Brief History of the Origins, Aims, and Operations of the Irish Presbyterian Jungle Tribes's Mission, with an Account of the Bheels: their Manners, Custom, Religion, etc.* Belfast: Committee of the Jungle Tribes' Mission.

Bland, Lucy (1995) *Banishing the Beast: Sexuality and the Early Feminists*. New York: New Press.

Boehmer, Elleke (2000) "'Immeasurable Strangeness' in Imperial Times: Leonard Woolf and W. B. Yeats." In *Modernism and Empire*, ed. Howard J. Booth and Nigel Rigby. New York: Manchester University Press, 93–111.

Bongie, Chris (1991) *Exotic Memoirs: Literature, Colonialism, and the Fin de Siècle*. Stanford, CA: Stanford University Press.

Booth, Howard J., and Nigel Rigby (2000) *Modernism and Empire*. New York: Manchester University Press.

Brantlinger, Patrick (1996) *Fictions of State: Culture and Credit in Britain, 1694–1994*. Ithaca, NY: Cornell University Press.

Bristow, Joseph (1991) *Empire Boys: Adventures in a Man's World*. London: Unwin Hyman.

Brody, Jennifer DeVere (1998) *Impossible Purities: Blackness, Feminity, and Victorian Culture*. Durham, NC: Duke University Press.

Brown, David (1999) *Walter Scott and the Historical Imagination*. London: Routledge & Kegan Paul.

Brown, Paul (1985) "This Thing of Darkness I Acknowledge Mine: *The Tempest* and the Discourse of Colonialism." In *Political Shakespeare: Essays in Cultural Materialism*, ed. Jonathan Dollimore and Alan Sinfield. Ithaca, NY: Cornell University Press.

Buckingham. J. S. (1830) *History of the Public Proceedings on the Question of the East India Monopoly*. London: Hurst, Chance & Co.

Burchell, Graham, Colin Gordon, and Peter Miller (1991) *The Foucault Effect: Studies in Governmentality*. Chicago, IL: University of Chicago Press.

Butler, Josephine (1885) *The Present Aspect of the Abolitionist Cause in Relation to British India: A Letter to my Friends*. London: Pewtress & Co.

The Cadet: A Poem in Six parts Containing Remarks on British India. By a Late Resident in the East (1814), 2 vols. London: Robert Jennings.

Caine, Barbara (1997) *English Feminism 1780–1980*. Oxford: Oxford University Press.

Calder, Jenni (1976) *Women and Marriage in Victorian Fiction*. Oxford: Oxford University Press.

Campbell, John (1864) *A Personal Narrative of Thirteen Years' Service Amongst the Wild Tribes of Khondistan for the Suppression of Human Sacrifice*. London: Hurst & Blackett.

Canning, Albert S. G. (1910) *Sir Walter Scott Studied in Eight Novels*. London: T. Fisher Unwin.

Carrington, Charles (1955) *Rudyard Kipling: His Life and Work*. Harmondsworth: Penguin.

Carson, Penelope (1991) "Missionaries, Bureaucrats and the People of India 1793–1833." In *Orientalism, Evangelicalism and the Military Cantonment in Early Nineteenth-Century India*, ed. Nancy G. Cassels. Lewiston: Edwin Mellen Press, 125–55.

Carstairs, R. (1895) *Human Nature in Rural India*. London: William Blackwood & Sons.

Carstairs, R. (1912) *The Little World of an Indian District Officer*. London: Macmillan.

Caruth, Cathy (1995) "Introduction to 'Recapturing the Past.'" In *Trauma: Explorations in Memory*, ed. Caruth. Baltimore, MD: Johns Hopkins University Press, 151–7.

Caruth, Cathy (1996) "Traumatic Departures: Survival and History in Freud." In *Trauma and Self*, ed. Charles B. Strozier and Michael Flynn. Lanham, MD: Rowman & Littlefield, 29–43.

Chakrabarty, Dipesh (2000a) "Postcoloniality and the Artifice of History: Who Speaks for the 'Indian' Pasts?" In *Provincializing Europe*. Princeton, NJ: Princeton University Press, 27–46.

Chakrabarty, Dipesh (2000b) *Provincializing Europe*. Princeton, NJ: Princeton University Press.

Chatterjee, Partha (1993) "The Colonial State." In *The Nation and its Fragments: Colonial and Post-Colonial Histories*. Princeton, NJ: Princeton University Press.

Chatterjee, Partha (1996) "The Disciplines in Colonial Bengal." In *Texts of Power: Emerging Disciplines in Colonial Bengal*, ed. Chatterjee. Calcutta: Centre for Studies in Social Sciences.

Cheem, Aliph (pseud.) [Captain Yeldham of the 18th Hussars] (1871) *Lays of Ind*. Bombay: Thacker, Vining & Co.

Chevrillon, Andre (1897) *Romantic India*, trans. William Marchant. London: Heinemann.

Clark, Gail C. (1985) "Imperial Stereotypes: G. A. Henty and the Boys' Own Empire." *Journal of Popular Culture* 18, 43–52.

Clifford, James (1988) *The Predicament of Culture: Twentieth-Century Ethnography, Literature, and Art*. Cambridge, MA: Harvard University Press.

Corbett, Mary Jean (1992) *Representing Femininity: Middle-Class Subjectivity in Victorian and Edwardian Women's Autobiographies*. New York: Oxford University Press.

Crawford, F. Marion (1893) *The Novel: What It Is*. London: Macmillan.

Croker, B. M. (1901) *Angel: A Sketch in Indian Ink*. London: Methuen.

Crosby, Christina (1992) "Reading the Gothic Revival." In *Rewriting the Victorians: Theory, History, and the Politics of Gender*, ed. Linda Shires. New York and London: Routledge, 101–15.

Cunningham, A. R. (1973) "The 'new woman' fiction of the 1890s." *Victorian Studies* 17, 111–28.

Cvetkovich, Ann (1992) *Mixed Feelings: Feminism, Mass Culture, and Victorian Sensationalism*. New Brunswick, NJ: Rutgers University Press.

Dandeker, Christopher (1990) *Surveillance, Power and Modernity*. New York: St. Martin's Press.

Darby, Phillip (1987) *Three Faces of Imperialism: British and American Approaches to Asia and Africa 1870–1970*. New Haven, CT: Yale University Press.

David, Deirdre (1995) *Rule Britannia: Women, Empire, and Victorian Writing*. Ithaca, NY: Cornell University Press.

Davin, Anna (1978) "Imperialism and Motherhood." *History Workshop* 5, 9–65.

Dawson, C. Amy (1892) *Idylls of Womanhood*. London: William Heinemann.

Dawson, Graham (1994) *Soldier Heroes, British Adventure, Empire, and the Imagining of Masculinities*. London: Routledge.

De Groot, Joanna (1989) "Sex and Race." In *Sexuality and Subordination*, ed. Susan Mendus and Jane Rendall. New York: Routledge, 89–128.

Desh-u-Lubun Ocharik (1830) *Letter to the Author of a View of the Present State and Future Prospects of Free Trade and Colonization of India*. 2nd edn. London: Smith, Elder & Co.

De Silva, Mervyn (1963) Introduction to Part II. In Leonard Woolf, *Dairies of Ceylon 1908–1911*. London: Hogarth Press, xlviii–lx.

Disraeli, Benjamin ([1845] 1995) *Sybil*. Ware: Wordsworth Classics.

Dixon, Robert (1995) *Writing the Colonial Adventure: Race, Gender, and Nation in Anglo-Australian Popular Fiction, 1875–1914*. Cambridge: Cambridge University Press.

Donnelly, Michael (1991) "On Foucault's Uses of the Notion of 'Biopower'." In *Michel Foucault, Philosopher*, trans. Timothy J. Armstrong. New York: Routledge, 199–203.

Donner, Wendy (1991) *The Liberal Self: John Stuart Mill's Moral and Political Philosophy*. Ithaca, NY: Cornell University Press.

Dowie, Menie Muriel (1893) *Women Adventurers: The Lives of Madame Velasquez, Hannah Snell, Mary Anne Talbot and Mrs. Christian Davies*. London, n.p.

Duncan, Ian (1993) "Scott's Romance of Empire: *The Tales of the Crusaders*." In *Scott in Carnival: Selected Papers from the Fourth International Scott Conference*, 1991, ed. J. H. Alexander and David Hewitt. Aberdeen: Association for Scottish Literary Studies, 370–9.

Duncan, Sara (1909) *The Burnt Offering*. London: Methuen.

Dutt, Romesh Chunder (1897) *England and India: A Record of Progress During a Hundred Years 1785–1885*. London: Chatto & Windus.

The Eastern Question: The Three Great Perils of England (1887). London: n.p.

Ellis, Harriet Warner (1862) *Toils and Triumphs, or, Missionary Work in the World's Dark Places*. London: n.p.

Ellis, Harriet Warner (1883) *Our Eastern Sisters and their Missionary Helpers*. London: Religious Tract Society.

Ellis, William, ed. (1833) *The Missionary or Christian's New Year's Gift*. London: Seeley & Sons.

Elridge, C. C. (1973) *England's Mission: The Imperial Idea in the Age of Gladstone and Disraeli 1868–1880*. Durham: North Carolina University Press.

Endelman, Todd M. (1979) *The Jews of Georgian England 1714–1830: Tradition and Change in a Liberal Society*. Philadelphia: Jewish Publication Society of America.

Evans, De Lacy (1829) *On the Practicability of an Invasion of British India and on the Commercial and Financial Prospects and Resources of the Empire*. London: n.p.

Ewald, François (1991) "A Power without an Exterior." In *Michel Foucault, Philosopher*, trans. Timothy J. Armstrong. New York: Routledge, 169–75.

Ewen, Frederic (1984) *Heroic Imagination*. Secaucus, NJ: Citadel Press.

Examination of the Principles and Policy of the Government of British India. By a Gentleman in the Service of the Honourable the East India Company (1829). London: Hurst, Chance, & Co.

Felsenstein, Frank (1995) *Anti-Semitic Stereotypes: A Paradigm of Otherness in English Popular Culture, 1660–1830*. Baltimore, MD: Johns Hopkins University Press.

Finck, Henry T. (1899) *Primitive Love and Love-Stories*. New York: Charles Scribner's Sons.

Forster, E. M. (1920) "Missionaries." *The Athenaeum*, 22, 545–6.

Forster, E. M. (1924) *A Passage to India*. New York: Harcourt, Brace & Co.

Forster, E. M. (1927) *Aspects of the Novel*. New York: Harcourt & Brace.

Forster, E. M. ([1953] 1983) *The Hill of Devi and Other Indian Writings*, ed. Elizabeth Heine. London: Edward Arnold.

Forster, E. M. (1972) *The Life to Come and Other Stories*, ed. Oliver Stallybrass. London: Edward Arnold.

Forster, E. M. (1985) *Selected Letters of E. M. Forster*, vol. 2: *1921–1970*, ed. Mary Lago and P. N. Furbank. Cambridge, MA: Harvard University Press.

Forsyth, James (1871) *The Highlands of Central India: Notes on their Forests and Wild Tribes, Natural History, and Sports*. London: Chapman & Hall.

Foucault, Michel (1972) *The Archaeology of Knowledge*, trans. A. M. Sheridan Smith. New York: Pantheon.

Foucault, Michel (1977a) *Discipline and Punish: the Birth of the Prison*, trans. Alan Sheridan. New York: Pantheon.

Foucault, Michel (1977b) *Language, Counter-Memory, Practice*, ed. and trans. Donald Bouchard. Ithaca, NY: Cornell University Press.

Foucault, Michel (1978) *The History of Sexuality I: An Introduction*, trans. Robert Hurley. New York: Pantheon.

Foucault, Michel ([1981] 1988) "Technologies of the Self." In *Technologies of the Self: A Seminar with Michel Foucault*, ed. Luther H. Martin, Huck Gutman, and Patrick Hutton. London: Tavistock.

Foucault, Michel (1991) "Governmentality.' In *The Foucault Effect: Studies in Governmentality*, ed. Graham Burchell, Colin Gordon, and Peter Miller. Chicago, IL: University of Chicago Press, 87–104.

Foucault, Michel (1997) "The Birth of Biopolitics." In *Ethics, Subjectivity and Truth*, ed. Paul Rabinow. New York: New Press, 73–9.

Furbank, P. N. (1978) *E. M. Forster: A Life*, vol. 2: *1914–1970*. London: Secker & Warburg.

Garside, Peter (1993) "Meg Merrilies, the Gypsies, and India." In *Scott in Carnival: Selected Papers from the Fourth International Scott Conference, 1991*, ed. J. H. Alexander and David Hewitt. Aberdeen: Association for Scottish Literary Studies, 154–71.

Garwood, John (1859) *Our Plague Spot: In Connection with our Polity and Usages, as Regards our Women, our Soldiery, and the Indian Empire*. London: Thomas Cautley Newby.

Gilman, Sander (1991) *The Jew's Body*. New York: Routledge.

Gorra, Michael (1997) "Rudyard Kipling to Salman Rushdie: Imperialism to Post-colonialism." In *The Columbia History of the British Novel*, ed. John Richetti. New York: Columbia University Press, 631–57.

Graham, George (1878) *Life in the Mofussil, or, The Civilian in Lower Bengal. By An Ex-Civilian*, vol. 1. London: C. Kegan Paul & Co.

Grant, Robert (1813) *A Sketch of the History of the East India Company from its First Formation to the Passing of the Regulating Act of 1773*. London: Black, Parry, & Co.

Green, Martin (1979) *Dreams of Adventure, Deeds of Empire*. New York: Basic Books.

Green, Martin (1991) *Seven Types of Adventure Tale*. University Park: Pennsylvania State University Press.

Hall, Catherine (1991) *White, Male, Middle Class: Male Sexuality 1900–1950*. Cambridge: Polity Press.

Hamilton, Walter (1815) *The East India Gazetteer; Containing Particular Descriptions of the Empires, Kingdoms, Principalities, Provinces, Cities, Towns, Districts, Fortresses, Harbours, Lakes, etc of Hindostan*. London: John Murray.

Hardie, J. Kier (1909) *India: Impressions and Suggestions*. London: Independent Labour Party.

Hardiman, David (1994) "Power in the Forest: The Dangs, 1820–1940." *Subaltern Studies VIII*, ed. David Arnold and David Hardiman. Delhi: Oxford University Press.

Harootunian, Harry D. (1996) "The Benjamin Effect: Modernism, Repetition, and the Path to Different Cultural Imaginaries." In *Water Benjamin and the Demands of History*, ed. Michael P. Steinberg. Ithaca, NY: Cornell University Press, 62–87.

Harris, Abram L. (1964) "John Stuart Mill: Servant of the East India Company." *Canadian Journal of Economics and Political Science* 30, 185–202.

Harvey, David (1989) *The Condition of Postmodernity*. Oxford: Oxford University Press.

Harvie, Christopher (1983) "Scott and the Image of Scotland." In *Sir Walter Scott: The Long Forgotten Melody*, ed. Alan Bold. London: Vision Press, 17–42.

Hendricks, Margo (1994) "Civility, Barbarism, and Aphra Behn's *The Widow's Ranter*." In *Women, "Race," and Writing in the Early Modern Period*, ed. Hendricks and Patricia Parker. London: Routledge, 225–39.

Hennessy, Rosemary (1994–5) "Queer Visibility in Commodity Culture." *Cultural Critique* 29, 31–76.

Hennessy, Rosemary, and Rajeswari Mohan (1994) "The Construction of Woman in Three Popular Texts of Empire: Towards a Critique of Materialist Feminism." In *Colonial Discourse and Post-Colonial Theory*, ed. Patrick Williams and Laura Chrisman. New York: Columbia University Press, 462–78.

Herdman, W. A. (1903) *Report to the Government of Ceylon on the Pearl Oyster Fisheries of the Gulf of Manaar*. London: Royal Society.

Hervey, H. (1912) *Nautch Girls: Cameos of Indian Crime*. London: Stanley Paul.

Heywood, T. (1830) *An Enquiry into the Impediments to a free Trade with the Peninsula of India*. London: T. Rodd.

Hobsbawm, Eric (1987) *The Age of Empire, 1875–1914*. London: Weidenfeld & Nicolson.

Hollis, Patricia, ed. (1979) *Women in Public 1850–1900: Documents of the Victorian Women's Movement*. London: George Allen & Unwin.

Hornell, James (1905) *The Biological Results of the Ceylon Pearl Fishery of 1904, with Notes on Divers and their Occupation*. Colombo: n.p.

Hornell, James (1907) *Report on the Operations on the Ceylon Pearl Banks: During the Fishing Season of 1907*. Colombo: The Ceylon Company of Pearl Fishers.

Hutchins, Francis G. (1967) *The Illusion of Permanence: British Imperialism in India*. Princeton, NJ: Princeton University Press.

Hyam, Robert (1990) *Empire and Sexuality: The British Experience.* Manchester: Manchester University Press.

Hyam, Robert (1992) *Britain's Imperial Century 1815–1914: A Study of Empire and Expansion.* Manchester: Manchester University Press.

India: A Poem in Three Cantos. By a Young Civilian of Bengal (1834) London: John R. Priestly.

Jackson, John (1829) *A Treatise on the Capability of our Eastern Possessions to Produce Those Articles of Consumption and Raw Material for British Manufacture, for which We Chiefly Depend on Foreign Nations; and the Incalculable Advantages of a Free Trade to and Settlement in India to All Classes of His Majesty's Subjects.* London: Smith, Elder & Co.

Jameson, Fredric (1990) "Modernism and Imperialism." In *Nationalism, Colonialism, and Literature.* Intro. by Seamus Deane. Minneapolis: University of Minnesota Press, 43–68.

JanMuhamed, Abdul (1985) "The Economy of Manichean Allegory: The Function of Racial Difference in Colonialist Literature." *Critical Inquiry* 12, 59–87.

Johnston, Charles (1900) *Kela Bai: An Anglo-Indian Idyll.* London: Doubleday & McClure.

Johnstone, J. K. (1954) *The Bloomsbury Group: A Study of E. M. Forster, Lytton Strachey, Virginia Woolf, and their Circle.* London: Secker & Warburg.

Kaplan, Cora (1986) "Pandora's Box: Subjectivity, Class and Sexuality in Socialist Feminist Criticism." In *Sea Changes: Essays in Culture and Feminism.* London: Verso, 147–76.

Keegan, William (1889) *Sirdhana (An Account of the Begum Somre and her Family).* London: n.p.

Kent, Susan K. (1987) *Sex and Suffrage in Britain 1860–1914.* Princeton, NJ: Princeton University Press.

Kincaid, Dennis (1938) *British Social Life in India 1608–1937.* London: George Routledge & Sons.

Kipling, Rudyard ([1901] 1998) *Kim.* New York: Oxford University Press.

Kipling, Rudyard, and C. Wolcott Balestier ([1892] 1921) *The Naulahka: A Novel of East and West.* Garden City, NY: Doubleday.

Knighton, W. (1854) *Forest Life in Ceylon.* London: Hurst & Blackett.

Knox, Robert (1681) *An Historical Relation of the Island of Ceylon in the East Indies.* London: n.p.

Koestenbaum, Wayne (1989) *Double Talk: The Erotics of Male Literary Collaboration.* New York: Routledge.

Kopf, David (1969) *British Orientalism and the Bengal Renaissance: The Dynamics of Indian Modernization.* Berkeley: University of California Press, 1969.

Koundoura, Maria (1998) "Multiculturalism or Multinationalism?" In *Multicultural States: Rethinking Difference and Identity,* ed. David Bennett. New York: Routledge, 69–87.

Krishnaswamy, Revathi (1998) *Effeminism: The Economy of Colonial Desire.* Ann Arbor: University of Michigan Press.

Kumar, Deepak (1997) *Science and the Raj 1857–1905.* Delhi: Oxford University Press.

Lach, Donald F., and Edwin J. van Kley (1993) *Asia in the Making of Europe,* vol. 3. Chicago, IL: University of Chicago Press.

Lago, Mary (1995) *E. M. Forster: A Literary Life.* New York: St. Martin's Press.

Lane, Christopher (1995) *The Ruling Passion: British Colonial Allegory and the Paradox of Homosexual Desire.* Durham, NC: Duke University Press.

Lane, Christopher (1997) "Betrayal and its Consolations in *Maurice,* 'Arthur Snatchfold,' and 'What Does it Matter?' A Morality." In *Queer Forster,* ed. Robert K. Martin and George Piggford. Chicago, IL: University of Chicago Press, 167–92.

Lane, Christopher (1998) "Savage Ecstasy: Colonialism and the Death Drive." In *The Psychoanalysis of Race,* ed. Lane. New York: Columbia University Press, 282–304.

Langbauer, Laurie (1990) *Woman and Romance: The Consolations of Gender in the English Novel.* Ithaca, NY: Cornell University Press.

Lauber, John (1966) *Sir Walter Scott.* New York: Twayne.

Lawrence, D. H. ([1920] 1987) *Women in Love*. London: Penguin.

Lays of a Subaltern. By "The Subaltern" (1895) Lahore: Civil and Military Gazette Press.

A Letter to the Proprietors of East India Stock (1769). London: W. Nicoll.

Ledger, Sally (1997) *The New Woman: Fiction and Feminism at the Fin de Siècle*. Manchester: Manchester University Press.

Ledger, Sally, and Roger Luckhurst (2000) *The Fin de Siècle: A Reader in Cultural History c. 1800–1900*. Oxford: Oxford University Press.

Levine, Philippa (1987) *Victorian Feminism 1850–1900*. Gainesville: Florida University Press.

Levine, Philippa (2003) *Prostitution, Race, and Politics: Policing Venereal Disease in the British Empire*. New York: Routledge.

The Life and Adventures of Shigram-Po, Cadet in the Service of the Hon'ble East India Company on the Bengal Establishment. By the Author of "Occasional Poems" (1821) Calcutta: Government Gazette Press.

Lloyd, David, and Paul Thomas (1998) *Culture and State*. New York: Routledge.

Lloyd, Trevor (1991) "John Stuart Mill and the East India Company." In *A Cultivated Mind*, ed. Michael Laine. Toronto: University of Toronto Press, 44–79.

Lowe, Lisa (1991) *Critical Terrains: French and British Orientalisms*. Ithaca, NY: Cornell University Press.

Lyall, Alfred (1894) *The Rise and Expansion of British Dominion in India*. 3rd edn, London: John Murray.

Lyall, Alfred (1907) *Verses Written in India*. 6th edn, London: Routledge.

Macaulay, Thomas Babington (1860) *Miscellaneous Writings*. London: Longman.

McClintock, Anne (1995) *Imperial Leather: Race, Gender and Sexuality in the Colonial Contest*. New York: Routledge.

McCosh, John (1856) *Advice to Officers in India*. London: W. H. Allen & Co.

MacDonald, Robert (1994) *The Language of Empire*. Manchester: Manchester University Press.

McDowell, Frederick P. W. (1982) *E. M. Forster*. Rev. edn, Boston, MA: Twayne.

Mackenzie, John M. (1986) *Imperialism and Popular Culture*. Manchester: Manchester University Press.

Mackenzie, John M. (1987) "The Imperial Pioneer and Hunter and the British Masculine Stereotype in Late Victorian and Edwardian Times." In *Manliness and Morality*, ed. J. A. Mangan and James Walvin. Manchester: Manchester University Press, 176–98.

McKeon, Michael (1987) *The Origins of the English Novel 1600–1740*. Baltimore, MD: Johns Hopkins University Press.

McMaster, Graham (1981) *Scott and Society*. Cambridge: Cambridge University Press.

Macmillan, Margaret (1988) *Women of the Raj*. New York: Thames & Hudson.

Macpherson, Samuel Charters (1865) *Memorials of Service in India: From the Correspondence of the Late Major Samuel Charters Macpherson*, ed. William Macpherson. London: John Murray.

Malchow, H. L. (1996) *Gothic Images of Race in Nineteenth-Century Britain*. Stanford, CA: Stanford University Press.

Mangan, J. A., and James Walvin, eds (1987) *Manliness and Morality: Middle-Class Masculinity in Britain and America 1800–1940*. Manchester: Manchester University Press.

Marcus, Jane (1992) "Britannia Rules the Waves." In *Decolonizing Tradition: New Views of Twentieth-Century "British" Literary Canons*, ed. Karen R. Lawrence. Urbana: University of Illinois Press, 136–62.

Marshall, P. J. (1968) *Problems of Empire: Britain and India 1757–1813*. London: George Allen & Unwin.

Martin, John Sayre (1976) *E. M. Forster: The Endless Journey*. Cambridge: Cambridge University Press.

Martin, Robert K., and George Piggford (1997) "Introduction: Queer, Forster?" In *Queer Forster*, ed. Martin and Piggford. Chicago, IL: Chicago University Press.

Mayhew, Henry (1851–62) *London Labour and London Poor: A Cyclopedia of the Conditions and Earnings of Those that Will Work and Those that Cannot.* London: n.p.

Mazlish, Bruce (1975) *James and John Stuart Mill: Father and Son in the Nineteenth Century.* Oxford: Transaction Books.

Mehta, Uday Singh (1999) *Liberalism and Empire: A Study in Nineteenth-Century Liberal Thought.* Chicago, IL: University of Chicago Press.

Merivale, Herman (1839) *Introduction to a Course on Colonization and Colonies.* London: Longman, Orme, Brown, Green.

Metcalf, Thomas R. (1995) *Ideologies of the Raj. The New Cambridge History of India* III, 4. Cambridge: Cambridge University Press.

Mill, John Stuart (1981) *Autobiography and Literary Essays*, ed. John M. Robson and Jack Stillinger. Toronto: University of Toronto Press.

Mill, John Stuart (1982) "England and Ireland." In *Essays on England, Ireland, and the Empire*, ed. John M. Robson. Toronto: University of of Toronto Press, 505–32.

Mill, John Stuart (1990) *Writings on India. Collected Works of John Stuart Mill*, vol. 30, ed. John M. Robson, Martin Moir, and Zawahir Moir. Toronto: University of Toronto Press.

Mill, John Stuart (1993) *On Liberty and Utilitarianism*, intro. Alan M. Dershowitz. New York: Bantam Books.

Millet, Marcus W. (1914) *Jungle Life in Ceylon.* London: Methuen & Co.

Milligan, Barry (1995) *Pleasures and Pains: Opium and the Orient in Nineteenth-Century British Culture.* Charlottesville: University of Virginia Press.

Mitchell, John (1805) *An Essay: By John Mitchell.* Edinburgh: William Blackwood.

The Modern Marriage Market. By Marie Corelli, Lady Jeune, Flora Annie Steel, and Susan, Countess of Malmesbury (1898). London: Hutchinson & Co.

Moir, Martin (1990) "Introduction." In John Stuart Mill, *Writings on India*, ed. John M. Robson, Martin Moir, and Zawahir Moir. Toronto: University of Toronto Press, vii–liv.

Moor, Edward (1794) *A Narrative of the Operations of Captain Little's Detachment.* London: n.p.

Moore, G. E. ([1903] 1951) *Principia Ethica.* Cambridge: Cambridge University Press.

Moore, R. J. (1966) *Liberalism and Indian Politics 1872–1992.* London: Edward Arnold.

Moore, R. J. (1983) "John Stuart Mill at East India House." *Historical Studies* 20, 497–519.

Moore-Gilbert, Bart (1997) *Postcolonial Theory: Contexts, Practices, Politics.* New York: Verso.

Mufti, Aamir, and Ella Shohat (1997) "Introduction." In *Dangerous Liasions: Gender, Nation, and Postcolonial Perspectives*, ed. Anne McClintock, Mufti, and Shohat. Minneapolis: University of Minnesota Press, 1–12.

Mukherjee, Ramakrishna (1974) *The Rise and Fall of the East India Company.* New York: Monthly Review Press.

Nautch Women: An Appeal to English Ladies on behalf of their Indian sisters (1893). Madras: Christian Literature Society.

Niranjana, Tejaswini (1992) *Siting Translation: History, Post-Structuralism, and the Colonial Context.* Berkeley: University of California Press.

Oak, V. V. (1925) *England's Educational Policy in India.* Madras: B. G. Paul.

Opinions on the Nautch Question. Collected and Published by the Punjab Purity Association (1894). Lahore: New Lyall Press.

Our Plague Spot in Connection with our Polity and Usages, as Regards our Women, our Soldiery, and the Indian Empire (1859). London: n.p.

Owen, David (1994) *Maturity and Modernity: Nietzsche, Weber, Foucault and the Ambivalence of Reason.* New York: Routledge.

Page, Norman (1997) *E. M. Forster's Posthumous Fiction*. Victoria, BC: University of Victoria Press.

Parekh, Bhikhu (1994) "Superior People: The Narrowness of Liberalism from Mill to Rawls." *Times Literary Supplement*, February 25, 11–13.

Parekh, Bhikhu (1997) "Liberalism and Colonialism: a Critique of Locke and Mill." In *The Decolonization of Imagination: Culture, Knowledge and Power*, ed. Jan Nederveen Pieterse and Parekh. Delhi: Oxford University Press, 81–98.

Parry, Benita (1998) *Delusions and Discoveries: India in the British Imagination 1880–1930*. New York: Verso.

Patton, James Blythe (1898) *Bijli the Dancer*. London: Methuen.

Paxton, Nancy (1992) "Mobilizing Chivalry: Rape in British Novels about the Indian Uprising of 1857." *Victorian Studies* 36.1, 5–30.

Paxton, Nancy (1996) "Secrets of the Colonial Harem: Gender, Sexuality, and the Law in Kipling's Novels." In *Writing India 1757–1990*, ed. Bart Moore-Gilbert. Manchester: Manchester University Press, 139–62.

Paxton, Nancy (1999) *Writing under the Raj: Gender, Race, and Rape in the British Colonial Imagination, 1830–1947*. New Brunswick, NJ: Rutgers University Press.

Payne, Charles Wynne (1947) *The Eastern Empire. Ceylon. First series*. London: G. Odell.

Peebles, Patrick (1981) "Governor Arthur Gordon and the Administration of Sri Lanka." In *British Imperial Policy in India and Sri Lanka 1858–1912: A Reassessment*, ed. Robert I. Crane and N. Gerald Barrier. Columbia, MO: South Asia Books, 84–106.

Peeps at Ceylon Life and People. By the Wife of a Missionary (1885). London: Religious Tract Society.

Peggs, James (1832) *India Cries to British Humanity*. 3rd edn, London: Simpkin & Marshall.

Penny, F. E. (1898) *The Romance of the Nautch Girl: A Novel*. London: Swan Sonnenschein & Co.

Perrin, Alice (1905) *The Waters of Destruction*. London: Chatto & Windus.

Phillips, Kathy J. (1994) *Virginia Woolf Against Empire*. Knoxville: University of Tennessee Press.

Pietz, William (1993) "Fetishism and Materialism: The Limits of Theory in Marx." In *Fetishism as Cultural Discourse*, ed. Emily Apter and Pietz. Ithaca, NY: Cornell University Press, 119–51.

Pocock, J. G. A. (1985) *Virtue, Commerce, and History: Essays on Political Thought and History*. New York: Cambridge University Press.

Pollins, Harold (1982) *Economic History of the Jews in England*. Rutherford, NJ: Farleigh Dickinson University Press.

Porter, Dale H. (1970) *The Abolition of the Slave Trade in England, 1784–1807*. New York: Archon Books.

Porter, Dennis (1994) "*Orientalism* and its Problems." In *Colonial Discourse and Post-Colonial Theory*, ed. Patrick Williams and Laura Chrisman. New York: Columbia University Press, 150–61.

Pradhan, S. V. (1976) "Mill on India: A Reappraisal." *Dalhousie Review* 56, 5–22.

Ragussis, Michael (1995) *Figures of Conversion: The Jewish Question and English National Identity*. Durham, NC: Duke University Press.

Rangarajan, Mahesh (1996) *Fencing the Forest: Conservation and Ecological Change in India's Central Provinces 1860–1914*. Delhi: Oxford University Press.

Ransom, John S. (1997) *Foucault's Discipline: The Politics of Subjectivity*. Durham, NC; Duke University Press.

Rickards, Robert (1814) *The Speeches of Robert Rickards, Esq. in the Debate in Parliament on the*

Renewal of the Charter of the Hon. East India Company, 1813. London: Whittingham & Rowland.

Rickards, Robert (1829) *India, or, Facts Submitted to Illustrate the Character and Condition of the Native Inhabitants. With Suggestions for Reforming the Present System of Government.* London: Smith, Elder & Co.

Ridgeway, Sir West (1903) *Administration of the Affairs of Ceylon, 1896 to 1903: A Review.* Colombo: n.p.

Roberts, Morley (1891) *Songs of Energy.* London: Lawrence & Bullen.

Roberts, Morley (1899) A *Son of Empire: A Novel.* London: Hutchinson & Co.

Robertson, Fiona (1994) *Legitimate Histories: Scott, Gothic and the Authorities of Fiction.* Oxford: Clarendon Press.

Robertson, Thomas Campbell (1829) *Remarks on Several Recent Publications regarding the Civil Government and Foreign Policy on British India.* London: John Murray.

Rose, Jacqueline (1998) *States of Fantasy.* Oxford: Oxford University Press.

Rosenbaum, S. P. (1987) *Victorian Bloomsbury: The Early History of the Bloomsbury Group*, vol. 1. New York: St. Martin's Press.

Roth, Cecil (1978) *A History of the Jews in England.* Oxford: Clarendon Press.

Rouse, Joseph (1994) "Power/Knowledge." In *The Cambridge Companion to Foucault,* ed. Gary Gutting. Cambridge: Cambridge University Press, 92–114.

Rowbotham, Judith (1989) *Good Girls Make Good Wives: Guidance for Girls in Victorian Fiction.* Oxford: Blackwell.

Rowney, Horatio B. (1882) *The Wild Tribes of India.* London: De La Rue & Co.

Roy, Parama (1998) *Indian Traffic: Identities in Question in Colonial and Postcolonial India.* Berkeley: University of California Press.

Ruskin, John, ed. (1885) *Bibliotheca Pastorum*, vol. IV: *A Knights Faith: Passages in the Life of Sir Herbert Edwardes.* London: George Allen.

Russell, R. V. (1916) *The Tribes and Castes of the Central Provinces of India*, 4 vols, vol. 2. London: Macmillan.

Ryan, Alan (1973) "Two Concepts of Politics and Democracy: James and John Stuart Mill." In *Machiavelli and the Nature of Political Thought.* London: Croom Helm.

Ryan, Michael (1989) *Politics and Culture: Working Hypotheses for a Post-Revolutionary Society.* Baltimore, MD: Johns Hopkins University Press.

Said, Edward (1979) *Orientalism.* New York: Vintage.

Said, Edward (2002) "*Kim* as Imperialist Novel." In *Kim,* ed. Zohreh T. Sullivan. New York: W. W. Norton, 337–50.

Salaman, Malcolm C. (1892) *Woman: Through a Man's Eyeglass.* London: William Heinemann.

Sarkar, Sumit (1983) *Modern India.* Delhi: Oxford University Press.

Scott, David (1995) "Colonial Governmentality." *Social Text* 43, 191–220.

Scott, Walter ([1827] 2000) *Chronicles of the Canongate,* ed. Claire Lamont. Edinburgh: Edinburgh University Press.

Scurry, James (1824) *The Captivity, Sufferings and Escape of James Scurry who was Detained a Prisoner during Ten Years in the Dominions of Hyder Ali and Tippoo Sahib.* London: Henry Fisher.

Seeley, J. R. ([1885] 1971) *The Expansion of England,* ed. John Gross. Chicago, IL: University of Chicago Press.

Sharpe, Jenny (1993) *Allegories of Empire: The Figure of Woman in the Colonial Text.* Minneapolis: University of Minnesota Press.

Shires, Linda (1992) "Afterword: Ideology and Subject as Agent." In *Rewriting the Victorians,* ed. Shires. New York and London: Routledge, 147–65.

Showalter, Elaine (1990) *Sexual Anarchy: Gender and Culture at the Fin de Siècle.* New York: Viking.

Silverman, Kaja (1992) *Male Subjectivity at the Margins*. New York: Routledge.

Simcox, A. H. A. (1912) *A Memoir of the Khandesh Bhil Corps 1825–1891*. Bombay: Thacker & Co.

Simons, Jon (1995) *Foucault and the Political*. London: Routledge.

Singh, Hira Lal (1963) *Problems and Policies of the British in India, 1885–1898*. Bombay: Asia Publishing House.

Singh, Jyotsna (1996) *Colonial Narratives/Cultural Dialogues: "Discoveries" of India in the Language of Colonialism*. New York: Routledge.

Singh, K. S. (1994) *The Scheduled Tribes*. Delhi: Oxford University Press.

Sinha, Mrinalini (1995) *Colonial Masculinity: The "Manly Englishman" and the "Effeminate Bengali" in the Late Nineteenth Century*. Manchester: Manchester University Press.

Skaria, Ajay (1996) "Writing, Orality and Power in the Dangs, Western India, 1800–1920." *Subaltern Studies IX*, ed. Shahid Amin and Dipesh Chakravarty. Delhi: Oxford University Press.

Skidelsky, Robert (1983) *John Maynard Keynes*, vol. 1. London: Macmillan.

Smith, Anthony (1998) *Nationalism and Modernism*. New York: Routledge.

Solomon, John I. (1914) *A Memorandum of the Pearl Fisheries of Ceylon*. Rangoon: n.p.

Sorenson, Jane (1997) "Writing Historically, Speaking Nostalgically: The Competing Languages of Nation in Scott's *The Bride of Lammermoor*." In *Narratives of Nostalgia, Gender, and Nationalism*, ed. Jean Pickering and Suzanne Kehde. New York: New York University Press, 30–51.

Spenser, Edmund (1983) "A View of the Present State of Ireland, Discoursed by Way of a Dialogue Between Eudoxus and Irenius." In *Elizabethan Ireland: A Selection of Writings by Elizabethan Writers on Ireland*, ed. James P. Myers, Jr. New York: Archon Books, 60–125.

Spivak, Gayatri C. (1999) *A Critique of Postcolonial Reason: Toward a History of the Vanishing Present*. Cambridge, MA: Harvard University Press.

Stallybrass, Oliver (1972) "Introduction" to E. M. Forster, *The Life to Come and other Stories*, ed. Stallybrass. London: Edward Arnold, vii–xxi.

Stewart, Maaja A. (1993) *Domestic Realities and Imperial Fictions: Jane Austen's Novels in Eighteenth-Century Contexts*. Athens: University of Georgia Press.

Stokes, Eric (1959) *The English Utilitarians and India*. Oxford: Clarendon Press.

Stoler, Ann L. (1995) *Race and the Education of Desire*. Durham, NC: Duke University Press.

Stone, Wilfred (1966) *The Cave and the Mountain: A Study of E. M. Forster*. Stanford, CA: Stanford University Press.

Strachey, Lytton ([1914] 1933) "Bonga Bonga in Whitehall." In *Characters and Commentaries*. London: Chatto, 175–80.

Suleri, Sara (1992) *The Rhetoric of English India*. Chicago, IL: University of Chicago Press.

Sullivan, Edward (1858) *Letters on India*. London: Saunders & Otley.

Sullivan, Zohreh T. (1993) *Narratives of Empire: The Fictions of Rudyard Kipling*. Cambridge: Cambridge University Press.

Sussman, Herbert (1995) *Victorian Masculinities*. Cambridge: Cambridge University Press.

Sutherland, John (1995) *The Life of Walter Scott*. Oxford: Blackwell.

Sutherland, J. A. (1989) *The Longman Companion to Victorian Fiction*. Harlow: Longman.

Taussig, Michael (1987) *Shamanism, Colonialism, and the Wild Man*. Chicago, IL: University of Chicago Press.

Taussig, Michael (1993) "*Maleficium*: State Fetishism." In *Fetishism as Cultural Discourse*, ed. Emily Apter and William Pietz. Ithaca, NY: Cornell University Press, 217–47.

Taylor, P. Meadows (1872) *Seeta*, 3 vols, vol. 1. London: Henry S. King & Co.

Tharu, Susie, and K. Lalita (1991) *Women Writing in India: 600 B.C. to the Present*. New York: Feminist Press.

Tickner, Lisa (1988) *The Spectacle of Women*. Chicago, IL: University of Chicago Press.

Tolan, Rachel (1995) "Colonizing and Transforming the Criminal Tribesman: The Salvation Army in British India." In *Deviant Bodies*, ed. Jennifer Terry and Jacqueline Urla. Bloomington: Indiana University Press, 78–108.

Trelawny, Edward John ([1831] 1974) *Adventures of a Younger Son*, 3 vols. London: Oxford University Press.

Turley, David (1991) *The Culture of English Antislavery, 1780–1860*. London: Routledge.

Twelve Years' Military Adventure in Three Quarters of the Globe: or, Memoirs of an Officer who Served in the Armies of His Majesty and of the East India Company, between the years 1802 and 1814, in which are Contained the Campaigns of the Duke of Wellington in India (1829), 2 vols. London: Henry Colburn.

Viswanathan, Gauri (1989) *Masks of Conquest: Literary Study and British Rule in India*. New York: Columbia University Press.

Viswanathan, Gauri (1998) *Outside the Fold: Conversion, Modernity, and Belief*. Princeton, NJ: Princeton University Press.

The Voluntary Exile: A Political Essay in Verse (1784). London: n.p.

Vron Ware, Veronica (1992) *Beyond the Pale: White Women, Racism and History*. London: Verso.

Wagenknecht, Edward (1991) *Sir Walter Scott*. New York: Continuum.

Welsh, James (1830) *Military Reminiscences: Extracted from a Journal of Nearly Forty Years' Active Service in the East Indies*, 2 vols. London: Smith, Elder, & Co.

Westmacott, Charles M. (1825) *The English Spy: An Original Work, Characteristic, Satirical, and Humorous. Comprising Scenes and Sketches in Every Rank of Society, being Portraits of the Illustrious, Eccentric, and Notorious*, part 16. London: Sherwood Jones.

Williams, Raymond (1980) "The Significance of 'Bloomsbury' as a Social and Cultural Group." In *Keynes and the Bloomsbury Group*, ed. Derek Crabtree and A. P. Thirwall. London: Macmillan, 40–67.

Wilson, Duncan ([1978] 2003) *Leonard Woolf: A Political Biography*. London: Palgrave Macmillan.

Wolcot, John (1783) *More Lyric Odes to the Royal Academicians by Peter Pindar, a Distant Relation to the Poet of Thebes and Laureate to the Academy*. London: n.p.

Woolf, Leonard ([1913] 1981) *The Village in the Jungle*. New York: Oxford University Press.

Woolf, Leonard (1920) *Mandates and Empire*. London: British Periodicals.

Woolf, Leonard (1921) *Economic Imperialism*. London: Swathmore Press.

Woolf, Leonard ([1921] 1963) "Three Stories on Ceylon by Leonard Woolf." In *Diaries of Ceylon 1908–1911: Records of a Colonial Administrator*, ed. Woolf. London: Hogarth Press.

Woolf, Leonard (1928) *Imperialism and Civilization*. London: Hogarth Press.

Woolf, Leonard (1960) *Sowing: An Autobiography of the Years 1880–1904*. London: Hogarth Press.

Woolf, Leonard (1989) *Letters of Leonard Woolf*, ed. Frederic Spotts. New York: Harcourt.

Woolf, Virginia (1925) *Mrs Dalloway*. New York: Harcourt.

Woolf, Virginia (1931) *The Waves*. New York: Harcourt.

Wright, Arnold (1891) *Baboo English as 'Tis Writ. Being Curiosities of Indian Journalism*. London: T. Fisher Unwin.

Young, Robert C. (1990) *White Mythologies: Writing History and the West*. New York: Routledge.

Young, Robert C. (1995) *Colonial Desire: Hybridity in Theory, Culture, and Race*. New York: Routledge.

Zastoupil, Lynn (1988) "J. S. Mill and India." *Victorian Studies* 32.1, 31–54.

Žižek, Slavoj (1989) *The Sublime Object of Ideology*. London: Verso.

Žižek, Slavoj (1998) "Love thy Neighbor? No, Thanks!" In *Psychoanalysis of Race*, ed. Christopher Lane. New York: Columbia University Press, 154–75.

Index

administration: in Ceylon 169; colonial
3–4, 11–12, 64–5, 71, 80, 119–20,
138–9, 164–5
adventure, tales, colonial 92–3
adventurers, women 57–8
Adventures of a Younger Son (Trelawny) 20,
21, 39, 43, 44, 52, 53, 192
alterity: colonial 50, 59, 72, 73–4; in D. H.
Lawrence 184; in E. M. Forster 136;
figures of 8, 14, 21, 34, 51, 55–6; Jewish
42; in Walter Scott 55, 58
ambivalence: textual 9–10
Anglo-Indian romance 21, 90, 91–7, 100,
107, 114, 121, 194; and the frontier
sensibility 103
Anstey, F. 4; *Baboo Jabberjee* 179, 184–6
anti-Semitism 38, 54–5
Arnold, Mathew 7, 18–19, 189
Aspects of the Novel (Forster) 126, 133, 142
Austen, Jane: *Sense & Sensibility* 12
Autobiography (John Stuart Mill) 24–5, 29,
61, 62–4, 67, 68, 69, 72–7, 78, 80, 81,
89, 193

baboo (*also* babu): 3, 5, 6–7, 11, 12–13,
16–17, 25, 31, 35, 184–6, 188; in *Baboo
Jabberjee* 184–6; civility of 13;
competition 2, 4; hybridity of 9; in *Kim*
4, 6–7, 12–13, 17, 19; language of 5,
188
Behn, Aphra 7
Bengal 5, 7
Bengali 18
Benjamin, Walter 132–3
Bentham 74
Bhabha, Homi 9–10, 20, 48, 75; on John
Stuart Mill 67
Bildungsroman 24, 67, 193

biopolitics 25, 27–8
biopower 23, 171–2
Bloomsbury 146–7, 151, 153, 157–8, 164;
aesthetics 150
bureaucracy: bureaucratic work 153, 175;
in *A Son of Empire* 101; colonial 23–4,
70, 85, 185; in Leonard Woolf 147

cadet: colonial 43–6, 194
Calcutta Review 2–5, 16–19, 92, 187, 188, 189
Cambridge Apostles 151
Caruth, Cathy 153–4, 198
character: Indian 86–7
Chatterjee, Partha 31, 187
Christianity 134–5, 137, 141
citizenship 3; *see also* nation, nationality
civic virtue 10
civil 5; conduct 178; discourse 9; identity
10; rule among aboriginal peoples 130;
self 8; services 2, 4, 7, 119–20, 194;
society 129
civility: and civil governance 64; colonial
power relations, implicit in 8; definition
of 7, 9, 10, 19–20, 33, 125; and
discipline 11, 61; in Edmund Spenser
10; and education 1–4; elusiveness of 5,
8, 12, 125, 143, 157, 21; genealogy of
32; and gentlemanly behavior 100; in
Jane Austen 12; and language 5, 6, 7;
and liberalism 25; and metropolitan
identity 8, 31, 34, 149; missionary 24,
124; and naturalization 16; normative
role of 10–11, 15–17,18, 19–20, 23, 42,
60, 178; "sly" 9, 20; social behavior and
7, 10, 12; *see also* norm, normativity
civilization 132, 197; idea of 17; in
Lawrence 182; rivalry between
civilizations 102